THE BEST OF ETHNIC
HOME COOKING

MARY POULOS WILDE

WARNER BOOKS

A Warner Communications Company

Warner Books Edition

This Warner Books edition is published by arrangement with
J. P. Tarcher, Inc. 9110 Sunset Blvd. Los Angeles, CA 90069

Warner Books, Inc., 666 Fifth Avenue, New York, NY 10103

 A Warner Communications Company

Printed in the United States of America
First Warner Books Trade Paperback Printing: September 1987
10 9 8 7 6 5 4 3

Library of Congress Cataloging-in-Publication Data

Wilde, Mary Poulos.
    The best of ethnic home cooking.

    Reprint. Originally published: Los Angeles :
Tarcher, 1981.
    Includes indexes.
    1. Cookery, International. I. Title.
[TX725.A1W454 1987]   641.59   87-10634
ISBN 0-446-38493-3 (pbk.) (U.S.A.)
    0-446-38494-1 (pbk.) (Canada)

PRAISE FOR MARY POULOS WILDE'S INTERNATIONAL FESTIVAL OF FOOD

"Those who never knew the delights of their Jewish grandmother's matzo balls, their Polish grandmother's pierogi, or a sauerbraten that's linked to the family's German background have a second chance to sample their culinary heritage in *The Best of Ethnic Home Cooking*."
—*Chicago Sun-Times*

"Mary Poulos Wilde's award-winning cookbook is a remarkably eclectic and well-researched collection."
—*Slimmer*

"Lucid introductions to each dish constitute a veritable short course in comparative culture."
—*Raleigh News & Observer*

"A must for anyone who really loves the taste, the fragrance, and the joy of sharing wonderful foods."
—*Lafayette Journal & Courier* (Indiana)

"Utterly charming."   —John Clancy,
                              Cookbook Author/Executive Chef,
                              Time-Life "Food of the World Series"

"A good many foreign cultures are represented....The recipes range from simple to sophisticated, and they are written with clear, concise directions."
—*Publishers Weekly*

To Betty and Jim Poulos,
Whose ethnic home cooking
I still love best

CONTENTS

ACKNOWLEDGMENTS

I am truly grateful to the following folks who were so generous with their time, recipes, suggestions, and words of encouragement: June Alpert, Mary Hall Angel, Mary Lou Brady, Jane Jordan Browne, Molly Custrini, Genevieve Davis, Andrew Ettinger, Robin Fields, Gregg and Martha Fox, Janice Gallagher, Derek Gallagher, Susan Glazer, Joyce Goldberg, Jessie Groshart, Hilda Josefsberg, Cindy Leonetti, Jacqueline Lewerke, Miriam Marks, Ruth Modlin, Bessie Martin, Vicki Pasternack, Betty Poulos, Susan Roth, Dr. Jim Siedel, Audrey Wildman, Fay Wildman, and my husband, Larry.

INTRODUCTION: IN SEARCH OF THE PERFECT PIEROGI

A while back, I set out to make Polish potato *pierogi* as a treat for a transplanted New York friend, which wasn't easy because I'd never seen—much less tasted—one of these dumplings. The New Yorker had complained that *pierogi* in Los Angeles restaurants were nothing like the ones his aunt used to make. "Why don't you give me your aunt's recipe," I suggested, "and I'll learn to make them for you." But it wasn't that simple. Like so many ethnic cooks, the Manhattanite's aunt never used a recipe and never wrote one down. Her formula was lost forever.

After rummaging through an assortment of authentic (even translated) Polish cookbooks, I came across precious few recipes that even sounded close.

With my pal's description of these buttery bites in mind (". . . kind of like a Jewish *kreplach*, or maybe a Chinese *won ton*—no, more like Italian *ravioli* only much bigger, but not quite as big as a Russian *pelmeny* . . ."), I tested my researched recipes. None produced the kind of pierogi my friend was yearning for.

After several more failed batches, it happened. I accidentally stumbled upon the magical method. Big, light noodle dumplings stuffed with a treasure trove of butter, onions, and potato. My chum was ecstatic. As he sat in my kitchen mopping up the remains of a mountain of sour cream with the last dumpling, he sighed, "Wouldn't it be terrific if you could get all the very best ethnic recipes—real home cooking—and put them together in one cookbook?"

I was more than a little intrigued by his offhand suggestion (as evidenced by the book you're holding). That was the beginning of a

9

two-year search for the cream of ethnic cookery as practiced in the kitchens of America's parents, grandparents, aunts, uncles, cousins, friends, and neighbors.

To start, I solicited family favorites from friends and relatives and their friends and relatives. It had a surprising rippling effect. Very soon I began getting recommendations from total strangers like, "My mother in Oshkosh has a second cousin whose brother-in-law used to work in an Armenian bakery. Would you like me to see if he has any good recipes?"

As the culinary contributions arrived, I tackled the job of testing and selecting dishes that would eventually appear in the book. I looked for reasonably authentic foods, which again was not a simple task. Trouble was, there were too many "right" ways to make many of the recipes—all of them different. One lady wrote, "The only way to make good red beans and rice is to simmer them together in the same kettle." Yet another cook insisted, "Adding rice directly to the beans will spoil the whole mess."

It became apparent that no recipe was the last word. In the world of ethnic cooking, there is a wide margin for creativity and individuality. Ethnic cooks seem to have an intense pride in their own brand of cooking and they wouldn't dream of knuckling under to some gastronomic guru.

Perusing *The People's Almanac*, I counted nearly 50 different ethnic groups in the U.S.A. If my book was going to be portable, there had to be some limits. For one reason or another, the ethnicities whose cooking is represented herein boiled down to Basque, Cuban, Jamaican, German, Greek, Hungarian, Italian, Irish, Polish, Swedish, Danish, Finnish, Russian, and recipes from America's Deep South.

This final list of ethnicities evolved slowly and with a great deal of consideration. Of course there will always be someone who wonders why there are no Indonesian recipes. Oriental cooking is an art unto itself and often requires special equipment, ingredients, and know-how. Therefore, I decided to leave Asian cuisines to the myriad of authoritative volumes already devoted to them.

Likewise, French cooking—even country French cooking—has been tackled in countless books and magazines. Instead this book offers an unusual blending of French and Spanish flavors in its selection of spirited Basque specialties gleaned from the West's Basque communities and festivals. Tempting, off-the-beaten-path concoctions like a splendidly seasoned Rabbit Stew, traditional Sheepherder's Bread baked high in a black iron kettle, plus spit barbeques, buffet salads, and a parade of homemade sweets. There are recipes enough to throw your own Basque festival. All you need are the red berets.

Then there's Mexican cooking. I love it. But I decided not to lead you down the trampled path to yet another version of enchiladas. Rather than grapple with one more guacamole, I sought out some of the lesser known treats of Latin American cooking. There's a delightful sampling of Cuban and Jamaican cookery and their relatives, Cajun and Creole specialties. Dishes like a tangy, intricately spiced Cuban Pot Roast, a magnificent Caribbean Black Bean Soup, recipes for homemade Jamaican Breads, salads of tropical fruits with spicy dressings, and many wonderful soups and stews.

All in all, this book presents a unique and diverse cross section of nationalities, cooking styles, and flavors. And as a result of thoughtful selection, there are plenty of recipes from each ethnicity to create varied menus.

Having the scope of the cookbook in clear focus, there was a lot of weeding to be done. First to go were things like Mrs. Berman's Jewish lasagne with American cheese. "Sure it's ethnic," she argued. "It's Italian, only much better!" Also discarded were Hungarian goulash made with four kinds of canned soup, Jewish lo mein, assorted casseroles with potato chip toppings, a dozen or more cakes made with pudding or frosting mixes, and the all-time authentic rip-off—a Hawaiian appetizer made with canned wiener slices and pineapple chunks threaded on frilly toothpicks.

Since homemade food is best when it's handmade, I excluded most convenience and processed items. Good ethnic cooking is traditionally done from scratch.

One of my goals was to compile a compendium of family favorites, reproduced in the original fashion—long before there was high technology. Therefore, most all the dishes on these pages can be produced in a moderately well stocked kitchen without the use of expensive equipment, machines, or specialized pots and pans. However, when preparation time can be cut by the use of a blender or food processor, instructions are offered.

These ethnic recipes can be created using top-quality ingredients you may well have on your shelves. There is generally no need for odd, hard-to-get items. For reasons of economy and accessibility, most ethnic cooks do not stock their pantries with imported delicacies. That's one reason why ethnic cooking in America differs from the original "foreign" version. Immigrants were forced to abandon many of their native ingredients and substitute regional American fare instead. A whole new realm of cooking resulted, far removed from "international" or "haute cuisine."

When any of these foods can be enhanced by an exotic flavor or ingredient, sources for mail order are provided at the back of this book.

In ferreting out prized family recipes, the best versions of popular standards and classic dishes were selected, including real Homemade Egg Pastas, a spectacular rendition of Creole Gumbo File, and a monumental Sauerbraten with Potato Dumplings.

There is also a substantial collection of atypical preparations—the kind you'd sample only in the home of an ethnic friend. Sicilian Christmas Cake, Basque Rabbit Stew, and Greek Easter Bread are among these less familiar specialties.

Overall, there's a balance of foods that are quick and easily prepared as well as those that are more challenging and complex. From a simple Hungarian Cucumber Salad to intricate Homemade Phyllo Dough, there are recipes to please cooks on many levels.

Finally, *The Best of Ethnic Home Cooking* is filled with festive foods just right for entertaining. After all, who wants to bake up a luscious Polish Walnut Torte from scratch and not have someone to appreciate it?

Entertaining Ethnic

Once you choose an occasion, whether it's a bona fide holiday or just the urge to cook, consider this: put away your silver fish forks and forget all that stuff about paper doilies under sherbet glasses and panties on the lamb. This is food you serve right out of the kettle. It's gathering everyone in the kitchen for a relaxed buffet. Serving good food and plenty of it, but making just one or two courses. Like a homemade soup and bread party with just good wine, cheese, and a lovely dessert. These are meals you serve either family-style or at a big, carefree buffet.

A no-fuss, no-frills approach to entertaining doesn't have to be crass or colorless. Quite the contrary, it can induce some of the liveliest responses.

But a guest can't relax while trying to balance a delicate cup and saucer on his or her knee.

If you have attractive casual dinnerware, use it. Colorful extra large napkins can easily be made at home by stitching big squares of bright fabric and fringing the edges.

For serving pieces, use wooden spoons, copper kettles, black iron skillets, heavy Dutch ovens, earthenware crocks, casseroles and bowls, or large wooden carving boards—anything suitably earthy and comfortable.

Table accents might include a big basket of assorted homemade breads, a small bushel of colorful fresh fruits and vegetables that you can eat later, or any kind of ethnic collection you might have like a group of German beer steins. Big leafy batches of fresh rhubarb or Swiss chard tied in bundles with floral ribbons; inexpensive mats, trinkets, and ornaments from local ethnic import shops and bazaars; all make an enticing atmosphere.

Have you ever seen a staid executive-type cut loose with a vigorous Greek handkerchief dance? It's truly amazing what mirth and spirit music can add. Ethnic recordings are available in everything from Highland flings to Russian balalaika ballads. *The Yellow Pages* might offer some sources. Otherwise, refer to the Ethnic Mail Order Bazaar at the back of this book.

 # Appetizers

The term "appetizer" is loosely used here to group together foods that *can* precede a meal. Some are light snacks meant to be cocktail nibblers, while others can be served in a variety of ways.

Since ethnic family dinners usually begin with the main dish itself (maybe a salad or soup), appetizers as such are most often reserved for guests, holidays, and special occasions.

This does not mean that the following recipes should be considered for celebrations only. On the contrary, most of the foods in this chapter are regular fare, in one way or another.

For instance, *Jewish gefilte fish,* while a traditional sit-down first course, can also be served as a refreshing summertime luncheon.

Dolmathes (stuffed grape leaves) are served often in many Greek homes, not just as appetizers and starters, but also as snacks, light lunches, and sometimes as a vegetable side dish with meats and poultry.

Tirokopita (Greek spinach and cheese tarts), in addition to being offered before dinner, are also popular as snacks, lunches, and they're a delightful substitute for bread at festive dinners.

Finally, the *Polish zakaski buffet,* a bountiful feast in itself, can be considered a whole meal. Its components—the delectable pickles, relishes, and spreads—make fine complements for main dishes, soups, stews, fresh-baked breads, and salads.

Stuffed Grape Leaves

DOLMATHES (DOL-*MAH*-THES)

Makes 3 to 4 dozen

The herb-scented rice and meat filling is encased in tender leaves of the grape vine to make these understandably treasured delicacies. They are divine appetizers served with wine or glasses of iced *ouzo*. For an enticing first course, place three or four on a small plate with healthy chunks of lemon, and some black Calamata olives, or spoon some tangy Egg and Lemon Sauce (*see* index) over the tiny rolls and offer bread for dunking.

Grape leaves packed in salt brine are available in jars from most Greek or Middle Eastern import grocers, and they can even be found on the shelves of many supermarkets in the specialty section. Each jar contains as many as 50 leaves, but you should not stuff the leaves that are coarse, tough, or torn. Therefore, the amount of *dolmathes* you can get out of one jar is variable, but figure on about 40.

Dolmathes can be made a couple of days in advance.

FILLING

½ to ¾ pound (225 to 340 g) lean ground beef or lamb or a combination of the two
2 large onions, finely chopped
3 large cloves of garlic, finely chopped
2 tablespoons (30 ml) tomato paste
¼ cup (60 ml) chopped fresh dill weed, or 2 tablespoons (30 ml) dried dill
½ cup (125 ml) fresh parsley, finely chopped
3 or 4 sprigs of fresh mint, finely chopped
Juice of 1 lemon
1 cup (250 ml) long grain white rice (not instant)
½ cup (125 ml) pine nuts, pistachios, chopped walnuts, or chopped pecans
1 cup (250 ml) water or light meat stock
Salt and pepper to taste

Crumble the meat in a skillet and stir over medium heat until the meat loses most of its pinkness. Add the onions and garlic and continue to cook until the meat is well done and the onions and garlic are soft. Tilt the skillet and spoon off as much fat as possible. Stir in all remaining ingredients except water and bring to a simmer. Pour in water and cover the skillet. Let simmer for about 10 minutes, or until most of the moisture is absorbed. The rice should still have a bite—it should be about half done. Remove from heat and cool.

LEAVES

12   ounce (336 g) jar of grape leaves, or about 50 fresh
     grape leaves

If you want to use *fresh grape leaves* make sure that the vines are free from all pesticides. You can identify grape vines by their curled tentacles or by using a reliable botanical guide. Pick only the second and third leaves from the top of each vine. These are the right size. The top leaf is too small and any leaves lower than the third leaf are too tough. Choose leaves that are unblemished and untorn. Rinse the fresh picked leaves under warm water, and place them one on top of another in a stack, each with the shiny dark side down. Place this entire stack in a kettle of rapidly boiling water. After about 40 seconds turn the entire stack over very gently with tongs or two wooden spoons, being careful not to poke holes in the leaves. Allow the vine leaves to stay in the hot water for another half minute or so, then transfer them all at once to a colander and drain until you are ready to use them.

If you use *commercial grape leaves* packed in salt brine, rinse them in several changes of cold water and drain. Pick over the leaves, setting aside any leaves that are too small, too large and tough, or torn. The leaves should just about cover your open hand. If any have tough stems up into the leaf, carefully cut them out using a small sharp knife. Do not discard the rejects. Lay the selected leaves, one on top of another in a stack, with their dark, shiny side down and with their points and stems running in the same direction. This will make it easier when you begin to fill them. Lay the stack of leaves in a colander to drain until you are ready to use.

PROCEDURE

Line the bottom of a Dutch oven (or any other heavy kettle with a lid) with the rejected grape leaves. Overlap them and bring them a couple of inches (about 50 mm) up the side of the kettle. This will serve to protect the stuffed leaves from scorching, sticking, or burning. Place about 1 heaping teaspoon (5 ml) of filling on the dull side of a leaf, on the lower half of the stem end in the center. Fold the stem end up and over the filling, fold in the sides of the leaf, then roll the leaf up to make a neat package. Do not wrap the rolls too tightly because the rice will expand some during cooking. Also, make sure that the filling is totally encased or it will leak out into the stock later on. As the stuffed grape leaves are completed, lay them side-by-side in

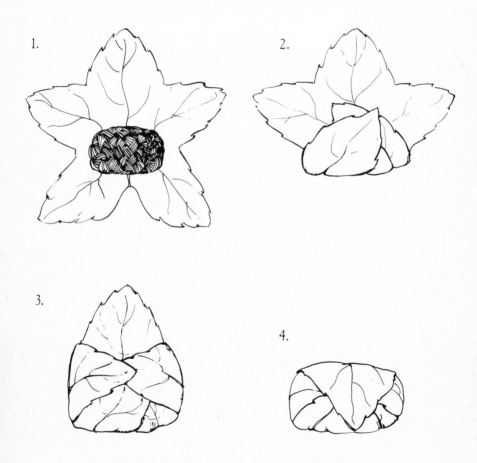

1.

2.

3.

4.

a circular pattern until the bottom of the kettle is covered. The dolmathes should be snug, but not crammed. When one layer is finished, start on a second in the same circular manner. Proceed until all the filling and/or leaves have been used. Cover the stuffed grape leaves with water or light meat stock. Weight them down in the kettle using a heavy plate. This is to prevent the rolls from unraveling during the cooking process. The plate should be barely covered with liquid—if not, add more to the kettle. Bring the kettle to a boil, cover, and reduce the heat to a simmer. Cook for about 1½ hours until most of the liquid is absorbed. Remove the dolmathes from the heat and let them stay in the kettle, covered, until they are completely cooled. They will keep in the refrigerator in this manner for a couple of days. Carefully remove them from the kettle using your fingers or two spoons.

Greek Spinach and Cheese Tarts
TIROKOPITA
Makes about 60 appetizers

These crisp, triangular tarts can be made in big batches, then frozen for later convenience. Flash freeze after baking, then seal them in airtight plastic bags. This lets you use only the exact amount needed each time.

Tirokopita are as delicious warm from the oven as they are at room temperature. Serve them with soups, salads, and main courses instead of bread; offer them as hot appetizers to be washed down with iced Greek ouzo; or present them as a luncheon main course with salad and wine.

For added flavor and crispness, sprinkle the tarts with sesame seeds before baking.

½ to ¾ pound (225 to 340 g) unsalted butter, melted in the top of a double boiler and kept warm over hot water

2 pounds (900 g) commercial or Homemade Phyllo Dough (*see* index)

1 recipe Filling from Greek Deep Dish Spinach and Cheese Pie (*see* index)

On a large work surface, set out the butter (in the top of a double boiler over hot water), a large pastry brush, the filling, a large baking sheet, and the *phyllo* dough. Lay the dough out on a sheet of plastic wrap and cover with another sheet of plastic. Lay a damp kitchen towel over all to keep the dough moist and pliable. As you remove each sheet of phyllo, carefully recover the stack. Brush the top of the first phyllo sheet with a thin coating of melted butter. Remove the sheet from the stack and lay it out flat. Then fold in thirds lengthwise (letter-style), brushing the top of each fold with butter. Place a heaping teaspoon (5 ml) of filling on the lower end of the

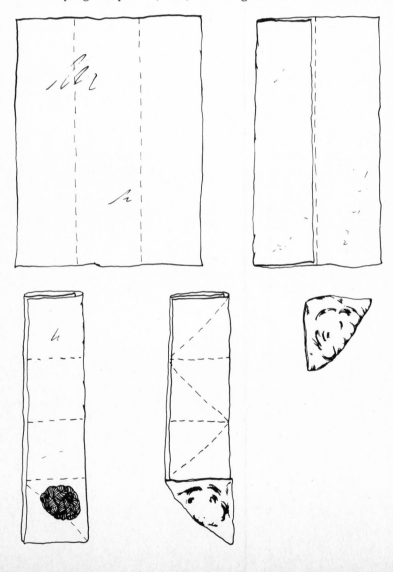

dough about 2 inches (50 mm) up from the bottom and slightly to the right. Fold the lower left corner of the dough up and over to the right to encase the filling in a triangle. Continue to fold, military flag-style, until you have a triangle-shaped pillow. Brush the outside with melted butter and place on the baking sheet, seam side down. Repeat this process, using up all of the dough and filling. Bake in a 375° F. oven for about 15 minutes until the appetizers are golden brown.

TO FREEZE
Flash freeze tirokopita either baked or unbaked, then place in plastic bags and seal tightly. To reheat frozen tirokopita, place directly on a cookie sheet and bake in a 350° F. oven for 25 to 30 minutes for unbaked tarts, and about 18 to 20 minutes for the prebaked appetizers. Break one in half to see if the filling is hot.

Jewish Chopped Liver
Serves 8 as a first course or 10 to 12 as an appetizer

Beef livers produce somewhat stronger, heavier results than chicken livers. I prefer a combination of both, but that's entirely a matter of personal taste.

Pack the pâté into a covered glass or earthenware crock and refrigerate up to 3 days before serving.

Nothing tastes better with chopped liver than slices of fresh, homemade bread (rye, black, pumpernickel, etc.) with crisp scallions, radishes, and celery sticks to nosh on the side.

1   pound (450 g) chicken or beef livers
½   cup (125 ml) rendered chicken fat (approximate)
        (recipe follows)
3   large onions, chopped
3   hard-cooked egg yolks, mashed
     Pinch of sugar
     Salt and pepper to taste
     Dash of hot pepper sauce (optional)

Rinse the liver under cold, running water. Remove all membrane and visible fat. Drain on a paper towel and pat dry. In a large heavy skillet, heat 3 tablespoons (45 ml) of the rendered fat to start. Add the onions and sauté until they're golden, but do not brown. Add more fat if necessary to prevent sticking. Transfer the onions to a large mixing bowl. Either broil the liver until it is cooked through or heat another 3 tablespoons (45 ml) of chicken fat in the skillet and add the livers, which have been cut into 1½ inch (37 mm) chunks (cut the chicken livers in half). Sauté livers, stirring frequently until they have lost all pinkness throughout. To the bowl with the onions add the livers along with the mashed egg, a pinch of sugar, and salt and pepper to taste. Run the mixture through a food grinder (once for coarse texture, and twice for a fine texture—again a matter of personal taste). Add as much chicken fat as needed to bind the mixture. Place in a deep bowl, cover tightly, and refrigerate. For an appetizer, accompany with small rounds of rye and pumpernickel or crackers and offer assorted crisp raw vegetables (radishes, scallions, carrots, and celery sticks, etc.). For a first course, use a small ice cream scoop to form a ball of the liver. Place on a lettuce leaf, dab a bit of melted chicken fat over it, and garnish with crisp raw vegetables. Pass rye and pumpernickel at the table.

Also makes a great sandwich filling.

RENDERED CHICKEN FAT

Place raw chicken fat in a heavy saucepan. Heat over low flame and allow the fat to melt slowly until it's almost all liquid. Remove the few crisp pieces, called *gribbenes*, and store the fat in a sterilized airtight jar in the refrigerator until use. It will keep for many weeks.

 **Gefilte Fish**

Makes 25 pieces

My California friend Susan Roth has practically parted the Red Sea to get this recipe from her mother-in-law, June Alpert, a celebrated New York hostess.

June's gefilte fish are so special that, for Passover, she air freights these cloud-like cakes on ice all the way from Long Island to Los Angeles so her children can enjoy a bit of "home" on the holidays.

3 pounds (1350 g) whitefish filets, plus head, tail, skin, and bones
3 pounds (1350 g) pike filets, plus head, tail, skin, and bones
2 to 3 thick slices of onion
2 large onions, grated
3 eggs, well beaten
1 cup (250 ml) *cold* water
1½ tablespoons (22½ ml) matzo meal
Kosher salt and white pepper to taste
Cooked carrot slices
Red and white prepared horseradish

Place all of the fish scraps into a large kettle along with the thick slices of onion. Cover with cold water and bring to a boil. Lower heat, cover, and allow to simmer for 1 to 2 hours. Strain stock, discard scraps, return stock to the kettle, and season with kosher salt. Grind the filets in a food grinder or food processor. Place ground fish along with the grated onion in a large bowl and mix well. Add the beaten eggs a little at a time, alternating with the cold water. Mix in the matzo meal and a sprinkling of kosher salt and white pepper. Form the fish mixture into patties similar to thick hamburgers. Press them into oblong shapes about 3½ inches × 2½ inches (87 mm × 62 mm) and about 2 inches (50 mm) thick at the middle. Bring the stock to a rapid boil. Add the fish patties and reduce the heat to a gentle low simmer. Cook for 2 hours. Transfer the fish to a glass baking dish, cover tightly, and refrigerate until serving time. Serve cold and garnish each piece with a slice of cooked carrot and a sprig of fresh parsley. Pass the horseradish at the table and offer some whole matzos.

🌸 Polish Appetizers
ZAKASKI

Polish appetizers, or *zakaski* (za-*kah*-skee), are usually served in the living room on small plates accompanied by glasses of ice cold vodka.

A zakaski buffet usually includes a variety of cooked and smoked cold fish, assorted cold meats, pickled eggs, relishes, pickles, assorted breads with sweet or flavored butters, crisp raw or preserved vegetables—the list is endless.

Select a good vodka and put it in the freezer, along with the glasses, at least 3 hours before serving. Once opened, keep the vodka on ice.

Here are some foods you might include—many are available in delicatessens or specialty sections of supermarkets:

1. Crisp red and white radishes
2. Pickled Mushrooms*
3. Pickled Eggs*
4. Anchovy filets
5. Polish Cottage Cheese Spread*
6. Red or black caviar
7. Herring in sour cream
8. Little Polish sausages
9. Smoked salmon or whitefish
10. Black, brown, pumpernickel, and rye breads
11. Mustard Butter*
12. Sardines
13. Pickled Watermelon Rind*
14. Beet Relish*
15. Polish Creamed Mushrooms*
16. Fresh scallions
17. Pickled onions
18. Assorted cheeses
19. Sliced cold chicken
20. Smoked oysters, clams, or mussels
21. Olives
22. Shrimp
23. Tomato slices
24. Celery ribs, including tops

*See index for these recipes.

Beet Relish

Makes about 2 cups (500 ml)

Variations of beet relish are found in Russian, Jewish, and Polish homes. Here's the typical Polish version, to be served with Zakaski (*see* index) before the meal, or to accompany a main course.

2   bunches of fresh beets
     Grated white horseradish to taste
     Sugar to taste
2   tablespoons (30 ml) cider vinegar
     Juice from ½ lemon
     Salt and ground pepper
½   small onion, finely minced or grated

Clean and trim beets but do not peel. Place in a kettle and cover with water to which a bit of salt has been added. Bring to a good boil and cook until the beets are tender when pierced with the end of a small sharp knife. Drain beets, reserving the liquid for Borscht (*see* index) if you wish. Peel, then mince or grate the beets and combine with remaining ingredients. Cover tightly and refrigerate overnight. Serve slightly chilled.

Polish Cheese Spread

Makes about 2½ cups (625 ml)

Chopped scallions and sweet gherkins add character to this cool, creamy mixture.

Polish cheese spread comes to life lathered on thick slices of moist black bread then topped with bits of smoked fish, rounds of fresh cucumber, or chilled radishes—all washed down with gulps of freezing vodka.

Vary this spread by adding chopped herbs to your liking.

1   cup (250 ml) large curd cottage cheese
2   tablespoons (30 ml) sour cream or yogurt

1   cup (250 ml) scallions, finely chopped, including
        green tops
2   tablespoons (30 ml) sweet gherkins, finely chopped
    Salt and pepper to taste

Combine the cottage cheese and sour cream with an electric mixer; beat until smooth. Add the scallions, chopped gherkins, salt, and pepper and mix well by hand. Refrigerate for at least 2 hours before serving.

🥀 Pickled Eggs
Makes 1 quart (1000 ml)

Pink and piquant, these preserved eggs are often part of the Polish Zakaski (*see* index) buffet. Serve them halved, accompanied by black bread, good mustard, coarse salt, and ice cold beer.

They're quite nice to have on hand in the summer to slice over sandwiches, salads, and bowls of chilled Borscht or Polish Cold Beet and Cucumber Soup (*see* index).

1   cup (250 ml) beet juice (use liquid from cooked fresh
         beets or Rusell broth) (*see* index)
½   cup (125 ml) Chablis wine
2   cups (500 ml) cider vinegar or wine vinegar
3   garlic cloves, peeled and cut in half
8   to 10 peppercorns
2   sprigs of fresh dill (optional)
1   bay leaf
½   teaspoon (3 ml) allspice
3   or 4 whole cloves
6   to 8 hard-boiled eggs, shelled

Place all ingredients (except eggs) in a saucepan and bring to a boil. Cook, uncovered, for about 20 minutes. Put the eggs in a sterile quart (1000 ml) jar with lid. Pour boiling marinade over eggs, cover tightly, and refrigerate for up to a week before serving. To serve, slice the eggs in half lengthwise and arrange yolk side up on a serving dish.

Garnish with sprigs of fresh dill or parsley. The marinade can be used over again with fresh eggs, simply by bringing to a boil for a few minutes and following the above procedure.

Pickled Mushrooms

Makes about 1 quart (1000 ml)

Serve these pickled mushrooms with Zakaski (Polish appetizers—*see* index) before a substantial Polish feast, or offer them as part of an antipasto for a lively Italian treat. Herbs can be used to vary the flavor for your own brand of creative cooking.

Since there is no pressure canning method used here, these mushrooms are not meant to be kept for longer than a couple of days before serving, and they must be refrigerated.

2	pounds (900 g) fresh button mushrooms
¾	cup (180 ml) corn oil
½	cup (125 ml) white distilled vinegar
2	garlic cloves, minced
1	bay leaf
8	to 10 whole peppercorns
2	teaspoons (10 ml) salt
½	teaspoon (3 ml) dry mustard
	Pinch of sugar

Clean and trim mushrooms. Place in a kettle with enough water to cover. Add a bit of salt to the kettle and bring it to a boil. Boil gently until the mushrooms sink to the bottom. Drain thoroughly. In a small saucepan, combine the remaining ingredients and bring to a slow boil over medium heat. Simmer for a few minutes. Pack mushrooms into hot, sterilized jars. Pour boiling marinade over and seal tightly with a sterile lid. Cool completely and refrigerate for up to 3 days. Serve chilled.

VARIATIONS
Add two tablespoons (30 ml) minced parsley, basil, or oregano to marinade.

🌺 Pickled Watermelon Rind

Makes about 6 pints (3000 ml)

For me it's a thrill to open the pantry doors and see neat rows of sparkling, hand-labeled jars of homemade preserves, pickles, and relishes. One of my favorites is sweet pickled watermelon rind.

These crisp, succulent opaque cubes are a popular complement to some of the most unlikely and different ethnic dishes—everything from Slavic buffets to Southern fried chicken with black-eyed peas.

This spice-laden recipe is superb. I prefer thick, pungent pickles, but it's tricky to find thick-skinned watermelons. Look for stippled or striped melons, and try to buy melons sold by the piece so you can pick the ones with the very thickest rind. The popular dark green supermarket melon has been dismal disappointment with thin, limp skin. Don't worry about wasting the meat. This is the perfect opportunity to try the Italian Watermelon Ice (*see* index).

½	large, thick-skinned watermelon [about 6 to 7 pounds (2700 to 3150 g)]
¾	cup (180 ml) salt
½	cup (125 ml) lime juice
4	quarts (4000 ml) cold water
2½	quarts (2500 ml) ice cubes
8	cups (2000 ml) sugar
3	cups (750 ml) distilled white vinegar
3	cups (750 ml) water
2	to 3 slices, ¼ inch (6 mm) thick, fresh ginger
2	tablespoons (30 ml) whole cloves
4	or 5 cinnamon sticks broken into pieces
6	sterile pint (500 ml) jars with canning lids and rings

Scoop out the watermelon meat leaving just the barest hint of pink on the rind. Using a heavy, sharp knife, cut the rind into manageable chunks (4 or 5 pieces). Peel away the green outer skin and cut the rind into 1 inch (25 mm) cubes. In a large stainless steel or enamel kettle, mix the 4 quarts (4000 ml) of cold water with the lime juice and salt. Stir to dissolve. Add the ice cubes and the watermelon rind. Cover and soak 6 to 8 hours. Drain and rinse thoroughly under cold running water. Cover with cold water, set the kettle on a high flame, and bring to a boil. Cook until just tender when pierced with a fork, about 10 minutes. The rind must be firm—do not overcook. Drain and set aside.

Combine the sugar, vinegar, and 3 cups (750 ml) of water plus the spices which have been tied together in a clean cheesecloth bag. Bring to a boil and simmer for several minutes. Remove from heat and cool. Add the watermelon rind to the syrup with spice bag, cover, and soak overnight.

PACKING

The next day, bring the kettle to a boil and simmer until the rind is translucent but still firm (about 10 minutes). Pack the rind into hot, sterilized pint-sized (500 ml) canning jars, adding a piece of the cinnamon stick and a bit of ginger to each jar. Ladle hot syrup to within ½ inch (12 mm) of jar tops. Wipe rims of jars with a clean damp cloth to be sure they are scrupulously clean and free from syrup. Place lids on jars according to their manufacturer's directions. Place upright in a kettle of boiling water (enough to cover over the lids with at least an inch (25 mm) of water). From the moment the kettle returns to a boil, time chunks according to your altitude: 1000 feet (30,480 cm) or under—10 minutes. Add 1 minute for each additional 1000 feet (30,480 cm) of altitude. Keep the kettle boiling gently but steadily throughout the processing time, adding boiling water if necessary to keep the water level up. Carefully remove the jars with canning tongs. Keep the jars in an upright position at all times, otherwise you may disturb the seal with some of the syrup. Tighten the rings if necessary and allow the jars to cool completely. Check to see that each jar is sealed properly by following the lid manufacturer's directions. Label the jars, including the date, and store in a cool, dry, dark place for at least 1 month before serving. Serve chilled.

Danish Cheese Mold

The vigorous flavors of Camembert and blue cheese are tempered with whipped cream to make a light, yet full flavored cheese bombe.

Beset with toasted whole nuts, this decorative mound is a handsome, help-yourself platter surrounded with an assortment of flatbreads, crackers, and thinly sliced rye and pumpernickel bread.

¼ pound (112 g) Camembert cheese with crust, at room temperature
¼ pound (112 g) blue cheese
1 cup (250 ml) heavy cream
   Roasted, unsalted almonds or filberts

Press the cheeses through a food mill into a mixing bowl and beat with electric beaters until smooth. In a cold mixing bowl, whip the cream with electric beaters until it is very stiff. If you underbeat it, the cream will break down too easily. Fold the whipped cream into the cheese mixture and spoon into an oiled mold. Refrigerate several hours. Dip the mold in warm water momentarily, then slip the cheese mold out onto a pretty serving plate. Garnish with nuts and surround with assorted cream crackers.

Cured Fresh Salmon Filets
GRAVLAX

The open-faced sandwich is elevated to new heights when this delicacy is added.

In addition to an assortment of really good breads, creamery butter, and sliced sweet onions, offer with icy aquavit and cold beer chasers.

Refrigerated in oil, *gravlax* will keep for up to 2 weeks.

1 whole fresh red salmon [about 3 to 4 pounds (1350 to 1800 g)]
⅔ cup (170 ml) coarse (kosher-type) salt
1 teaspoon (5 ml) coarse ground black pepper
½ cup (125 ml) dried dill weed
⅓ cup (85 ml) granulated sugar

Scale the fish, then remove its head, tail, fins, and bones, leaving the fish in one piece. Rinse the fish under cold running water and pat dry. Combine the salt, pepper, dill weed, and sugar. Rub the inside of the fish well with the salt mixture. Press the sides together, sandwiching the salt in between. Spread the remaining salt mixture over the entire outside skin of the salmon. Lay the whole fish in a large glass baking dish that has been sprinkled with more coarse kosher salt. Weight the fish down using a large platter with some heavy cans on top. Refrigerate for 24 hours, undisturbed. To serve the fish, remove excess salt. Slice with a very sharp knife crosswise diagonally into thin slices. Serve cold or at room temperature on buttered slices of rye, pumpernickel, black bread, Swedish rye crisps, or hard breads.

HOW TO STORE GRAVLAX
Place the fish in a sterile jar with lid that is large enough to accommodate the filets comfortably. Pour a good quality olive oil into the jar, submerging the salmon completely.* Stir with a table knife to release any trapped air bubbles. Put the lid on tightly and store in the refrigerator. To use, drain each piece on a paper towel and pat dry.

❧ Alabama Cheese Straws
Makes 4 to 5 dozen

These Southern specialties are great cocktail nibblers. Keep them fresh longest in an airtight container or cookie jar.

  1   pound (450 g) grated, aged, sharp cheddar cheese, at room temperature
  6   tablespoons (90 ml) butter or margarine, at room temperature
  2   cups (500 ml) sifted all-purpose flour
  ½   teaspoon (3 ml) salt
  ½   teaspoon (3 ml) red pepper or a few drops Tabasco sauce

---

*The oil develops an interesting flavor and, used on crisp lettuce and onion salads, it is quite pleasing. If you're so inclined, add a sprig of dill and a clove of peeled garlic to the jar as well.

½ teaspoon (3 ml) Worchestershire sauce
Paprika for garnish

For best results, the cheese and butter must be softened and at room temperature. Place them in a mixing bowl and add the remaining ingredients except the paprika. Blend well with a wooden spoon. Pinch off marble-sized pieces and flatten with your hands. Place side-by-side on an ungreased baking sheet. Mash a criss-cross pattern in the top of each with a dinner fork. They should be about 1½ inches (37 mm) in diameter. Bake at 375° F. until the cheese straws are lightly browned. Sprinkle with paprika, cool, and store in airtight containers.

🌺 Red Pepper Cocktail Jam
Makes 8 cups (2000 ml)

Serve this ruby red jewel of a preserve as a cocktail appetizer with soft cream cheese and crackers—or offer it with homemade corn bread and butter. Red pepper jam makes a lovely condiment with roast meats and poultry and a spectacular glaze for baked ham.

Some folks like it hot—that is, full of hot peppers and Tabasco sauce. As for me, the jam has more possibilities left sweet and sour. But for those who like a kick in the pants, stir in some hot peppers just before you serve the jam or pass Tabasco sauce on the side.

Cook the jam until it is really thick. Since there's no pectin in this preserve, it must have lots of body. Don't open the jam too soon—it really improves with age.

1 dozen big, ripe-but-firm red bell peppers
1 tablespoon (15 ml) salt
2 cups (500 ml) white distilled vinegar
2½ cups (625 ml) sugar (white or brown)

Scrub, stem, and seed the peppers and chop them finely, with a knife or in a food processor (do not over-process). Place the peppers in a bowl and sprinkle with salt. Let stand overnight covered loosely with a clean kitchen towel. Drain the peppers thoroughly. Place in a large, heavy saucepan and add the vinegar and sugar. Bring to a boil and then reduce heat to a simmer. Stirring occasionally, cook until very thick. Spoon boiling preserves into hot, sterilized jelly jars leaving ½ inch (12 mm) headspace. Wipe rims of jars with a clean damp towel. Seal with hot, sterilized lids and rings. Cool jars. When the lids pop down, a seal is good. Store in a cool, dark pantry or cupboard. Let age for a few weeks before serving.

Soups & Stews

Nothing characterizes the heart of ethnic home cooking better than a simmering kettle of soup or stew. Simple to prepare, nourishing, flavorful, and sometimes exotic, this stick-to-your-ribs kind of family fare can be made well in advance and kept on the back burner for late comers.

And what could be more economical? Cooks of every ethnicity have favorite ways of turning the least bit of meat, bones, and even leftovers into a big, hearty broth that will satisfy a hungry family.

The following pages are brimming with inviting concoctions from classic soups to start off a festive dinner to thick, rich main dishes that require little more than a basket of bread and a bottle of wine. There are combinations of meats, sausages, fresh vegetables, assorted beans and peas, rice, lentils, nuts, fish, shellfish, homemade noodles, tender pasta, and plump, light dumplings.

Some are flavored with lager, wine, herbs, or spices. Others are peppery or piquant. Still others are soothing and smooth with the addition of frothy fresh eggs or thick cream.

The great majority of slow simmered meat and vegetable soups and stews benefit greatly from overnight refrigeration. This allows the variety of flavors to blend and harmonize. It also aids in the removal of excess fat, since it can easily be skimmed off the surface while hard and congealed.

However, there are a few exceptions. Soups with egg or cream in the broth, for instance, must be reheated with patience and care to avoid boiling which would curdle them immediately. And fish soups should be served freshly made. That's when the fish is most tender and the broth still light and delicate.

Before you begin to simmer up any of these recipes, I'd like to leave you with these thoughts: in many ways, a soup or stew is like an empty canvas awaiting the painter's brush. The artist may be using all the same colors again and again, but each painting will turn out differently. And so it is with the ethnic cook.

Never be intimidated into thinking a recipe is final.

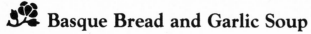 Basque Bread and Garlic Soup
Makes 8 servings

The amount of garlic used here depends on two things: (1) the freshness and strength of the garlic, and (2) your own penchant for this vigorous flavoring. Bear in mind that the actual cloves are removed long before the soup is served.

½	cup (125 ml) imported Spanish olive oil
8	to 10 large garlic cloves, peeled and bruised
2	quarts (2000 ml) strong beef or lamb stock
2	cups (500 ml) stale French bread crumbs, toasted
	Salt and freshly ground pepper to taste
2	ounces (56 g) sherry
4	eggs, well beaten
	Fresh lime wedges

Heat the oil in a heavy skillet and add the garlic. Sauté until nicely browned on all sides, remove with a slotted spoon, and discard garlic. In a soup kettle, bring the garlic-flavored oil and the stock to a brisk boil. Stir in the bread crumbs and reduce heat to a simmer. Add salt and pepper to taste plus the sherry and remove from the heat. Whisk in the beaten eggs and serve immediately, garnished with wedges of fresh lime to squeeze over the soup.

🌺 Basque Rabbit Stew

Makes 4 to 6 servings

On the western plains, this stew features fresh, wild cottontails simmered in a heavy iron kettle over an open fire. Since the rabbit you have access to may not be quite as fresh, the cooking time might need to be adjusted to produce meltingly tender results.

This stew is characterized by healthy doses of garlic and jalapeño peppers, so feel free to get as spicy as you like.

Basque Sheepherder's Bread (*see* index), cheese, olives, and a dry, red Spanish Rioja wine are all that's needed here.

2	to 3 pounds (900 to 1350 g) rabbit pieces
	Salt and pepper
¼	cup (60 ml) olive oil
4	garlic cloves, minced
1	large, green bell pepper, diced
	Chopped jalapeno peppers to taste (optional)
2	onions, peeled and cut in ½ inch (12 mm) wedges
4	medium-sized potatoes, peeled and cut in eighths
1	bay leaf
1	teaspoon (5 ml) crumbled dried thyme
3	tablespoons (45 ml) minced fresh parsley
½	cup (125 ml) dry red wine

Wipe the rabbit with a clean, damp kitchen towel. Salt and pepper both sides. Heat the olive oil in a heavy Dutch oven. Brown the rabbit on all sides and transfer to a platter. Turn the heat down and add the garlic, bell pepper, jalapeños, and onions to the oil. Simmer slowly until the vegetables are soft, stirring often. Return the rabbit to the pan along with the potatoes, bay leaf, thyme, parsley, and wine. Cover tightly and simmer slowly for about 45 to 60 minutes, or until the rabbit and potatoes are tender.

✿ Basque Seafood Stew

BACALAO
Makes 4 to 6 servings

The key to the flavor and creaminess of this stew lies in slow, careful simmering.

Serve *bacalao* with a freshly baked loaf of Basque Sheepherder's Bread (*see* index), a dry red Spanish Rioja wine, and some boiled new potatoes on the side.

1	pound (450 g) salt cod
¼	cup (60 ml) good olive oil
2	onions, peeled and finely minced
1	large onion, peeled and sliced
3	or 4 garlic cloves, peeled and chopped
4	ounce (112 g) jar fire-roasted Spanish pimentos, cut into strips
2	small ripe tomatoes, peeled, seeded, and chopped
1	large green bell pepper, seeded, stemmed, and cut into ¼ inch (6 mm) strips
1	cup (250 ml) diced celery, including tops
	Chopped jalapeño peppers to taste (optional)
¼	cup (60 ml) minced fresh parsley
	Crushed red pepper to taste
1	teaspoon (5 ml) crushed dried oregano
1	bay leaf
1	teaspoon (5 ml) crushed dried thyme
2	pounds (900 g) shelled seafood (any combination of shrimp, crab, or lobster)

Starting the day before, soak the cod in cold water. Change the water no fewer than four times. Prod the fish to find and remove all bones. The next day, cover the fish with fresh water and bring to a slow simmer. After a few minutes, taste the water. If it is salty, pour off the water and repeat this process until the fish no longer gives off salt. Pour off the water and drain well. Set aside. In a heavy Dutch oven or flameproof casserole, combine the olive oil, onions, garlic, pimento, tomatoes, peppers, and celery. Bring to a slow simmer. Cover and cook over low heat, shaking the pan occasionally, until the vegetables are very soft. Cut the cod into stew-like pieces and add to the kettle, along with the parsley, red pepper, and herbs. Cover and simmer very slowly for about 30 minutes, gently shaking the casserole occasionally. Add remaining seafood and simmer, covered, for an additional 5 to 10 minutes. Remove bay leaf. Serve directly out of the casserole, spooning some of the pan juices over each serving.

Caribbean Black Bean Soup
Makes 6 to 8 servings

Akin to America's Southern version, this enchantingly spicy pottage combines the best elements of both Creole and Caribbean cookery.

With minor adjustments in the flavorings, this recipe doubles with great success. And oversized batches can be frozen in airtight containers. Thaw in the refrigerator before reheating.

- 1 pound (450 g) black beans, washed and picked over
- 2 quarts (2000 ml) cold water
- 4 thick slices of bacon
- 3 large onions, finely chopped
- 3 cloves of garlic, peeled and chopped
- 1 large green bell pepper, scrubbed, seeded, and diced
- 1 cup (250 ml) celery, chopped, including tops
- 2 large ripe tomatoes, peeled, seeded, and chopped, or 1 cup (250 ml) canned equivalent
- 1 teaspoon (5 ml) ground cumin
- ½ teaspoon (3 ml) thyme
- ¼ teaspoon (1.5 ml) marjoram
- 1 large bay leaf
- ½ teaspoon (3 ml) oregano
- ½ teaspoon (3 ml) sweet basil
- 2 cups (500 ml) diced smoked ham, or 2 whole smoked pork hocks
- ¼ cup (60 ml) sherry or rum (light or dark)
- 3 or 4 tablespoons (45 to 60 ml) red wine vinegar

Hot pepper sauce to taste
2   whole canned pimentos, chopped
Salt and pepper to taste

Cover the beans with the cold water and soak for several hours. Or, use the quick-soak method and bring the beans to a boil, cook for 2 minutes, then remove from the heat and let stand for about 2 hours before proceeding with recipe.

Render the fat from the bacon in the bottom of a heavy soup kettle. Cook until the bacon is quite brown. Remove bacon, crumble, and set aside. Add onions, garlic, green pepper, and celery to the bacon drippings and sauté until they soften and color slightly. Add the tomato and simmer for a few minutes. Grind the dried spices together using a mortar and pestle or crush and blend well using the back of a spoon. Drain the beans, reserving all of the liquids. Add the beans to the simmering vegetables along with the crushed herbs and spices. In a separate pan, bring the reserved liquid to a boil. Pour the boiling water into the kettle with the beans. Add the pork or ham hocks. Bring to a full boil then reduce heat to a gentle simmer, cover, and cook slowly for about 3 hours, stirring occasionally until the beans are quite soft and their skins have broken. During the last 30 minutes of cooking, stir in the sherry or rum, wine vinegar, hot pepper sauce, chopped pimentos, and salt and freshly ground black pepper to taste. Cool soup completely. If you used pork hocks in the soup, remove them from the kettle. Discard the rind and bone, dice meat, and return to kettle along with the crumbled bacon. Reheat before serving.

GARNISHES

Set out any (or all) of these garnishes and allow each guest to add his own: lemon or lime wedges, chopped hard-cooked egg, avocado slices, sour cream, jicama slices, sprigs of fresh cilantro, capers, chopped scallions including green tops, and/or chopped fresh tomato (seeded and drained).

🌸 German Onion Soup

Serves 4 to 6

Smokey bacon, garlic, herbs, beer, sour cream, potatoes, and yes, onions! This makes, I think, the ultimate onion soup.

To start a meal, top the soup with freshly made croutons from day-old black bread. Or, pass a basket of warm bread with butter at the table.

For a satisfying main course, surround steaming bowls of soup with a board of cheeses, a plate of steamed sausages, cold mugs of beer, and for dessert, a fresh fruit compote.

4	thick slices of smoked bacon
4	large yellow onions, peeled and thinly sliced
1	garlic clove, minced
¼	teaspoon (1.5 ml) crushed dried marjoram
¼	cup (60 ml) minced parsley
1	quart (1000 ml) strong beef stock, or 2 cups (500 ml) stock with 2 cups (500 ml) dark beer
5	medium potatoes, boiled and skinned
	Salt and pepper to taste
	Vinegar to taste
1	pint (500 ml) sour cream
	Hot Croutons (*see* index)

In a heavy-bottomed soup kettle, fry the bacon until it is crisp and brown. Remove from the kettle, drain on paper toweling, crumble, and set aside. Cook the onions and garlic in the bacon fat, stirring often, until the onions are limp and a nice brown color. Add the marjoram, parsley, and beef stock and bring to a boil. Simmer, uncovered for about 20 minutes. Rice the potatoes through a food mill and add directly to the simmering soup. Simmer another few minutes. Taste for salt and pepper, and add the vinegar to your taste . . . it should have just a slight bite. Remove the soup from the heat. Mix some of the hot soup into the sour cream to warm it, then whisk the sour cream into the soup. Warm the soup slightly if necessary, but do not let it boil. Serve immediately topped with hot croutons and crumbled bacon.

German Pea Soup with Bacon

Makes 6 to 8 servings

For the most part, this thick soup is too stout to be relegated to first course status. Instead, make it the main attraction accompanied by sausages, beer, homemade Sour Beer Bread (*see* index), and a freshly baked Strudel (*see* index) for dessert.

1	pound (450 g) dried split green peas
½	pound (225 g) smoked bacon, diced
1	carrot, scraped and chopped
1	celery rib, cleaned and chopped
2	onions, chopped
1	garlic clove, minced
½	teaspoon (3 ml) crushed dried marjoram
¼	teaspoon (1.5 ml) crushed dried thyme
	Pinch of sage
	Salt and pepper to taste
1	quart (1000 ml) strong meat stock

Rinse the peas in a colander, then place in a stainless steel kettle and cover with cold water. Let stand overnight or, for faster soup, bring to a boil for 2 to 3 minutes, drain, and rinse. Fry the bacon in a heavy-bottomed soup kettle. When nicely brown and most of the fat rendered, remove the bacon from the kettle with a slotted spoon and drain on paper toweling. Add the carrot and celery and sauté for a few minutes. Then add the onion and sauté until the onion is limp and golden. Add the garlic, spices, a bit of salt and pepper, and the peas. Cover with the boiling stock. Reduce heat to a slow simmer and cook, stirring occasionally, until the peas are very, very soft (1½ to 2 hours). Add more stock if necessary. Return bacon to kettle, adjust seasoning, and serve hot.

🌺 Greek Chicken Avgolemono Soup

Makes 8 to 10 servings

This tangy, fragrant soup was standard Sunday fare in our home when I was growing up. Mother varied it by adding either rice or orzo and, occasionally, instead of adding the chicken to the soup, she would slice it and serve it on the side.

Orzo macaroni is shaped like extra large grains of rice, and it is available in cellophane packages at most Greek and Middle Eastern import grocers as well as the specialty section of many supermarkets. It has a smooth texture and a "bite" that is quite a treat in this soup.

3	pounds (1350 g) chicken, including neck and giblets
1	small bunch of parsley
1	small whole onion
6	to 8 whole peppercorns
3	or 4 stalks of celery
2	cloves of garlic, peeled
	Salt to taste
1½	cups (375 ml) long grain white rice (not instant), or 1 cup (250 ml) orzo macaroni
	Juice of 2 lemons, strained
3	eggs, well beaten, at room temperature

Place the chicken, with neck and giblets, in a large soup kettle. Cover with about 5 quarts (5000 ml) of water. Bring to a boil, skimming the surface constantly until no more foam rises. Add parsley, onion, peppercorns, celery, garlic, and a bit of salt. Cover and simmer about 45 minutes until the chicken is tender. Lift the chicken, neck, and giblets from the stock and place on a platter to cool completely. Skin the chicken. Pull all of the meat off the bones and cut into bite-sized pieces. Pull the meat from the chicken neck and chop the giblets. Set all of the meat aside. Discard the skin, bones, fat, and sinew. Strain the broth through a wire sieve. Press the juice out of the vegetables using the back of a wooden spoon. Discard the vegetables. Cool the stock and skim the fat off the top. Return the broth to a rapid boil. Sprinkle rice or orzo into the broth and boil, uncovered until tender—about 20 minutes. Test for doneness in the last 5 minutes of cooking. When the rice or orzo is soft, stir the chicken meat back into the kettle. Whisk the lemon juice into the eggs. With the soup still boiling, add a bit of the hot soup to the egg mixture and stir to warm the eggs and prevent them from curdling. Whisk the egg mixture into the boiling soup, then remove the soup from heat immediately. Serve hot accompanied with bread, butter, and olives. If you must reheat this soup, do it very gently and be careful not to let it boil, otherwise the eggs will curdle and separate.

Papou's Greek Stew

Makes 6 to 8 servings

From the island of Crete, my mustachioed grandfather, John Poulos, came many years ago with nothing more than a wealth of spirit and heritage.

As a coal miner in Wyoming, he was able to ease the family's meager existence by coaxing an abundance of home-grown vegetables from the barren soil. Without benefit of recipes or books, he knew instinctively how to create magnificent rounds of yeast bread and kettles of thick, aromatic stew. Much of what he cooked was seasoned with the rich red wine he made by stomping purple grapes and fermenting them in oak barrels, the way his ancestors had done for centuries.

His love for food and wine and life was evident in every aspect of his life . . . and it has transcended generations, cultures, and continents.

Today, my father ferments the robust wine and cultivates the vegetables that my mother combines in this stew . . . just like Papou used to make.

¼   cup (60 ml) imported olive oil
2   pounds (900 g) lean lamb or beef stew meat
6   or 7 cloves of garlic, peeled
2   medium-sized yellow onions, peeled and quartered
    Salt and pepper
1   cup (250 ml) dry red wine
6   ounces (168 g) canned tomato paste

2   cups (500 ml) water or stock
1   bay leaf
1   teaspoon (5 ml) cinnamon
    Peel of 1 orange or tangerine, fresh or dried
4   red-skinned potatoes, quartered
1   bunch of young carrots, scraped and cut into chunks
5   or 6 young stalks of celery, cleaned and cut diagonally
      into chunks
½   pound (225 g) fresh, mature green beans, with ends
      and strings removed, cut in half
¼   pound (112 g) imported Calamata olives

Heat the olive oil in a large heavy kettle. Add the lamb and brown on all sides (about 10 to 15 minutes). Add the garlic, onion, a little salt and pepper, and cook until the onion and garlic are soft. (If you don't want to eat the whole garlic buds when the stew is done, remove them. Many Greeks prefer to eat the whole cooked cloves and consider them to be very healthful and strengthening. Garlic does become sweeter the longer it is cooked—still it's an acquired taste.) Add the wine, tomato paste, water, bay leaf, cinnamon, and tangerine or orange peel. Stir with a long wooden spoon to blend and let the meat simmer slowly with the spices for about an hour or until the lamb is tender. Add the potatoes, carrots, and celery and simmer for about 15 minutes. Then add the green beans and simmer, covered, for 15 minutes until the vegetables are tender but not too soft. Add the olives and cover. Remove from the heat and allow to stand for at least an hour. Reheat just before serving.* Remove the bay leaf and citrus peel and serve the stew in deep wide dishes. Offer a tossed green salad and good bread for dunking, as well as chunks of feta cheese and a jug of deep red wine.

*The stew is at its best when made several hours (or even a day) ahead.

🌹 Greek Rabbit Stew

Makes 6 to 8 servings

Follow the recipe and procedure for Papou's Greek Stew (*see* index), substituting 2 to 3 pounds (900 to 1350 g) of fresh, young rabbit pieces for the lamb.

🌹 Greek Lamb and Lentil Soup

Makes 10 to 12 servings

This soup is thick and hearty—a big meal when it includes good homemade bread and a fruit dessert. Like many meat and vegetable stews, it tastes best after it has been refrigerated overnight, then reheated gently.

Freeze any leftovers in airtight containers. To vary the flavor of leftovers, add a dollop of sour cream or thick plain yogurt to each serving, and some crushed hot peppers if desired.

HEARTY LAMB STOCK
- 3 pounds (1350 g) meaty lamb bones (shank or leg bones are best)
- 3 or 4 whole cloves of garlic, outer papery layer removed
- 1 bay leaf
- 10 to 12 peppercorns
- 3 or 4 stalks of celery
- 1 small bunch of parsley
- 1 large whole onion, peeled of its outer papery layer
- 1 large carrot, scraped
- Salt

Place the bones in a large stock pot. Cover with water and bring slowly to a boil, skimming the surface constantly until no more foam comes to the top. Unless you prefer to strain the stock when it is done, tie the garlic, bay leaf, peppercorns, celery, and parsley together in a cheesecloth bag tied with kitchen twine. Add the onion and carrot to the boiling broth. Cover and simmer for at least 2 or 3 hours. Remove the cheesecloth bag and its contents along with the onion and carrot. Transfer the bones to a platter and, when they are cool, strip the meat off, remove marrow, and set these aside. Discard bones. Skim the fat off the top of the stock. You should have about 3 to 4 quarts (3000 to 4000 ml) of stock. Salt to taste. Set aside.

SOUP

- 1   pound (450 g) spicy pork sausage, bulk or links
- ¾   pound (340 g) lamb stew meat, cut into ½ inch (12 mm) cubes
- 2   large onions, chopped
- 5   or 6 cloves of garlic, peeled and finely chopped
- 1   pound (450 g) brown lentils, washed and picked over
- 3   to 4 quarts (3000 to 4000 ml) of hearty lamb stock or other strong meat stock
- 1   bay leaf
- ½   teaspoon (3 ml) dried or 1 to 1½ teaspoons (5 to 8 ml) fresh thyme
- 1   teaspoon (5 ml) dried oregano
- ¼   teaspoon (1.5 ml) dried marjoram
- 2   carrots, scraped and grated
- 3   medium-sized boiling potatoes, scrubbed and cut into ¾ inch (18 mm) cubes

Salt and freshly ground pepper to taste

Crumble bulk sausage into chunks; slice link sausage into ¾ inch (18 mm) pieces. In a large, heavy stock pot or soup kettle, brown the sausage. Transfer cooked sausage to a piece of paper towel to drain. In the fat, brown the lamb well. Add the onions and stir-fry until they are limp, then add the garlic and continue to cook until the onions are quite soft, but not brown. Return the meat and marrow from the bones to the kettle. Add the lentils to the kettle and pour in the lamb stock. Bring to a rapid boil. Add the bay leaf, thyme, oregano, and marjoram. Cover and simmer for about 1½ hours, until the lentils are very soft. Add the carrots and potatoes and continue to simmer for another 30 minutes until the potatoes are very soft. Add salt and pepper to taste. For best flavor, cool the soup and skim any fat from the surface. Reheat before serving.

Hungarian Cauliflower Soup
Makes 6 servings

I first happened upon this soup in a little Hungarian restaurant in Denver. For years afterward I searched for a recipe that was as thick, creamy, and bursting with cauliflower. Here's the recipe of the soup I finally devised using bits and pieces of a dozen versions. Freshly baked wheat or rye bread with sweet butter and thin slices of aged cheese are blissful companions.

1	medium-sized head of cauliflower
2	cups (500 ml) water (approximate)
1	teaspoon (5 ml) salt
7	tablespoons (105 ml) butter
7	tablespoons (105 ml) flour
1	quart (1000 ml) milk, warmed
½	cup (125 ml) sour cream, at room temperature
	Salt and white pepper to taste
1	cup (250 ml) cheddar cheese, grated (approximate)
	Sweet Hungarian paprika

Trim the cauliflower and break it into flowerlets. Bring the water and salt to a boil. Add the cauliflower, and cook until tender. Drain, reserving liquid. Mash about half the flowerlets and cut the remaining half into small pieces. Make a roux: melt the butter in the bottom of a heavy soup kettle and add the flour a bit at a time, stirring continuously over low heat until the flour just begins to color. Do not brown it! Slowly add the warm milk, stirring continuously until the mixture is smooth. Add the cauliflower and heat until the soup is thick and creamy. Stir a ladle of the hot soup into the sour cream to warm it, then pour the sour cream mixture back into the soup. Add some of the reserved broth if soup is too thick. Taste for seasoning and add salt and white pepper if desired. Serve immediately, topping each bowl with a sprinkling of cheese and a dash of paprika. Hot Homemade Croutons (*see* index) are delicious with this soup.

🌹 Hungarian Goulash Soup

Makes 6 servings

This is what goulash soup should be. A thick, colorful collage of tender meat and abundant vegetables seasoned to the hilt with the likes of caraway, garlic, and sweet paprika. Homemade Csipetke Noodles are added near the end—the final flourish for an authentic Hungarian classic.

 2   tablespoons (30 ml) corn oil
 1   onion, chopped
 2   ribs of celery, diced
 1   tablespoon (15 ml) crushed caraway seeds
 1   pound (450 g) lean beef chuck, cut into 1 inch
       (25 mm) pieces
 2   cloves of garlic, minced
 3   teaspoons (15 ml) sweet Hungarian paprika
 1   small green bell pepper, diced
 8   ounces (224 g) canned tomatoes, well drained
 1   teaspoon (5 ml) tomato paste
     Pinch of marjoram
 1   quart (1000 ml) beef stock (if you substitute canned
       stock, omit salt from this recipe)
 2   large red-skinned potatoes, peeled and diced
 1   carrot, scraped and diced
     Salt and pepper
     Csipetke Noodles (*see* index)

Heat the corn oil in the bottom of a large heavy soup kettle. Add the chopped onion, celery, and caraway seeds and sauté until the onion is limp and the celery barely soft. Add the meat, garlic, and paprika. Toss until the meat has lost all of its redness. Add the green pepper, tomatoes, tomato paste, marjoram, and salt very lightly. Add the quart (1000 ml) of stock, bring to a boil, then reduce heat. Cover and simmer for about 2 hours, stirring occasionally. Add diced potato and carrot and simmer an additional 40 minutes. Allow the soup to cool. Skim any fat off the surface. Taste for seasoning, and add salt and pepper if desired. Return to a simmer. Add the cooked Csipetke Noodles and serve hot.

Hungarian Veal Stew with Mushrooms and Sour Cream

Makes 6 to 8 servings

This delightful main dish is perfectly balanced by a crisp green salad vinaigrette, freshly baked Black Bread (*see* index), a fruity white wine and for dessert, a spectacular Walnut Torte (*see* index).

2   to 4 tablespoons (30 to 60 ml) corn or peanut oil
1   large onion, chopped
2   pounds (900 g) veal shoulder, cut into small strips
     (2 inches × ¼ inch × ¼ inch—50 mm × 6 mm
     × 6 mm)
1   green bell pepper, stemmed, seeded, and cut into 1
     inch (25 mm) chunks
2   cloves of garlic, minced
½   pound (225 g) fresh white mushrooms, cleaned and
     cut into thick slices
2   tablespoons (30 ml) fresh parsley, finely minced
¼   teaspoon (1.5 ml) crushed dried marjoram
1   tablespoon (15 ml) tomato paste
½   cup (125 ml) dry white wine
1   cup (250 ml) stock
     Salt and pepper
½   cup (125 ml) sour cream at room temperature

Heat the oil in a heavy saucepan. Add the onion and sauté until the onion just begins to soften. Add the veal strips and sauté until all the strips have lost their pinkness. Add the bell pepper, garlic, mushrooms, parsley, and marjoram and sauté for another 3 minutes. Blend the tomato paste, wine, and stock. Stir into the veal stew and bring to a good simmer. Taste for seasoning and add salt and pepper if desired. Cover loosely and simmer gently for about 40 minutes, or until the veal is tender, stirring occasionally. Stir some of the hot sauce from the stew into the sour cream to warm it, then slowly pour the sour cream mixture into the stew, stirring continuously, and simmer another 2 or 3 minutes. Serve hot over plain white rice or noodles.

Hungarian Sauerkraut Soup

Makes 6 servings

Here is soup quickly made and especially suited for blustery winter weather. Warm black bread with butter and mugs of beer make it a simple but satisfying meal.

4	thick slices of lean smoked bacon, diced
6	smoked sausage links, cut in thirds
1	medium-sized onion, finely chopped
1	cup (250 ml) cooked smoked ham, diced
2	cups (500 ml) tarhonya (egg barley), boiled and drained according to package (egg barley)
2	tablespoons (30 ml) sweet Hungarian paprika
½	teaspoon (3 ml) crushed caraway seeds
2	cloves of garlic, crushed
2	pound (900 g) jar sauerkraut, drained
4	cups (1000 ml) chicken stock
½	cup (125 ml) sour cream

In the bottom of a heavy soup kettle, brown bacon and sausage links slowly and carefully over medium low heat. Add onion to the fat and sauté until limp. Tilt the kettle and spoon off most of the fat leaving about 2 tablespoons (30 ml). Return to heat and add the ham and the boiled tarhonya, tossing just to brown. Add paprika, caraway seeds, and garlic and simmer another 5 minutes. Add the sauerkraut and the chicken stock. Bring to a boil, reduce heat, and simmer uncovered for about 30 minutes. Add some of the hot liquid to the sour cream and then slowly pour the sour cream mixture back into the hot soup. Serve immediately.

Irish Beef Stew with Lager

Makes 6 servings

Because this stew is simmered in a lazy oven, it needs no tending. It's just perfect for a busy weekend.

Hot homemade soda biscuits with butter and honey and cinnamon baked apples drenched with thick, cold cream make this a homey, yet guest-pleasing autumn dinner.

½	cup (125 ml) flour
	Salt and pepper
1	teaspoon (5 ml) allspice
1½	pounds (675 g) marbled beef stew meat
¼	cup (60 ml) shortening
4	carrots, peeled and chopped
2	large onions, coarsely chopped
2	cloves of garlic, chopped
2	large onions, peeled and quartered
¼	cup (60 ml) minced fresh parsley
1	teaspoon (5 ml) crushed dried rosemary
1	teaspoon (5 ml) crumbled thyme
¼	teaspoon (1.5 ml) dried marjoram
1	bay leaf
1	cup (250 ml) lager
1	packet beef bouillon
	Salt and freshly ground pepper to taste
2	1 inch (25 mm) thick slices day-old French bread
	Dijon mustard

Combine flour, salt and pepper, and allspice in a brown paper bag. Add a few cubes of meat at a time and shake to coat. In a heavy Dutch oven, heat the shortening until it ripples. Fry the meat in the fat until it is brown and crisp on all sides. Transfer to a plate and set aside. Add the chopped carrot, chopped onions, and garlic to the kettle and cook, stirring often, until they are soft and slightly brown. Drain off most of the fat from the pan. Return the beef to the pan and add the quartered onions, herbs, lager, bouillon, and a bit of salt plus some grindings of fresh pepper. Spread the bread slices on both sides with the mustard and place them on top of the beef. Cover and set in a 275° F. oven for about 4 hours, or until the beef is very tender and the bread has disintegrated. Serve hot over buttered egg noodles or with boiled potatoes and peas on the side.

🌺 Baked Irish Lamb Stew
Makes 6 to 8 servings

So simple—a carefree oven casserole of lamb, potatoes, and onions heartily spiked with herbs. All you need add is a crisp salad and crusty bread.

12 medium-sized red-skinned potatoes, peeled
4 large onions, peeled and quartered
3 to 4 pounds (1350 to 1800 g) boneless, trimmed lamb (neck or shoulder) cut into 1 inch (25 mm) cubes
½ pound (225 g) lean thickly sliced bacon, diced
   Generous amount of crumbled thyme (1 teaspoon (5 ml) or more)
2 to 3 tablespoons (30 to 45 ml) minced parsley
   Salt to taste
   Freshly ground pepper
3 cups (750 ml) Hearty Lamb Stock (*see* index)
1 bay leaf

Slice half the potatoes very thin and layer them on the bottom of a large Dutch oven or casserole. Slice the onions ½ inch (12 mm) thick and layer half of the onions on top of the potatoes. Arrange the lamb cubes and bacon over the onions and season generously with the thyme, parsley, salt, and pepper. Cover with the remaining sliced onions. Arrange the remaining potatoes, left whole, over the onions and pour in the lamb stock. Sprinkle the top with more salt and pepper and tuck the bay leaf into the casserole. Cover with a tight-fitting lid or aluminum foil and place in a preheated 350° F. oven for about 2½ hours, or until the meat is very tender and the bottom potatoes have cooked down into a sauce. This stew is best when made the day before you intend to serve it. Refrigerate it overnight, skim any fat from the casserole and reheat in a 350° F. oven until the center is hot.

TO SERVE

Remove the bay leaf. Ladle into soup bowls and serve with Irish Soda Bread (*see* index) and butter and cold beer. You may divide the stew into courses by serving the broth first then following it with the meat and vegetables.

VARIATIONS

1. Add peeled carrots, turnips, and celery cut into 2 inch (50 mm) chunks to the pot in the last 45 minutes of cooking.

2. Add one package of frozen peas (thawed) to the kettle in the last 15 minutes of cooking.

Italian Chick Pea and Pasta Soup
Makes 6 to 8 servings

This soup is very thick and stew-like—a real stick-to-your-ribs kind of meal. I find that it's too hearty to be served with a dinner. Instead, I like to round out the meal with a salad, bread, and cheese, and a good dry wine. Ricotta Coffee Dessert (*see* index) makes a scrumptious finale.

⅓ cup (85 ml) good olive oil
4 cloves of garlic, peeled and finely chopped
½ cup (125 ml) finely minced fresh parsley
2 teaspoons (10 ml) crushed dried rosemary
4 large tomatoes, peeled, seeded, and chopped
32 ounces (900 g) canned chick peas, with liquid
1 quart (1000 ml) meat stock
1 pound (450 g) elbow macaroni, or other small pasta
   Salt and pepper to taste
   Grated Parmesan cheese

Heat the olive oil in the bottom of a large soup kettle. Add the garlic, parsley, and rosemary and simmer for a few minutes. Add the tomatoes, chick peas, and stock and simmer uncovered over low heat for about 15 minutes. Turn the heat up to a boil and add the macaroni. Return to a boil, then turn the heat down so that the macaroni simmers gently until it is almost tender. Stop cooking before the pasta is soft. Turn off the heat and let the soup stand covered for a few minutes. Add salt and pepper to taste. Serve with lots of grated cheese.

Minestrone

Makes 6 to 8 servings

This fresh garden vegetable soup can be savored either hot or at room temperature.

3	tablespoons (45 ml) butter or olive oil
1	onion, peeled and finely chopped
2	cloves of garlic, peeled and finely chopped
	Veal or beef shank bone
2	carrots, scraped and diced
2	stalks of celery, diced, including leafy tops
5	large, ripe tomatoes, peeled, seeded, and chopped
4	large boiling potatoes, diced
1	leek, cut in half, cleansed in several changes of cold water, then chopped
2	cups (500 ml) fresh green beans, cleaned and cut in ¾ inch (18 mm) pieces
3	quarts (3000 ml) light homemade meat stock, boiling
3	small fresh zucchini, well scrubbed, trimmed, and sliced into ¼ inch (6 mm) rounds
½	pound (225 g) fresh spinach leaves, washed and stemmed
1½	cups (375 ml) fresh sweet peas or one 10 ounce (280 g) package frozen thawed peas
2	cups (500 ml) elbow macaroni or other small pasta
½	cup (125 ml) fresh minced parsley

½   cup (125 ml) fresh sweet basil leaves, or 3 to 4 table-
    spoons (45 to 60 ml) dried basil
½   teaspoon (3 ml) crushed dried rosemary
½   teaspoon (3 ml) crushed dried oregano
¼   teaspoon (1.5 ml) ground sage
    Salt and pepper to taste
    Plenty of freshly grated Parmesan cheese

In a large soup kettle, heat the oil, add the onion and garlic, and simmer until the onion is soft and transparent but not brown. Put the shank into the kettle. Add the carrot and celery and when they begin to soften (in about 4 minutes), add the chopped tomatoes. Next, add the potatoes, leek, and green beans, and bring to a good simmer. Pour the boiling stock into the kettle and continue to simmer uncovered over low heat. At this point add about half the total amount of each of the herbs to the soup. When the vegetables are still somewhat resistant to the bite, add the zucchini, spinach, peas, and macaroni to the soup, keeping it simmering all the while. When the macaroni is tender, stir in the remaining herbs and adjust the salt and pepper. Simmer another minute or two. Discard the veal bone (if any marrow is left, put it back into the soup). Sprinkle each serving with plenty of Parmesan cheese and pass extra cheese at the table.

Italian Seafood Stew

CIOPPINO
Makes 6 to 8 servings

Cioppino is a seafood fancier's fantasy, a lusty soup-stew. Even though it probably originated in San Francisco, it is perfectly Italian in spice and sentiment.

Feel free to vary the fish according to your taste and the availability of fresh seafood in your area.

All you really need to enjoy this stew is a hearty appetite and a great big napkin. But I would add a crisp romaine and onion salad, a basket of crusty bread for sauce sopping, and a good dry wine.

    2   tablespoons lemon juice
1½   pound (675 g) live lobster, or 2 large crabs
    ½   pound (225 g) raw, medium-sized shrimp, in the shell
    1   pound (450 g) fresh mussels or clams, well scrubbed
        Fish scraps, including tails, heads, and bones
    1   large yellow onion, coarsely chopped
    1   cup (250 ml) chopped celery, including tops
    ½   cup (125 ml) dry white wine
    ¼   cup (60 ml) good olive oil
    1   onion, finely chopped
    3   to 4 cloves of garlic, finely chopped
    1   bay leaf, crumbled
    1   teaspoon (5 ml) each of crumbled dried thyme,
            oregano, and sweet basil
    ¼   cup (60 ml) minced fresh parsley
    ⅛   teaspoon (.5 ml) powdered saffron
    8   large, ripe tomatoes, peeled, seeded, and chopped
    2   pounds (900 g) raw fish filets (rock cod, red snapper,
            ling cod, etc.)
        Salt and crushed red pepper to taste
        Fresh lemons

In a large kettle, bring 1 quart (1000 ml) of lightly salted water to a rapid boil. Add the lemon juice. Drop the live lobster or crab into the boiling water and cook for about 5 minutes. Remove and cool. Add shrimp to the water and cook briefly—no longer than 1½ minutes. Remove immediately and cool with cold running water. Pour about 1 inch (25 mm) of the hot water into another kettle and steam the mussels or clams until their shells open. Discard the ones that do not open. Pour this water back into the other stock. Add the fish scraps, coarsely chopped onion, celery, white wine, and simmer, uncovered for about 20 minutes. Strain and set stock aside. Heat the olive oil in the bottom of a large soup kettle. Add the onion, garlic, bay leaf, oregano, basil, parsley, and saffron and sauté until the onions are soft and limp. Stir often to prevent sticking or scorching. Add the chopped tomatoes and simmer for several minutes. Pour in the reserved fish stock and bring to a boil. Correct the seasoning. Shell the lobster and crab if you wish, and cut the meat into chunks. If you'd rather, you can cut them into chunks while leaving them in the shell. But be sure to have the proper utensils on hand to make them easy to eat. Shell and devein the shrimp. Cut the raw fish filets into chunks. Add the lobster or crab and the raw fish to the bubbling kettle and simmer for about 5 to 8 minutes. Add the shrimp and clams or mussels and just heat through. Place a piece of each kind of fish into a large soup bowl, ladle the broth over all, and garnish with chunks of fresh lemon. Serve very hot.

❦ Italian Spinach and Meatball Soup
Makes 6 to 8 servings

Here is the essence of home cooking. A fine, flavorful broth full of good things—and available only from your kitchen. You won't find this soup in cans or on the usual restaurant menu. It's a light repast with bread, olives, cheese, and wine, and makes a pleasing first course as well.

1	pound (450 g) ground meat (any combination of lean beef, veal, and pork)
1	egg
½	cup (125 ml) Parmesan cheese, freshly grated
¼	cup (60 ml) fine bread crumbs
¼	cup (60 ml) onion, finely chopped
	Dash of ground nutmeg
	Butter or olive oil
3	cloves of garlic, finely chopped
1	large onion, finely chopped
2	tablespoons (30 ml) flour
2	quarts (2000 ml) strong meat stock, boiling
1	pound (450 g) fresh spinach, washed, stemmed, and drained
½	pound (225 g) pastina, or other small pasta
	Salt and crushed red pepper to taste

Combine the ground meat, egg, cheese, bread crumbs, ¼ cup (60 ml) onion, and nutmeg in a mixing bowl. Blend well with your hands and shape into little meatballs, about ¾ inch to 1 inch (18 mm to 25 mm) in diameter. Brown them in a little hot oil until they are well colored on all sides. Drain on a paper towel. In the bottom of a soup kettle, heat 2 tablespoons (30 ml) of olive oil and sauté the garlic and onion slowly until they begin to disintegrate, but do not let them brown or burn. You may need to add a tiny bit of the stock as they cook. Sprinkle the flour over the onions and cook for a couple of minutes until the flour begins to color. Pour the boiling meat stock into the kettle and bring to a boil, stirring to blend well. Add the pastina and the spinach and simmer until the macaroni is tender. Adjust the seasoning. Return the meatballs to the soup and heat through. Serve hot and pass some grated cheese at the table.

VARIATION
When the soup is finished, two well beaten eggs and a dash of nutmeg may be whisked into the bubbling broth. Remove from heat immediately and serve hot. This makes a creamy soup.

🌹 BORSCHT

There are practically as many variations of *borscht* as there are folks who love it. Eastern European in origin, borscht simply is a healthful, deep claret-colored soup based on fresh beets which is served hot or cold. The similarities end here.

Certain kinds of borscht are creamy with the addition of a frothy egg whisked into the bubbling broth. Other versions feature a steaming hot boiled potato without the jacket drenched with ice cold beet broth and mounded with thick sour cream. What's more, this fragrant soup changes with the addition of chopped egg, chopped and seeded cucumber, chives, lemon rind, and even tiny shrimp.

Still another version, Rusell Borscht (*see* index) is soured by fermenting beets and water in a heavy earthenware crock for up to 3 or 4 weeks. This is the traditional soup and stock for the Jewish Passover holiday.

Recipes for some of the very best variations of this age-old soup follow the basic recipe.

Basic Borscht

Makes 6 to 8 servings

This soup is laden with fresh beets.

2   bunches of beets (8 or 10 medium-sized beets)
1   large onion, finely chopped
2½ to 3 quarts (2500 to 3000 ml) cold water
½   teaspoon (3 ml) salt
    Juice of 1½ lemons, or to taste
2   tablespoons (30 ml) sugar, or to taste

Trim the beets; remove tops and peel away the tough outer skin. Finely chop or grate the beets and place in a large soup kettle along with the onion. Cover with the water and bring the kettle to a boil. Add a little salt and some of the lemon juice. Reduce heat to a simmer and cook, covered, for about 1 hour until the beets are tender. Skim the soup of any foam. Add sugar, lemon juice, and salt to taste and simmer a bit longer. Chill and serve with a steaming whole boiled potato, big dollops of sour cream, chopped scallions, and chunks of moist black bread with butter.

Creamy Borscht

Follow recipe for Basic Borscht (preceding recipe). When the soup is done and the seasoning corrected, remove the soup from the heat. Beat two eggs in a large bowl until they are frothy. Add some of the hot soup gradually to the eggs. Whisk into the soup. Chill and serve with plenty of sour cream.

 Rusell Borscht

JEWISH FERMENTED BEET STOCK
Makes 8 to 12 servings

RUSELL BEETS
10   pounds (4500 g) fresh beets
     Cold spring water

Trim, clean, and peel the beets. Cut into 1½ inch (37 mm) chunks and place in a clean, sterilized 2 gallon (8 l) earthenware or glass crock with a lid. Cover with water to within 2 inches (50 mm) of the top of the crock. Set in a cool, dark place where the crock will go undisturbed. Put the lid on slightly ajar to allow some air to get in. Place a clean kitchen towel over the crock and tie in place with some kitchen twine. Let stand for 1 week.

Remove the towel and lid and skim the surface until no foam remains. To see if the beets are fermenting, dip a clean glass into the center of the crock. Hold the juice up to the light. It should be pink and cloudy. Stir the crock's contents with a long wooden spoon. Again cover with the lid slightly ajar and a new towel tied in place over all. Let stand for 3 to 4 weeks.

Finally the juice should be a clear deep claret, with the pleasant fragrance of good wine vinegar.

SOUP
2   to 3 cups (500 to 750 ml) rusell beets, finely chopped
2   quarts (2000 ml) rusell beet juice
1   onion, finely chopped
1   teaspoon (5 ml) salt, or to taste
3   tablespoons (45 ml) sugar, or to taste
    Juice of 1 lemon, or to taste

Combine the rusell beets, rusell beet juice, onion, and salt in a soup kettle. Bring to a boil, reduce heat, cover, and cook until the beets are tender (about 45 minutes). Add the sugar and lemon juice and simmer for another few minutes. Adjust the flavor to suit your taste. Serve hot or cold with a boiled potato and sour cream.

Creamy Rusell Borscht

Complete the recipe given for Rusell Borscht (preceding recipe). After the seasonings have been adjusted, whisk two eggs until frothy. Add some of the hot soup gradually to the eggs, whisking continually so the eggs won't curdle. Then remove the soup from heat. Whisk in the egg mixture gradually. Do not let the soup come to a boil again. Serve hot or cold with a boiled potato and sour cream.

VARIATIONS

You can vary the soup with accompaniments. For instance, you might offer chopped boiled egg with the hot rusell borscht. With cold rusell borscht, chopped cucumbers, chopped green onions, or chives are very tasty.

Clear Chicken Soup

This is it, folks . . . Jewish penicillin! Enough has been written to attest to the miraculous healing powers of this proverbial concoction that it's a wonder Jews ever get colds in the first place. Alas, they do. My husband is living proof. But sometimes I think he brings on the sniffles just so he can sip this heavenly golden brew. He swears it helps. Well, anyway, it couldn't hurt.

If you intend to follow this lovely light soup with a main course of tender boiled chicken, select 3 pounds (1350 g) of young, meaty chicken parts to boil for the stock. However, if you want just soup with a strong, yellow broth, buy bony pieces of chicken. Many poultry shops sell necks, wings, backs, and giblets at very low prices and these seem to make the very best tasting soup. I save the bony parts from many batches of chicken and store them in my freezer. I add a few of them to the kettle whenever I make chicken stock.

3 pounds (1350 g) of chicken pieces
1½ cups (375 ml) chopped celery, including core and tops
1½ cups (375 ml) coarsely chopped onion

3   carrots, scraped and chopped
2   or 3 large cloves of garlic, peeled but left whole
    Several sprigs of fresh parsley and a bunch of fresh
        dill weed tied together with kitchen string (dried
        dill weed can be used)
1   fresh parsley root
8   to 10 whole peppercorns
    Salt to taste

Place the chicken pieces in a large stainless steel or enamel kettle. Cover with cold water and bring to a slow boil over medium heat. Just as the kettle begins to boil, start skimming off the foam with a fine mesh strainer. Continue to do this until the foam stops rising to the top. Add the remaining ingredients to the kettle, cover, and simmer over low heat for 1 hour or until the chicken is tender. If you are using bony parts that will not be served for anything else, you can let the soup simmer for an additional hour or more. Remove the chicken pieces. Pour the soup through a wire mesh strainer and press down hard with the back of a wooden spoon to extract all the juice from the pulp. Discard the pulp. Skim all the fat off the top of the broth. Return the broth to the kettle. Add Matzo Balls (*see* index) or Kreplach (*see* index) to the soup, cook each accordingly, and serve hot.

Mushroom and Barley Soup with Boiled Flanken
Makes 10 to 12 servings

Many Jewish restaurants offer versions of this popular soup as the prelude to a multicourse dinner. In my opinion, it's much too hearty for a starter. With tender meat sliced and served on the side, it becomes a satisfying main dish. If possible, obtain some marrow bones from your butcher. They will give added flavor. At the table offer good mustard, coarse kosher salt, homemade wholemeal bread with butter, and some crisp raw vegetable sticks. Homemade Honeycake (*see* index) and a pot of tea is a blissful ending.

STOCK

- 2 tablespoons (30 ml) vegetable oil
- 1 teaspoon (5 ml) salt (or to taste)
- 4 to 5 pounds (1800 to 2250 g) of beef flanken with bones
- 1 to 2 pounds (450 to 900 g) marrow bones (optional)
- 1 small bay leaf
- 3 or 4 cloves of garlic, peeled
- 8 to 10 whole peppercorns
- 2 large onions, finely chopped
- 1 cup (250 ml) celery, finely chopped
- 1 large carrot, scraped and finely chopped
- 5 or 6 healthy sprigs of fresh parsley, chopped

SOUP

- 1 cup (250 ml) pearl barley
- 1 cup (250 ml) dried mushrooms
- 1 pound (450 g) fresh mushrooms, cleaned and chopped
- 4 tablespoons (60 ml) butter
- 5 to 6 tablespoons (75 to 90 ml) flour
- 1½ cups (375 ml) milk, warm
  Salt and pepper to taste

In a large heavy kettle, heat the oil until it ripples. Salt the meat lightly and brown it in batches. Brown the marrow bones in the same manner. When the meat and bones are a deep, rich color, put them all back into the kettle along with their juices. Cover with boiling water and bring to a boil. Tie the bay leaf, garlic, and peppercorns together in clean piece of cheesecloth. Hit it once or twice with a kitchen mallet to release the flavors, and add it to the kettle along with remaining ingredients for stock. Cover and simmer for about 2 to 2½ hours until the meat is tender. Lift the flanken from the kettle, wrap in foil, and set aside. Remove the marrow bones, return any marrow to the kettle, and discard the bones. Discard the spice bag. Return the stock to a rapid boil. Add the pearl barley and dried mushrooms to the kettle. Reduce heat to a steady simmer, cover, and cook for about 30 minutes, stirring occasionally. Meanwhile, prepare the fresh mushrooms. Heat the 4 tablespoons (60 ml) of butter in a skillet large enough to hold the mushrooms. Add the mushrooms and sauté until they are dark and limp. Sprinkle flour over the mushrooms, stirring continually until the liquid in the pan thickens. Gradually add the warm milk, stirring continuously. Bring to a boil, stirring, until the mixture becomes thick and creamy. Stir the mushroom mixture into the soup. Simmer for 30 to 40 minutes, until the barley is very soft. Reheat the flanken wrapped in foil in a slow oven. Ladle the soup into soup bowls, and serve the flanken on the side. Pass red and white horseradish, crusty bread and butter, and crisp raw vegetables like scallions, radishes, and celery sticks.

Cold Beet and Cucumber Soup

CHLODNIK
Serves 6 to 8

This Polish *chlodnik* (who-*owed*-nik) is delicious and quite unusual. It's a pretty azalea pink with a tart, refreshing flavor—perfect for hot weather. Serve it ice cold with some warm, crusty black bread and plenty of sweet butter.

1	medium-sized bunch of beets, including tops
2½	quarts (2500 ml) water
	Salt
2	cups (500 ml) sour cream or yogurt, or 1 cup (250 ml) of each
6	scallions, finely chopped, including green tops
1	large cucumber, peeled and diced
1	small bunch radishes, cleaned and sliced
2	tablespoons (30 ml) dill pickle juice
1	tablespoon (15 ml) fresh lemon juice
1	large Polish dill pickle, finely chopped
2	tablespoons (30 ml) dill weed
1	lemon, scored and thinly sliced
2	hard-cooked eggs, finely chopped
6	ounces (168 g) tiny bay shrimp, rinsed and drained

Select beets that are medium-sized and have a shock of healthy green tops. Remove the tops and wash them in a sink full of warm water to which a good shake of salt has been added. Rinse them in cool water and set aside. It's very important that the tops are scrupulously clean. Scrub the beets with a stiff-bristled vegetable brush and rinse them well. Do not peel. Put the beets and tops into a soup kettle, cover them with water, and add about 1 teaspoon (5 ml) of salt. Cover and bring to a boil, then reduce the heat and cook for about 30 minutes, or until the beets are tender when pierced with a sharp knife point. Allow the beets and the liquid to cool. With a slotted spoon, remove the beets and tops from the kettle and reserve the liquid. Peel and dice the beets. Mince the beet tops. Place the beets and minced tops in a large covered bowl or kettle. Place the sour cream and/or yogurt in a blender. Add about 4 cups (1000 ml) of the reserved liquid and blend at low speed until completely mixed. Add this mixture to the beets, along with the chopped scallions, diced cucumber, sliced radishes, dill pickle juice, lemon juice, chopped dill pickle, dill weed, and salt to taste. Mix thoroughly and refrigerate for 5 to 6 hours. This soup will improve with age up to 3 days.

TO SERVE

Score the lemon using a small, very sharp knife. Cut V-shaped grooves the length of the lemon, about ½ inch (12 mm) apart all the way around. Then slice the lemon into thin rounds crosswise. Ladle the cold soup into chilled bowls and float a lemon slice on each. Sprinkle with the chopped egg and a few shrimp. Pass extra sour cream at the table.

Swedish Yellow Split Pea Soup with Pork
Makes 6 to 8 servings

The pork shoulder is simmered slowly, then sliced thin and served on the side with horseradish, brown mustard, and coarse salt.

Bowls of thick, porridge-like soup come steaming hot to the table with chunks of buttered cracker bread and mugs of ice-cold beer.

  1   pound (450 g) yellow split peas, washed and picked
        over
  2   pounds (900 g) lean, boneless pork shoulder
  3   or 4 link sausages, sliced thin
  3   onions, peeled and chopped
  3   carrots, scraped, trimmed, and grated
  3   leeks, trimmed and soaked in several changes of cold
        water, then chopped
       Salt and pepper to taste
1½   teaspoons (8 ml) marjoram
  2   teaspoons (10 ml) dried parsley
  1   teaspoon (5 ml) dried thyme
  ½   cup (125 ml) cubed, cooked ham

Place all the ingredients except the ham in a large stock pot or soup kettle and cover with cold water. Bring to a slow boil, cover and simmer slowly for about 3 hours until the peas are very soft and the pork is tender. In the last half hour, add the ham and taste for seasoning. Remove the pork shoulder from the kettle and slice it thinly. Serve the soup in deep bowls and offer the pork slices on the side.

🏵 GUMBO

A true Black American original, this stew-like soup is said to have been named for the Congolese word for okra, *quingombo*.

Gumbo is thickened with a roux and either okra or a fine powder made of ground, dried sassafras leaves called filé, which is available in most specialty grocery stores around the country. Okra is cooked right along with the soup, while filé is nearly always added at the very end. Three cups (750 ml) of fresh chopped okra has the thickening power of about 1 tablespoon (15 ml) of filé.

The roux for a gumbo takes plenty of time and patience and the cook has got to stick with the pot. The flour, cooked in an equal amount of hot fat, must be stirred and attended until it is a deep brown color. If the mixture should burn, throw it out and start all over.

Gumbo can accommodate an infinite assortment of shellfish, sausage, poultry, or ham. The combination and quantity are a matter of personal taste. When adding raw oysters the gumbo will become thinner because of their inherent moisture. Therefore, you may want to thicken the soup before you add any oysters.

Serve gumbo hot in wide shallow bowls of boiled white rice. A skillet of crisp cornbread dripping with butter is the best accompaniment. For dessert, have a warm Peach Cobbler (*see* index) with cream and a dash of Southern Peach Brandy (*see* index).

🌺 Chicken and Okra Gumbo

Makes 4 to 6 servings

2	to 3 pounds (900 to 1350 g) frying chicken, cut in eighths
	Salt and pepper
	Flour
¼	cup (60 ml) peanut oil
	Bacon grease
¼	cup (60 ml) all-purpose flour
1½	pounds (675 g) fresh okra, washed and stemmed
1	onion, chopped
2	cloves of garlic, minced
2	large ripe tomatoes, peeled, seeded, and chopped
1	large green bell pepper, seeded, stemmed, and chopped
½	teaspoon (3 ml) crushed rosemary
½	teaspoon (3 ml) crushed thyme
4	tablespoons (60 ml) minced parsley
2½	quarts (2500 ml) boiling chicken stock
	Salt and pepper to taste

Wipe the chicken with a clean, damp kitchen towel and dry it with paper towels. Salt and pepper lightly on both sides and dredge the pieces in flour. In a large, heavy kettle, heat the fats and brown the chicken well on both sides. Transfer chicken to a heated platter. Add enough flour to the hot fat to make a roux. Stir constantly until the mixture browns. Add okra, onion, garlic, tomatoes, green pepper, and herbs to the roux and simmer for about 10 minutes. Return the chicken to the kettle and pour in the boiling stock. Cover and simmer for about 1 to 1½ hours until everything is very tender. For a thicker gumbo, leave lid off. If a thinner consistency is desired, add boiling water. Adjust the seasoning and serve over boiled white rice.

🌹 Creole Gumbo Filé

Makes 8 to 10 servings

½	cup (125 ml) peanut oil
½	cup (125 ml) all-purpose flour
2	large onions, peeled and chopped
3	cloves of garlic, peeled and chopped
1	large green bell pepper, scrubbed, stemmed, seeded, and chopped
3	or 4 stalks of celery, chopped
4	large, ripe tomatoes, peeled, seeded, and chopped (with liquid)
1	teaspoon (5 ml) crushed thyme
1	bay leaf
¼	cup (60 ml) minced fresh parsley
2	teaspoons (10 ml) paprika
	Salt and red pepper to taste
1	pound (450 g) sausage, cut in 1 inch (25 mm) pieces (use either Louisiana hot sausage, smoked sausage, or any garlic or hot-flavored pork sausage)
½	pound (225 g) good smoked ham, cut in ¾ inch (18 mm) cubes
8	to 10 chicken wings
2½	quarts (2500 ml) boiling homemade chicken stock, plus a little more if needed
1	pound (450 g) medium shrimp, shelled and deveined
1	pound (450 g) crab meat
6	cups (1500 ml) raw oysters with liquid
1	tablespoon (15 ml) filé powder

In a large, heavy saucepan, heat the peanut oil until it ripples. Add the flour to make a roux. Stir constantly, adjusting the heat when necessary, until the roux is deeply browned. Add the onions, garlic, pepper, and celery and simmer for about 20 to 25 minutes until the vegetables are very soft. Add the tomatoes and their liquid and simmer another 15 minutes. Add the thyme, bay leaf, parsley, paprika, a bit of salt (remember the ham and sausage are salty), and red pepper. Cover and continue to simmer. In a very large, heavy soup kettle, brown the sausages and ham in their own fat over low heat. Remove the tips from the chicken wings and discard. Cut the wings in two at the joint. When enough fat has been rendered from the sausages, add the chicken wings to the kettle and brown. Add the roux with all the vegetables and spices plus the boiling stock to the meat. Simmer carefully for about 1 hour. Add the shrimp, crab meat, oysters, and filé powder and simmer slowly for an additional 15 minutes. If the soup is too thick for you, add some boiling stock. Taste for seasoning. Serve hot over rice.

Seafood Gumbo

Makes 6 to 8 servings

2   pounds (900 g) medium-sized raw shrimp in shells, preferably with heads
1   large onion, sliced
3   tablespoons (45 ml) butter
3   tablespoons (45 ml) flour
2   tablespoons (30 ml) oil or butter
2   large onions, peeled and chopped
5   or 6 large, ripe tomatoes, peeled, seeded, and chopped (with liquid)
4   cloves of garlic, peeled and minced
1   bay leaf
½   teaspoon (3 ml) crushed rosemary
1   teaspoon (5 ml) paprika
    Salt and red pepper to taste
1   to 2 pounds (450 to 900 g) crab meat

4   to 6 cups (1000 to 1500 ml) raw oysters (with liquid)

1   tablespoon (15 ml) filé powder

Peel and devein the raw shrimp and take off heads. Place shells and heads in a large kettle and cover with about 2 quarts (2000 ml) of salted water. Add a sliced onion and bring to a boil. Cook for about 30 minutes. Strain and discard shells and heads. Reserve stock for gumbo. Melt 3 tablespoons (45 ml) of butter in a large saucepan. Add flour and make a roux, stirring until the mixture turns a deep, rich brown. Add the shrimp to the roux and simmer for a few minutes, stirring continually, and set aside. In a large, heavy kettle, heat the oil and sauté the chopped onion until it is limp. Add the tomatoes, garlic, bay leaf, rosemary, paprika, and salt and pepper and continue to simmer for 15 to 20 minutes. Add the shrimp and roux plus about 1½ quarts (1500 ml) or more of boiling shrimp stock. Bring to a simmer. Add crab meat and oysters and cook gently for about 15 minutes. Turn heat off and stir in filé powder. Let stand for about 10 minutes before serving. Ladle over hot boiled rice in shallow soup bowls.

 ## Southern Corn Chowder

Makes 6 to 8 servings

Thick and creamy, this chowder is the best way I know to take advantage of a bountiful yield of summer corn. This soup makes a fine lunch or a tasty first course. And it should always be served freshly made.

8   ears of summer corn, husked

4   tablespoons (60 ml) butter

2   large onions, finely chopped

1   large green bell pepper, seeded, stemmed, and diced

2   large boiling potatoes, peeled and diced

¼   cup (60 ml) fresh minced parsley

2   to 3 tablespoons (30 to 45 ml) all-purpose flour

1   quart (1000 ml) milk

1   pint (500 ml) heavy cream
    Salt and white pepper to taste
    Butter
½   pound (225 g) bulk sausage, or several slices of
    bacon, browned, drained, and crumbled

Choose thick yellow corn (hog corn) for the best tasting chowder. Stand each husked ear on end and, using the blade of a knife, scrape down all the kernels. When the kernels have been removed, scrape the cob with the knife to extract as much of the "milk" as possible. In the bottom of a soup kettle, melt the butter and sauté the onions and pepper until they are very soft, but not brown. Stir them often and keep the heat low. Add the corn and sauté for a few minutes. Add the potatoes and parsley, cook for 2 to 3 minutes, then sprinkle with flour and stir until the mixture begins to thicken. Stir in the milk and cream and bring to a slow boil. Simmer gently for 30 to 45 minutes, stirring often. Salt and pepper to taste and stir in another lump of butter until it melts. Stir in the sausage or bacon. Serve very hot with bread and butter and hot pepper sauce if desired.

Southern Oyster Stew

Makes 6 to 8 servings

This soup is as soothing as it is tasty. I like it with crisp oyster crackers or warm buttered toast. It's at its peak when freshly made.

1   quart (1000 ml) milk
1   pint (500 ml) heavy cream
1   bay leaf
¼   pound (112 g) plus 6 tablespoons (84 g) butter
2   onions, finely chopped
3   stalks of celery, diced
1   clove of garlic, finely chopped
¼   cup (60 ml) fresh minced parsley
4   dozen raw oysters (with liquid)
    Salt and red or white pepper to taste

In a large saucepan bring the milk, cream, bay leaf, and ¼ pound (112 g) of butter to a gentle boil. Simmer while you prepare the remaining ingredients. In a large skillet, melt the remaining butter and add the onions, celery, and garlic. Cook slowly until the vegetables are soft, but not brown. Drain the oysters, reserving the liquid. Add the oysters and parsley to the skillet and sauté until the edges of the oysters begin to curl. Add the oyster liquid plus all the ingredients in the skillet to the simmering milk. Discard the bay leaf and stir in a big chunk of butter. Add salt and pepper and serve very hot.

 # Russian Cabbage Soup

SCHI
Makes 6 to 8 servings

A Russian home without *schi* is like a Jewish home without chicken soup. It's a staple. A tradition. And each cook has a version.

Feel free to spice the kettle to suit yourself. This version is best when made at least a day in advance and reheated.

2   pounds (900 g) meaty beef bones (crosscuts or shanks are best)
1   parsley root
2   leeks, trimmed, cut in half and soaked in several changes of cold water to remove all sand, then chopped
1   carrot, scraped, trimmed, and chopped
1   large onion, peeled and quartered
    Few sprigs of parsley
2   bay leaves
10   to 12 peppercorns
2   tablespoons (30 ml) butter
2   onions, peeled and chopped
2   cloves of garlic, peeled and finely chopped
2   tablespoons (30 ml) flour
1   large, firm head of green cabbage, shredded
2   large potatoes, peeled and cut in ¾ inch (18 mm) cubes

2   large, ripe tomatoes, peeled, seeded, and chopped
    Salt and pepper to taste

Cover the bones with cold water in a large soup kettle and bring to a slow simmer, skimming off all foam that rises to the surface. Add parsley root, leeks, carrot, onion, sprigs of parsley, bay leaves, and peppercorns. Cover and simmer slowly for 3 to 4 hours. Transfer meaty bones to a plate to cool. Strain the stock in a large wire sieve. Press down hard on the vegetables and herbs to extract their juices. Discard the vegetables, peppercorns, and herbs. Return the stock to the kettle and bring to a simmer. Strip meat from bones, plus any remaining bone marrow and return to the kettle. In a large skillet, melt the butter and sauté the chopped onions and garlic until very soft but not brown. Sprinkle with flour and stir until mixture browns. Pour a couple of ladles of hot soup into the skillet and cook for a few minutes until all ingredients are well blended. Pour this mixture into the soup. Add shredded cabbage and simmer, covered, for 15 minutes. Add the potatoes and simmer for an additional 15 minutes. Stir in the tomatoes, salt and pepper to taste, and simmer for 2 or 3 minutes. Serve hot.

 **Russian Kidney Bean and Walnut Soup**

Makes 6 to 8 servings

Good homemade black bread and a pot of sweet butter is a fine addition to this meal-in-a-kettle.

2   cups (500 ml) dried kidney beans, washed and
    picked over
2   quarts (2000 ml) cold water or meat stock
1   bay leaf
2   garlic cloves, finely chopped
3   tablespoons (45 ml) butter
2   large onions, peeled and finely chopped
2   teaspoons (10 ml) all-purpose flour
½   cup (125 ml) finely chopped walnuts
    Chopped or ground dried red peppers to taste

½   cup (125 ml) fresh parsley, finely minced
     Salt and freshly ground black pepper to taste
     Sour cream or yogurt

Cover the beans with the water or stock and bring to a boil. Add the bay leaf and finely chopped garlic and simmer slowly for about 2 hours until the beans are soft. In a large skillet, melt the butter and sauté the onions until they are very soft, but not brown. Sprinkle with the flour and cook, stirring continually, for 2 or 3 minutes until the mixture browns. Stir in some liquid from the soup and cook another minute or so to blend all ingredients. Pour this mixture into the simmering soup. Stir in the walnuts, red pepper, parsley, and salt and pepper. Simmer for another 25 minutes, stirring often. Remove the bay leaf and serve hot. Top each serving with a big dollop of thick sour cream or yogurt if desired.

 ## Russian Lamb and Coriander Soup

CHIKHIRTMA
Makes 6 to 8 servings

Saffron, lemon, and fresh coriander are the keys to this fine broth. Many Russians use mutton but, frankly, I find the flavor too gamy for my tender American palate. I use lamb instead.

Many versions of this soup use white vinegar instead of the freshly squeezed lemon. And it is possible to substitute dill weed or mint leaves for the fresh coriander.

 3   pounds (1350 g) very meaty lamb bones
 1   large onion, peeled and quartered
 2   cloves of garlic, peeled
10   to 12 whole peppercorns
 2   or 3 stalks of celery, including tops
      Several sprigs of fresh coriander
      Salt
 2   to 3 tablespoons (30 to 45 ml) butter
 2   onions, finely chopped
 1   tablespoon (15 ml) flour

½ teaspoon (3 ml) powdered saffron
   Pepper to taste
   Juice of 1 lemon, strained
2 eggs, well beaten, at room temperature

Cover the meaty bones with cold water in a large soup or stock kettle. Bring to a slow boil, skimming the surface until no more foam rises. Add the quartered onion, whole garlic, peppercorns, celery, and a few sprigs of coriander, plus a bit of salt. Cover, and simmer slowly for about 3 to 4 hours until the meat is very tender. Remove the meat from the broth and set it on a plate to cool. Strain the broth through a large wire sieve. Press down hard on the vegetables to extract their liquid. Discard the vegetables and peppercorns. Return the stock to the soup kettle. Strip the meat from the bones. Cut away pieces of fat and sinew. Cut the meat into bite-sized pieces, and return to the broth. In a skillet, melt the butter and sauté the onions until they are very soft, but not brown. Sprinkle the flour over the onions and cook, stirring until the mixture browns. Add a ladle of the broth to this skillet and simmer for 2 or 3 minutes, stirring occasionally. Add the the soup in the kettle to a boil. Pour the mixture in the skillet into the boiling soup. Cook for several minutes, stirring occasionally. Add the saffron and stir to dissolve. Season with salt and pepper to taste. Beat the lemon juice into the eggs. Add a spoonful of the hot soup and mix to warm the eggs. Whisk the egg mixture into the boiling soup. Remove from the heat immediately. Ladle into soup bowls and sprinkle each with some chopped fresh coriander or dill. Serve immediately. If you have to reheat this soup, do it very slowly, and never let the soup come to a boil, or the eggs will curdle.

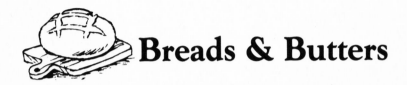 # Breads & Butters

Home-baked bread and the ethnic kitchen are practically synonymous. Earthy, honest, wholesome, and loving, the very essence of good home cooking is displayed in a simple loaf of bread.

This collection offers coarse, crusty breads, sweet doughs, and quick breads. There's one to enhance practically every dish throughout this book.

In an age of mass-produced sponge-like loaves, the creation of homemade bread has taken on the aura of being nearly an art form. Baking it for family and friends is considered to be a loving, giving gesture—a rare treat that never fails to find praise.

Good bread has texture and character. It is tangible nourishment for both body and soul.

In a warm fragrance-filled kitchen, when the scent of yeasty dough pervades the senses, one realizes that bread baking is truly one of life's most gratifying experiences.

If you're a seasoned bread baker, perhaps you'll discover some new taste treats within this chapter. And if you're inexperienced, here are some pointers that will soon have you rolling in dough:

1. Work in a pleasantly warm room, free from drafts. In other words, close all doors and windows.

2. Use fresh, dated yeast. I prefer dry active yeast which works at 110° F. to 115° F. Hotter temperatures kill the living yeast while cooler liquids make it sluggish.

3. Use a candy thermometer to test temperatures until you're experienced enough to test by feel.

4. Have all ingredients at room temperature, or even slightly warm. You can warm the mixing bowl and utensils with hot, running water, for instance. Never add anything cold to the dough.

5. Mix the dough in a large, heavy mixing bowl. Place a folded, damp kitchen towel underneath to keep the bowl from slipping.

6. If the board becomes too sticky during kneading, scrape it clean with a spatula and dust with fresh flour.

7. Don't try to work out your anger by kneading dough. It takes a good 15 to 20 minutes of quick, gentle kneading to sufficiently develop the gluten. Never tear or handle the dough harshly.

8. When it comes to rising, think of the dough as a living thing—a baby if you will. It needs to be protected from drafts and nursed in a warm spot. Here are some rising spots that work well:

The kitchen sink—Set the bread bowl into a sink half full of hot water. Do not get water into the bowl. Cover the bowl with a couple of thicknesses of toweling and add hot water periodically to keep the temperature up.

A closed oven—Either preheat your oven to 200° F. for a minute or two and then switch it off, or set a large shallow pan of boiling water on the bottom of a cold oven and place the bread bowl on a rack over the water. In either case, keep the door closed to retain the heat.

Whole grain and unusual flours can be obtained at many health food stores. You might also refer to the Yellow Pages for local flour mills. Ethnic bakeries will sometimes sell sacks of flour to retail customers.

Basque Sheepherder's Bread
Makes 1 large loaf

On the vast, dusty rangeland of Southern Wyoming where I was reared, you could ride for miles across a sea of sagebrush and find nothing but the occasional covered wagon of a Basque sheepherder's camp.

The Spanish Basques who tended the flocks were strong, fiercely proud men. Undaunted by harsh elements, relentless solitude, and prowling coyotes, they toiled to support their families back in Spain, and ultimately, to bring their relatives to America.

Basque men are by heritage good, inventive cooks as evidenced by this crusty, voluptuous bread. Concocted of the barest essentials and baked in the camp soup kettle, it rivals fine bakery bread in taste and texture.

A note of touching tradition: when the loaf is done, the herder slashes its top with the sign of the cross and offers the first slice to his revered companion, the sheepdog.

Out on the prairie, sheepherder's bread is baked in the embers of a lazy campfire. But I suggest you bake it at home in the range.

8   tablespoons (120 ml) soft butter or lard
½   cup (125 ml) granulated sugar
2   teaspoons (10 ml) salt
3   cups (750 ml) boiling water
2   packages active dry yeast
9   to 10 cups (2250 to 2500 ml) all-purpose flour
     Vegetable oil

In a big crockery bread bowl, combine butter, sugar, and salt. Add hot water and stir until mixture melts. Allow to cool to 110° F. to 115° F. (use a candy thermometer). Stir in the yeast, cover with a clean kitchen towel and place in a warm (80° F.), draft-free spot for about 15 minutes until the mixture is bubbly. Add 5 cups (1250 ml) of flour a bit at a time, stirring with a wooden spoon until you have a thick batter. Slowly stir in more flour until the dough is workable. Turn the dough out onto a floured board and knead for 10 minutes, adding flour when the dough gets sticky. Wash and dry the mixing bowl and paint it with a thin coating of vegetable oil. Place the dough in the bowl and turn to coat with oil on all sides. Cover the bowl with the towel, let rise in a warm (80° F.) spot for about 90 minutes until doubled in bulk. Punch down and knead on a floured board until the dough becomes a smooth ball. Cut a circle of foil to fit the bottom of a well seasoned 5 quart (5000 ml) cast iron or heavy aluminum Dutch oven. Paint the entire inside of the pan, including the underside of the lid, with vegetable oil. Place the dough into the kettle and cover with the lid. Let the dough rise about an hour until the dough pushes the lid up about ½ inch (12 mm). Watch closely. Bake *with the lid on* in a preheated 375° F. oven for 12 minutes. Remove the lid and continue to bake for 30 to 35 minutes until the loaf is golden brown and sounds hollow when thumped with your fingers. Turn the loaf out onto a rack to cool. Serve warm with sweet butter or slices of cheese.

🏵 Caribbean-Style Banana Bread

Makes one 9 inch × 5 inch × 3 inch
(22½ cm × 12½ cm × 7½ cm) loaf

This sweet, flavorful bread need not be served just for breakfast or snacks (while admittedly it is divine for both such occasions).

For a change, serve it as a foil for highly seasoned concoctions like spicy *Black Bean Soup* (*see* index) or peppery *Cuban Pot Roast* (*see* index).

This recipe doubles successfully and freezes without measurable loss of flavor.

½	cup (125 ml) butter
½	cup (125 ml) packed brown sugar
1	egg, well beaten, at room temperature
¼	cup (60 ml) Jamaican rum
1	teaspoon (5 ml) vanilla extract
2	cups (500 ml) all-purpose flour, unsifted
1	teaspoon (5 ml) baking powder
½	teaspoon (3 ml) soda
½	teaspoon (3 ml) salt
¾	teaspoon (4 ml) grated nutmeg
1¼	cups (310 ml) mashed, very ripe bananas
½	cup (125 ml) coarsely chopped walnuts
½	cup (125 ml) white seedless raisins (optional)
½	cup (125 ml) fresh, shredded coconut (optional)

Cream butter and sugar together. Beat in the egg until light and fluffy. Stir in rum and vanilla. Sift all dry ingredients together.

Add to the butter-sugar mixture, alternately with the mashed bananas, mixing well after each addition. Fold in the nuts and either coconut or raisins. Pour into a well buttered and floured loaf pan and spread batter evenly. Bake in a preheated 350° F. oven for about 1 hour and 15 minutes, until the bread shrinks from the sides of the pan and a straw inserted in the center comes out clean. Cool for about 30 minutes in the pan, then unmold and completely cool on a rack. Wrap tightly in plastic wrap or waxed paper and foil. Serve at room temperature with plenty of sweet butter.

Pumpkin Bread

Makes three 9 inch × 5 inch × 3 inch
(22½ cm × 12½ cm × 7½ cm) loaves

This is an interesting dinner bread with spicy foods like *Black Beans and Rice* (*see* index) or other highly seasoned dishes of meats, beans, or poultry.

Cooked, pureed red yams can be substituted for the fresh pumpkin with equal success.

Pumpkin bread freezes very well and can be stored for months. Serve it slightly warm with lots of soft sweet butter.

2	cups (500 ml) fresh or canned pumpkin puree
3	cups (750 ml) packed brown sugar
1	cup (250 ml) corn oil
4	eggs, at room temperature
2	teaspoons (10 ml) vanilla extract
3⅓	cups (835 ml) all-purpose flour
2	teaspoons (10 ml) baking soda
2	teaspoons (10 ml) salt
1	teaspoon (5 ml) baking powder
1½	teaspoons (8 ml) ground cinnamon
¼	teaspoon (1½ ml) cardamom
½	teaspoon (3 ml) ground cloves
½	teaspoon (3 ml) ground mace
½	teaspoon (3 ml) freshly grated nutmeg
½	teaspoon (3 ml) ground Jamaican ginger

½   teaspoon (3 ml) allspice
⅔   cup (170 ml) unsweetened pineapple juice, orange juice
    or coconut milk

OPTIONAL
1¾   cup (430 ml) coarsely chopped pecans or walnuts
    Grated coconut to taste
1   cup (250 ml) chopped, drained pineapple
1   cup (250 ml) chopped dates

Here is the procedure for preparing fresh pumpkin for use in this recipe. Cut the pumpkin in half with a large knife. Scrape out the seeds and strings. Place halves in a shallow baking dish, cut side down and cover tightly with foil. Bake at 350° F. for half an hour. Turn them right side up and continue to bake, tightly covered, about 1 hour or until they are tender. Cool completely. Scoop out all the meat and puree in a blender or food processor. One 2-pound pumpkin should yield about 2 cups (500 ml) of puree. Set aside.

In a large mixing bowl, beat together the brown sugar and oil. Add the eggs one at a time and beat well after each addition. Mix in the vanilla extract. Sift all dry ingredients together and beat into the batter gradually, alternating with the juice, until smooth. Stir in the pumpkin puree with a wooden spoon and fold in any of the optional ingredients. Pour into three well buttered and floured loaf pans and set on the middle rack of a preheated 350° F. oven until the bread tests done. Cool in pans on a rack for about 30 minutes, then unmold on the rack and cool completely. Serve fresh and warm with butter, or wrap in waxed paper and foil for the freezer.

🌸 Greek Easter Bread

Makes 2 braided or French-style loaves
or three 8 inch (200 mm) rounds

This is my mother's recipe—a slightly sweet, anise-flavored braid with gaily colored Easter eggs nestled into the dough.

Traditionally, this bread is served as part of Easter dinner with roast leg of lamb and all the trimmings. But we like it best toasted and buttered for breakfast.

Mom's first encounter with this bread wasn't enormously happy. "You wanna make your husband happy?" queried Meha, a well meaning but mostly meddling Greek neighbor. "I teach you to make the finest Easter bread."

Anxious to please her new husband, my newlywed, non-Greek mother stood by as Meha squandered every drop of flour, sugar, eggs, and a month's grocery money's worth of pure cream and butter. "You wanna make a bread right you gotta use only the best," Meha insisted.

When the cloud of flour lifted, every kettle in Mom's kitchen was stuffed with dough. Too much for Mom's oven, the two floury fraus carted the burgeoning batch off to the local baker and begged for space in his ovens.

That night Mother arranged the mountain of breads on the kitchen table, so Dad would see them first thing. She waited excitedly, sure that he would be proud and pleased.

Dad walked in the door, hung up his hat and huffed, "Where'd you get all this Easter Bread? I don't even like it!"

2	packages dry yeast
½	cup (125 ml) warm water (110° F. to 115° F.)
1	cup (250 ml) milk
⅔	cup (170 ml) sugar
¼	pound (110 g) soft butter
1	teaspoon (5 ml) salt
1	teaspoon (5 ml) oil of anise
1½	teaspoons (8 ml) whole anise seeds
½	teaspoon (3 ml) cinnamon or a few drops of cinnamon oil to taste (optional)
4	eggs at room temperature, well beaten
5	to 6 cups (1250 to 1500 ml) sifted all-purpose flour
8	or 9 hard-boiled eggs in their shells, dyed red with food coloring or Easter egg dye
1	egg, beaten with a little water for wash
	Sesame seeds

Sprinkle the yeast into the warm water and stir to dissolve. Let stand in a warm place. Scald the milk and set it aside to cool slightly. Combine the sugar, butter, and salt in a large bread bowl and cream well. Add the warm milk and stir to melt the butter completely. Add the oil of anise, anise seeds, and cinnamon. When this mixture falls below 115° F., add the dissolved yeast mixture and blend well. Add the beaten eggs and blend. Add the flour gradually, stirring first with a wooden spoon then mixing with your hands until you have a soft but not-too-sticky dough. Turn the dough out onto a lightly floured board and knead until it is smooth and elastic. Place the dough into an oiled bread bowl, cover with a slightly damp kitchen towel, and place in a warm spot (80° F.) away from drafts until it rises to double its original size. Punch the dough down, cover, and let rise again to double its bulk. Punch it back once more.

On a lightly floured surface, using oiled hands, shape the dough into loaves using any of the following methods.

For two braided loaves: Divide the dough into six equal parts. Working on a lightly floured surface, roll each part into a rope about 14 inches (350 mm) long. Lay three ropes side-by-side and braid them together. Pinch each end together and tuck under. Place each on a lightly greased cookie sheet.

For three round loaves: Divide dough into three equal parts. From each part, pull off a small handful of dough and set aside to use for braided trim. Form each third into a round loaf and place in lightly oiled 8 inch (200 mm) skillets, cake pans, or onto greased cookie sheets. Divide the three reserved trim pieces into thirds and roll into ropes about 18 inches (450 cm) long each. Lay three ropes side-by-side and braid. Repeat with remaining ropes until you have three braided lengths. Bring the ends of each braid together to form a circle and pinch together. Lay a braided circle on the top of each round loaf.

To make two "french" loaves: Divide the dough into two equal parts. Shape each into a loaf about 12 inches to 14 inches (300 mm to 350 mm) long. Place each on a lightly greased cookie sheet.

To finish all loaves: Make a pretty design by sinking dyed Easter eggs into each loaf. Don't bury the eggs, but push them down deep, because they will rise during baking.

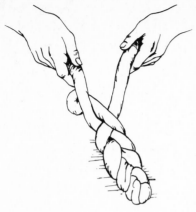

Brush each loaf with egg wash and sprinkle generously with sesame seeds.

Let the loaves rise until almost double in bulk. Bake in a preheated 375° F. oven for 25 to 30 minutes until the bread is richly browned and hollow-sounding when thumped with your fingers. Turn loaves onto a rack and cool thoroughly before serving.

🌹 Pita Bread

Makes 2 dozen

The making of homemade *pita* (sometimes called Middle Eastern pocket bread) is a fairly simple procedure, and the breads can be used in dozens of different ways.

Filled with grilled Greek Lamb Kebobs (*see* index), for instance, it makes an easy out-of-hand barbecue. Stuffed with melted cheese, it's· a wonderful accompaniment for soups and salads. Any kind of sandwich filling you can think of works beautifully in slit pockets. And halves broiled with butter, herbs, and grated cheese make a quick and delicious dinner bread. For appetizers, toast halves in the oven until crisp, then break into "chips" for dipping.

Stacked in plastic bags, pita freezes very well and can be thawed instantly in a warm oven.

    1   package active dry yeast
    2   cups (500 ml) warm water (105° F.)

1   tablespoon (15 ml) unsalted shortening
2   teaspoons (10 ml) sugar
6   cups (1500 ml) all-purpose white flour (approximate)
2   teaspoons (10 ml) salt
    Olive oil

Dissolve the yeast in the water in a large, warm mixing bowl. Add the shortening and sugar and mix with your fingers until everything is dissolved. Combine flour and salt. Gradually add to the yeast mixture, blending with a wooden spoon first, and then your hands until you have a nonsticky, workable dough. Add more or less flour if necessary. Lightly oil another warm mixing bowl (use a big earthenware bread bowl if you have one) and place the dough in it, turning once to coat with oil. Cover with a clean kitchen towel and let it rise in a warm (80° F.), draft-free spot to double its bulk, about 45 to 50 minutes. Punch the dough back, and using lightly oiled hands, divide the dough into 24 equal balls. Shape them into uniform spheres and place on a lightly floured surface. Cover with a clean kitchen towel and let them rest for about 25 minutes. On a lightly floured board, gently flatten a ball of dough with your fingers. Take care not to stretch, wrinkle, or puncture the dough from now on. Roll the dough easily into 6 inch to 7 inch (150 mm to 175 mm) rounds, again being very careful not to stretch the dough. Turn the dough slightly as you work to roll evenly in all directions.

Place on an ungreased cookie sheet, two or three at a time (or as many as will fit easily on your baking sheet) and bake in a preheated 475° F. oven for about 4 to 5 minutes. Turn over with a

spatula and bake an additional 2 minutes. The loaves should be puffed and slightly browned on both sides. Cool on a wire rack. Proceed with remaining dough.

Store, stacked one upon the other in securely tied plastic bags. The breads may be reheated before serving. A pocket should be formed in the center of each loaf. Split each on one side using a sharp small knife or fork. Fill with Souvlakia (*see* index) or other cooked meats, fish, chicken, tomatoes, lettuce, chopped cucumber, etc.

SESAME PITA
Sprinkle about 1 teaspoon (5 ml) of sesame seeds on the top of each round after it has been rolled out. Press the seeds into the dough gently with a rolling pin. Bake sesame side up first, then turn over and finish baking as directed above.

 # Peasant Black Bread
Makes 2 round loaves

2	packages active dry yeast
½	cup (125 ml) warm water (110° F. to 115° F.)
2¼	cups (560 ml) boiling water
1	teaspoon (5 ml) salt
¼	cup (60 ml) butter
⅓	cup (85 ml) blackstrap molasses
1	ounce (28 g) square unsweetened chocolate
1	teaspoon (5 ml) instant coffee
2	tablespoons (30 ml) crushed caraway seeds
1	teaspoon (5 ml) crushed fennel seeds
3	tablespoons (45 ml) cider vinegar
2	tablespoons (30 ml) grated onion
3½	cups (875 ml) all-purpose unsifted flour (approximate)
2	cups (500 ml) dark rye flour
	Corn oil
1	tablespoon (15 ml) instant coffee mixed with 3 tablespoons (45 ml) water
1	egg white mixed with 3 tablespoons (45 ml) water and ½ teaspoon (3 ml) salt
	Yellow corn meal

Sprinkle the yeast into warm water in a large bread or mixing bowl. Stir to dissolve and set aside. Combine salt, butter, molasses, chocolate, instant coffee, caraway seeds, fennel seeds, vinegar, and onion. Pour the boiling water over and stir to melt chocolate and butter and blend all ingredients. Cool to 110° F. Stir in the yeast plus 2 cups (500 ml) of the all-purpose flour. Beat until smooth. Add all of the dark rye flour and beat several minutes. Then add enough all-purpose flour to make a stiff dough—one that pulls away from the sides of the bowl. Turn out onto a floured board, cover with a clean, dry kitchen cloth and let the dough rest for 15 minutes. Knead the dough, adding flour as you go to keep it from being sticky. After 20 minutes of quick, gentle kneading the dough should be elastic and satiny. Shape into a smooth ball. Wash, dry, and rub the bread bowl with corn oil. Roll the dough over in the oil to coat. Cover with a kitchen cloth and set in a warm (80° F.) draft-free spot. Let rise to double its bulk, about 1¼ hours. Punch down, roll again in a bit of oil, cover, and let rise in the same warm, draft-free spot for another 40 minutes, until nearly double in bulk. Punch down and shape the dough into 2 round loaves. Butter two pie plates and sprinkle the bottoms with corn meal. Place 1 loaf in each pan, or bake the bread on either one large or two small cookie sheets prepared the same way. Cover with a clean, dry cloth and let rise until double, about 30 minutes. Poke two fingers into the dough at an inconspicuous spot. If the indentations stay, the bread is oven-ready. Brush each loaf first with some of the coffee wash, then with the egg white wash. Bake in a preheated 375° F. oven for about 35 minutes, or until the bread sounds hollow when thumped with your fingers.

🌹 European-Style Sour Beer Bread

Makes 2 round loaves

Tearing into a freshly baked loaf of this peasant-like crusty bread is a rare, earthy pleasure—but wait until you savor its tangy flavor!

With just some cheese and sweet butter, it makes a memorable picnic. And with a robust German feast, it smacks of heaven.

2 cups (500 ml) flat dark beer
½ cup (125 ml) corn meal
2 tablespoons (30 ml) butter
1 teaspoon (5 ml) salt
½ cup (125 ml) blackstrap molasses
2 packages active dry yeast
½ cup (125 ml) warm water (110° F. to 115° F.)
2 tablespoons (30 ml) honey
½ cup (125 ml) fresh wheat germ
½ cup (125 ml) whole wheat cereal
2 cups (500 ml) unsifted Graham flour
  or whole wheat flour
4½ cups (1125 ml) unsifted unbleached white flour, or
   substitute 1 cup (250 ml) gluten flour for 1 cup
   (250 ml) of the flour
   Corn oil
1 egg yolk beaten with 1 tablespoon (15 ml) water

Bring beer to steaming in a saucepan. Immediately remove from heat and gradually stir in corn meal, butter, salt, and molasses. Cool to around 95° F. In a big bread bowl, mix the water and honey, then stir in the yeast. Let stand for 10 minutes or until foamy. Stir in cooled beer mixture, wheat germ, cereal, whole wheat flour, and about 1 cup (250 ml) of white flour. Beat about 5 minutes until smooth. Gradually add enough white flour to make a stiff dough —one that pulls away from the sides of the bowl. Turn out onto a floured board and knead gently but thoroughly, adding unbleached flour as needed until the dough is smooth and satiny, about 15 to 20 minutes. Wash and dry the mixing bowl and rub it generously with corn oil. Shape the dough into a ball and turn in the bowl to coat all sides with oil. Cover with a clean kitchen towel and let rise in a warm (80° F.) draft-free spot for about 1¼ hours until double in bulk. Punch the dough down, cover, and let rise to nearly double in bulk, about 45 minutes. Punch the dough down once more and divide in half. Roll each piece into a ball and flatten slightly. Pull the sides down and under to make a smooth top and pinch the underside of the dough together to eliminate any gaps. Place the loaves on either one large baking sheet (3 inches to 4 inches (75 mm to 100 mm) apart) or on two smaller cookie sheets that have been oiled and sprinkled with corn meal. Cover with a clean, dry cloth and let rise in a warm, draft-free spot until doubled in size. Poke two fingers into the dough at an inconspicuous spot. If the indentations stay, the loaf is oven-ready. Using a very sharp, floured paring knife, slash the top of each loaf twice down and twice across about ½ inch (12 mm) deep. Brush with some of the egg wash. Bake in a preheated 350° F. oven for about 40 minutes or until bread is well browned and sounds hollow when tapped with your fingers.

 ## Westphalian Pumpernickel Loaf

Makes one 9 inch × 5 inch × 2 inch
(225 mm × 125 mm × 50 mm) loaf

No yeast, no rising, no kneading . . . and definitely no left-overs. The recipe for this dense, chewy German loaf comes by way of Derek Gallagher, a freelance publishing production wizard and bread-baking specialist.

Start this bread a day or two before you intend to serve it, and know that wrapped tightly and refrigerated, it will keep for days.

¼   cup (60 ml) granulated sugar
3   cups (750 ml) boiling water
4   cups (1000 ml) rye meal
1   cup (250 ml) cracked wheat
2   teaspoons (10 ml) salt
2   tablespoons (30 ml) corn oil

Put the sugar in a heavy black iron skillet and turn the heat fairly high until sugar is melted, stirring continually with a fork. Cook until sugar is burned black—a couple of minutes or so. Pour in the boiling water and stir to dissolve all the bits of sugar. Remove from heat and set aside. Combine rye meal, cracked wheat, salt, and oil in a mixing bowl. Add the cooled sugar syrup and mix well. Lay a piece of plastic wrap directly on the dough, patting it down to make an air-tight cover. Let the dough stand overnight at room temperature. Butter a glass loaf pan and press the dough into the pan, patting the surface to make it flat. Cover tightly with aluminum foil. Preheat oven to

200° F. Set a pan full of boiling water on the lowest rack. Put the bread on a rack over the water and bake for 4 hours. Turn the oven up to 300° F. and continue to bake for an additional 1½ hours until the bread is firm. Cool in the pan for a few minutes, then unmold onto a rack and cool completely. Wrap tightly in plastic wrap and chill thoroughly. Slice thinly and serve with sweet butter.

Irish Soda Bread
Makes 1 loaf

There are as many versions of Irish soda bread as there are Irish bakers. Some are sweetened with sugar and some are not. Some are studded with raisins or currants and some are plain. Some are spiced with caraway seeds or even cardamom and coriander.

But they all have a few things in common. For one thing the very heart of this biscuit-like loaf is the buttermilk, preferably thick and freshly churned. Each loaf has a cross slashed in its top to prevent the bread from splitting during the baking process. Soda bread is generally crusty and browned on top, and it is baked fresh—never stored for longer than a day.

Best of all, soda bread is quick to make, needs no rising time, and tastes divine with sweet butter.

4½	cups (1125 ml) all-purpose flour
1	teaspoon (5 ml) salt
4	tablespoons (60 ml) sugar
1	tablespoon (15 ml) double-acting baking powder
1	teaspoon (5 ml) baking soda
1	tablespoon (15 ml) caraway seeds (optional)
6	tablespoons (90 ml) sweet butter
2	eggs
1½	cups (375 ml) buttermilk

In a large mixing bowl, combine the flour, salt, sugar, baking powder, baking soda, and caraway seeds.

Using a pastry blender or two knives, cut in the butter as if you were making pie dough, until the mixture resembles crumbs—all coated with flour. Do not overmix.

Make a well in the center of the mixture. Beat the eggs well and set aside about 1 tablespoon (15 ml) of the beaten egg for the glaze. Add the buttermilk and mix well. Pour into the center of the flour mixture and mix quickly with a fork until a ball of dough is formed.

Turn out onto a floured board and using well floured hands, knead the dough eight or nine times—just until the dough is smooth. Do not knead too much or else the bread will become tough and heavy.

Form the dough into a ball and place in a well buttered 1½ quart (1500 ml) round casserole. Slash a cross about ¼ inch (6 mm) in depth into the top of the dough using a small sharp knife. Brush with the reserved beaten egg and place into a preheated 350° F. oven for 60 to 70 minutes until a skewer inserted into the center of the loaf comes out clean and the loaf sounds hollow when tapped. Cool on a wire rack.

VARIATIONS
If you wish, you can add raisins or currants to the bread.

Simply reduce the flour by ¼ cup (60 ml) and add either 1 cup (250 ml) seedless raisins or ¾ cup (180 ml) currants to the flour mixture before the butter is cut in. Bake as otherwise directed.

ALTERNATE BAKING METHOD

Shape the kneaded dough into a ball, flatten to about 2 inches (50 mm) thick, slash and glaze the top, and place on a well greased cookie sheet to bake. Bake at 350° F. for 60 to 70 minutes as directed above.

🌼 Finnish Peasant Bread

I come from Hanna, Wyoming, and as far back as I know, it has been a coal-mining town. High, flat and windy, Hanna was settled in the first part of this century by Greeks, Italians, Japanese, English, and Finns.

Each group lived in its own segregated neighborhood in those first years—their only commonality was that they were struggling immigrants who worked the treacherous underground coal caverns for the Union Pacific.

In the 1950s the mines shut down. The fading ethnic communities were totally abandoned leaving strings of boarded-up houses on tumbleweed lots.

Today, a few old timers still remember those early days—the people and the food.

This recipe for Finnish Peasant bread is like the heavy, coarse staple that sustained many a miner's family through those howling Wyoming winters long ago.

½	cup (125 ml) warm water (110° F. to 115° F.)
1	package active dry yeast
½	cup (125 ml) sugar
1	tablespoon (15 ml) molasses, plus a little more
⅔	cup (170 ml) butter or shortening
1½	teaspoons (8 ml) salt
2½	cups (625 ml) boiling water
1½	cups (375 ml) rye flour
1½	cups (375 ml) whole wheat flour
	All-purpose flour for kneading
2	tablespoons (30 ml) melted butter

Pour the warm water over the yeast in a glass measuring cup and set aside to dissolve. Place the sugar, molasses, butter, and salt in a large mixing bowl. Pour in the hot water and stir to dissolve. Let cool to 110° F. to 115° F. Stir in the dissolved yeast. Mix the rye and whole wheat flours together and gradually add to the liquids, stirring briskly with a wooden spoon or dough hooks of an electric mixer. Cover and let rise in a warm spot (80° F.) until double in bulk. Turn out onto a board dusted with all-purpose flour and knead in as much white flour as necessary to make a soft, nonsticky dough. Knead about 20 minutes or until the dough is smooth and satiny. Set in a lightly oiled bread bowl, cover with a kitchen cloth, and let rise in a warm, draft-free spot until double in size again. Using lightly floured hands and board, punch the dough back and shape into 2 round loaves and place each in a lightly oiled pie tin. Prick all over with a fork, brush the tops with melted butter, and let rise to double in bulk. Bake in a 400° F. oven for 15 minutes then lower oven heat to 350° F. and bake another 40 minutes until the dough is brown, rusty, and sounds hollow when thumped with your fingers. Serve in the traditional Finnish manner, cut into big wedges and buttered generously, and accompany with slices of good cheese.

Norwegian Herb-Nut Bread

Makes 1 loaf

Traces of savory herbs and the texture of chopped walnuts make this moist whole wheat bread wholesome enough to be a meal in itself.

Spread slices of warm bread with sweet creamery butter and have it with sliced Gouda or cheddar cheese and a big glass of cold buttermilk.

1	package active dry yeast
¼	cup (60 ml) warm water (110° F. to 115° F.)
½	cup (125 ml) scalded milk
¼	cup (60 ml) sugar
¼	cup (60 ml) sweet butter
1	teaspoon (5 ml) salt
¼	teaspoon (1½ ml) ground nutmeg

½   teaspoon (3 ml) each of crushed dried sweet basil,
      thyme, oregano, and rosemary
1   egg at room temperature, well beaten
2   to 2½ cups (500 to 625 ml) whole wheat flour
¼   cup (60 ml) finely chopped walnuts
      All-purpose flour for kneading

Dissolve the yeast in the water and let stand until it is spongy. In a large warm mixing bowl, pour the hot milk over the sugar, butter, salt, and herbs. Stir to melt the butter. When mixture cools to 110° F. to 115° F., stir in beaten egg and yeast mixture. Gradually add flour, stirring first with a wooden spoon or dough hooks if you're using an electric mixer. When you've added about half the flour, mix in the nuts. Add just enough flour to make a soft, nonsticky dough. Turn out on a board lightly dusted with all-purpose flour. Knead until the dough is satiny. Lightly oil a large, warm earthenware bowl and place the dough inside, turning once to cover with oil. Cover with a clean kitchen towel and let stand in a warm (80° F.) spot out of any drafts until it has doubled in size, about 1 hour and 10 minutes. Knock the dough back and shape into a loaf. Place in a buttered or oiled bread loaf pan and again set in a warm spot until it doubles in size, about 45 minutes this time. Bake in a 375° F. oven until the loaf is brown and sounds hollow when thumped with your fingers, about half an hour. Turn out to cool on a wire rack. Slice thickly, and store in a plastic bag to keep it moist. Serve with butter, cheese, or jam.

🌺 Crisp Corn Bread

*Makes one 9 inch to 10 inch (225 mm to 250 mm) bread
or 1 dozen muffins*

The crispiest and best corn bread is made in a heavy black iron skillet or pan especially designed to shape corn bread sticks.
      This Southern specialty is best hot from the oven and dripping with butter.

1½   cups (375 ml) yellow corn meal
¼   cup (60 ml) all-purpose flour
1   teaspoon (5 ml) soda

   1   teaspoon (5 ml) salt
   1   teaspoon (5 ml) sugar
   2   cups (500 ml) buttermilk or sour milk [milk plus 2
         tablespoons (30 ml) vinegar or lemon juice]
   1   egg, well beaten
       Bacon grease, lard, or shortening

Generously grease a 9 inch or 10 inch (225 mm to 250 mm) cast iron skillet or muffin pan and place it to heat in a 425° F. oven while you mix the bread. In a large mixing bowl, combine the dry ingredients, blending well. Add buttermilk and eggs and beat well. Pour into a hot, greased skillet and bake for 20 to 25 minutes at 425° F. Serve hot, cut into squares.

VARIATIONS
Here's a list of extras you might want to add to the batter:

1. ½ pound (225 g) spicy sausage, well browned, crumbled, and drained

2. Several pieces of bacon, crisply fried, drained, and crumbled

3. 1 small can diced green chiles, drained

4. Finely chopped green or red bell pepper

5. Crumbled cracklins—crisply deep-fried pork rinds

Hush Puppies
Makes about 2 dozen

These crisp fried corn meal cakes are best when eaten hot out of the skillet. For added flavor, fry them in the fat left from a mess of fried fish, sausage, or chicken.

Like biscuits, they ought to be served with a bucket of soft butter.

   1   cup (250 ml) yellow corn meal
   ½   cup (125 ml) all-purpose flour

2½   teaspoons (13 ml) baking powder
½   teaspoon (3 ml) salt
1   teaspoon (5 ml) sugar
1   egg
1   cup (250 ml) milk or buttermilk
2   tablespoons (30 ml) grated onion
     Dash of red pepper (optional)
     Shortening, oil, or fat for deep-frying

Combine all the dry ingredients in a mixing bowl and blend well. Add egg and enough milk to make a thick batter. Stir in the onion and pepper. Drop by spoonfuls into hot deep fat and brown on both sides, turning once. Drain momentarily and serve.

🌹 Southern Spoon Bread

Makes two 2 quart (2000 ml) soufflés

If you've got a kettle of black beans simmering on the stove and a batch of spoon bread rising in the oven, then your kitchen smells like a kitchen ought to.

This is spoon bread at its best. A smooth soufflé flavored with chiles, cheese, sour cream, and corn meal. Don't let it sit around and wait . . . it must be eaten hot out of the oven.

½   medium onion, finely chopped
4   tablespoons (60 ml) butter
3½   cups (875 ml) milk
1   cup (250 ml) white corn meal
1½   teaspoons (8 ml) salt
3   teaspoons (15 ml) baking powder
4   ounce (112 g) can diced mild green chiles, drained
2   teaspoons (10 ml) sugar
6   eggs, separated
½   cup (125 ml) buttermilk
1   cup (250 ml) grated cheddar or jack cheese
1   cup (250 ml) sour cream

Sauté the onions in 2 tablespoons (30 ml) of the butter until they are soft and golden, but not brown. Heat milk to boiling in a large saucepan. Stir in the onions. Keeping the milk boiling continually, gradually pour in the corn meal. Pour slowly enough to see the individual grains. Continue to boil gently, stirring often, until the corn meal is soft—not crunchy or grainy to the bite. Remove from heat. Stir salt, baking powder, chiles, sugar, and remaining butter into the corn meal. Blend well and cool completely, stirring occasionally. Lightly beat the egg yolks with the buttermilk. Add this mix to the cooled corn meal mixture gradually, stirring continually. Stir in the grated cheese. In a scrupulously clean deep mixing bowl, beat the egg whites with electric beaters on high speed until big bubbles form. Stop the beaters and add a pinch of salt. Resume beating at high speed until the whites stand in stiff peaks. Gently fold the beaten whites into the batter. Do not mix too well—the batter should be lumpy with egg whites. Pour into two well buttered 2-quart (2000 ml) soufflé dishes. Spoon dollops of sour cream here and there all around the bread. Bake in a 375° F. oven for about 30 minutes or until the spoon bread is set and lightly browned on top. Serve immediately. Spoon down deep into the soufflé for each serving. With black beans, spoon bread is a wonderful companion for meats and chicken.

Thin Russian Buckwheat Pancakes

BLINY
Makes 6 to 8 servings

Bliny makes the most elegant midnight supper. If you have several guests, set up a gas or electric burner and cook them at your serving table for each person.

Arrange a buffet of accompaniments from caviar to sour cream and offer plenty of iced vodka or champagne.

1½   packages active dry yeast
½   cup (125 ml) lukewarm water (110° F. to 115° F.)
2   cups (500 ml) sifted all-purpose flour
2   cups (500 ml) sifted buckwheat flour
3   eggs, separated, at room temperature

2   tablespoons (30 ml) sugar
1   teaspoon (5 ml) salt
3   tablespoons (45 ml) melted butter
2   cups (500 ml) warm milk (110° F. to 115° F.)
    Pinch of cream of tartar

In a large, heavy bread bowl, dissolve the yeast in the warm water and let it stand in a warm spot for a few minutes until it is spongy. Mix in all of the all-purpose flour plus one tablespoon (15 ml) of the buckwheat flour. Beat until smooth. Cover with a clean kitchen towel and set in a warm, draft-free spot for about 1 hour until the batter is bubbly. Beat the egg yolks with the sugar and salt. Mix into the batter along with the melted butter. Blend well. Gradually add the remaining buckwheat flour and beat until smooth. Mix in the warm milk a little at a time, blending well after each addition. Cover the bowl again and let batter rise in a warm spot to double its bulk. Beat it down and let rise once more. Meanwhile, place the egg whites in a deep mixing bowl and beat with electric beaters on high speed until the whites have formed big bubbles. Stop beaters and add a pinch of cream of tartar. Resume beating at high speed until the whites form stiff peaks. Gently fold the stiffly beaten whites into the risen batter with a spatula. Cover and let rise again. Heat a nonstick griddle to 375° F. Spoon the batter on the hot griddle [about 3 tablespoons (45 ml) per cake], and spread out a little with a spoon. When the cakes are lightly browned on the bottom, turn over with a spatula and brown on the other side. Stack on a warm plate, cover loosely with a clean, dry towel, and place in a warm oven until all the cakes are done. Serve the cakes hot with a selection of these traditional accompaniments: a big bowl of sour cream; red and black caviar; chopped cooked egg; mounds of sweet butter; thin slices of pickled or smoked fish; finely chopped onions; minced fresh parsley; and creamed cottage cheese.

🌹 Homemade Croutons

Good, but slightly dry bread
Butter

Trim the crust from day-old bread. Cut into cubes the size you want your croutons to be. Place the cubes on an ungreased baking sheet and toast in a 350° F. oven until they are golden brown. In a large skillet, melt 2 tablespoons (30 ml) of butter at a time. When the butter's foam begins to subside, add a batch of the toasted bread cubes and sauté lightly on all sides. Remove with a slotted spoon and drain on paper toweling. Continue, adding butter when necessary until all of the cubes are done. To make seasoned croutons, add the hot croutons directly to a bowl containing your desired seasonings, toss well, then transfer to a paper towel to cool. Suggested flavorings include combinations of grated cheese, Parmesan or Romano cheese, garlic powder, paprika, dried dill weed, dried parsley, oregano, etc. Minced fresh garlic and herbs can be added directly to the melted butter and sautéed along with the bread cubes. Plain toasted bread cubes make fine bread stuffing as well.

Warm, crunchy croutons laced with butter, and sometimes herbs, make spectacular use of aging breads (whole meal, rye, black, pumpernickel, white, etc.).

Sprinkle them over soups, salads, and even casseroles, but make them fresh every time. Fresh croutons without all those preservatives will not keep.

🌹 Anchovy Butter
Makes about ½ cup (125 ml)

Serve with warm, crusty French or Italian bread, or scoop off curls and place on hot broiled or poached fish.

½   cup (125 ml) sweet butter, softened at room
        temperature
4   anchovy fillets, ground in a blender or food processor

1½   tablespoons (18 ml) minced fresh parsley
1   clove garlic, minced

Combine all ingredients and blend in an electric blender, food processor, or with a mortar and pestle. When the mixture is creamy, pack into a butter pot, cover tightly, and refrigerate.

🌿 Herb Butter

Herb butters are delicious: to lather on slices of warm bread; to toss with tender homemade pasta, gnocchi, or pilaf; to spoon over baked potatoes or coat-boiled potatoes; and to flavor broiled fish, chicken, and meats. In addition to herbs, you can add finely minced anchovies or grated hard cheeses (Parmesan, Romano, Kefalotyri, etc.).

While fresh herbs are beyond compare, you can use dried herbs if you crush them well in a blender or with a mortar and pestle before adding them to the butter.

¼   pound (112 g) sweet butter, softened at room
        temperature
2   cloves of garlic, peeled and finely minced
2   tablespoons (30 ml) fresh parsley, finely minced
3   or 4 tablespoons (45 to 60 ml) fresh herbs, finely
        minced (sweet basil, tarragon, summer savory, sage,
        oregano, thyme, marjoram, chives, dill, rosemary)
Salt and white pepper to taste

Using an electric mixer or wooden spoon, combine all ingredients in a mixing bowl and beat until smooth, fluffy, and well mixed. Pack into a covered container and refrigerate until use.

🌺 Mustard Butter

To make this Polish favorite, simply beat together equal parts of softened butter and prepared mustard.

When spread on thin slices of black bread, this is a delicious foundation for a sandwich of smoked fish (smoked herring, for instance). Add sliced onion and red radishes and some ice-cold beer.

🌺 Sweet Mustard

Makes about ½ cup (125 ml)

Serve this with Scandinavian sandwiches, and most especially with thinly sliced Gravlax (*see* index), sliced sweet onion, and homemade Black Bread (*see* index).

    ¼   cup (60 ml) corn oil
    2   tablespoons (30 ml) prepared Dijon mustard
    2   tablespoons (30 ml) red wine vinegar
    ½   teaspoon (3 ml) salt
    1   teaspoon (5 ml) dried dill weed
    1   teaspoon (5 ml) sugar
        Few grindings of black pepper

Place corn oil in a jar with a tight-fitting lid. In a small dish or measuring cup, combine the remaining ingredients and blend thoroughly with a fork. Pour into the oil. Put the lid on tightly and shake until well blended. Chill and shake again if necessary before using. Serve in a small dish with a spoon.

Eggs & Cheese

Eggs, right out of the nest and flavorful, natural cheeses appear in a spectacular array of ethnic creations. These are ingenious examples of how ethnic cooking can be easy, light, and economical.

Out of necessity, immigrant cooks devised ways to use eggs and a little cheese to extend meats, sausages, herbs, fresh vegetables, nuts, grains, and leftovers to make a family feast.

Within this chapter are enticing dishes for almost any meal, including hearty brunch skillets, light lunches, inviting first courses, satisfying suppers, and even delicate desserts.

For those who live in the country, farm eggs with their thick, bright yellow yolks are usually accessible. But for city dwellers, the search for fresh, good-tasting eggs may lead to local farmer's markets and health food stores.

For the specialty cheeses recommended in some of the following dishes, check local sources or refer to the Ethnic Mail Order Bazaar at the back of this book.

🌺 Basque Omelet
Makes 6 to 8 servings

A perfect lazy weekend brunch—this omelet served with sliced fresh tomatoes, Basque Bean Salad (*see* index), crisp sourdough rolls with butter, and spicy Bloody Marys.

103

½   pound (225 g) chorizo, pepperoni, or any other hard garlic-flavored sausage, sliced into ⅛ inch (3 mm) rounds
3   tablespoons (45 ml) olive oil
1   medium-sized onion, chopped
1   green pepper, seeded, stemmed, and diced
1   large red-skinned potato, parboiled until just tender, then peeled and diced
2   chopped jalapeño peppers (optional)
8   eggs, lightly beaten
2   cups (500 ml) shredded jack cheese

In a small skillet, fry the sausage. Render most of the fat, but do not burn. Transfer to a paper towel and drain. In a large skillet (preferably well seasoned cast iron), heat the olive oil. Add the onion and green pepper and simmer slowly, stirring frequently until they are soft, but not brown. Add the diced potato and the jalapeño peppers (very hot, but good) and cook just to heat through, about 1 minute. Add the sausage, stir, and cook for 2 minutes. Spread the ingredients evenly across the bottom of the skillet. Pour beaten eggs over all, cover, and lower heat. Cook, checking frequently, until the eggs are almost set. Adjust the heat if necessary to prevent the bottom from becoming too brown. Do not stir. Sprinkle the shredded cheese evenly over the eggs. Remove from the stove top and slip the skillet under a hot broiler just long enough to melt the cheese (don't brown it). Slice into pie-shaped wedges and serve.

German Cheese Croquettes

These croquettes are a luscious breakfast or brunch treat. In addition, you could serve crispy fried bacon or sausages, buttered rye and pumpernickel toast, sliced fresh fruit or berries with cream, and hot coffee.

3   large baking potatoes, baked until meat is tender
1   pound (450 g) large curd cottage cheese, thoroughly drained (or buy dry cottage cheese)

2   eggs, well beaten
     Flour
¼   cup (60 ml) sugar, or to taste
1   teaspoon (5 ml) grated lemon zest (no white)
½   teaspoon (3 ml) ground cinnamon
½   teaspoon (3 ml) salt
½   cup (125 ml) seedless raisins, soaked and drained
     Butter or vegetable oil
     Fresh Applesauce (*see* index)

Scoop the meat out of the potato shells, discard skins (or reserve for another use), and spread the potato out on a board to dry a bit. Combine potato and cottage cheese in a food ricer or mill and sieve into a mixing bowl. Add the eggs and mix well, then add some flour gradually until the dough holds together. Season with sugar, lemon zest, cinnamon, and salt. Mix in raisins. Form into balls about the size of jumbo eggs, flatten a bit, and fry in hot butter or oil until golden on both sides. Serve immediately with fresh applesauce or assorted fruit preserves.

 ## German Onion Tart
Makes one 10 inch (250 mm) pie

This lively open-faced pie, like quiche, can be served on almost any occasion, from brunch to late night supper. While a baked pie can be frozen, this tart is at its best right out of the oven.

1   recipe Flaky Pie Crust (*see* index)*
4   thick slices smoked bacon
3   large onions, peeled and thinly sliced
     Salt and pepper
5   eggs
1   cup (250 ml) sour cream
     Chopped chives (optional)
2   teaspoons (10 ml) caraway seeds

*This recipe makes double the need, so divide the dough in half, wrap the unused portion in plastic wrap and freeze it for a later use.

Make the pie crust as directed in the recipe. Roll it out as directed and line a 10 inch (250 mm) glass pie plate. Flute the edges as directed, cover with a kitchen towel, and set aside while you make the filling. In a skillet, brown the bacon on both sides until it is crisp. Remove from the skillet, drain on paper toweling, crumble, and set aside. Add the sliced onions to the skillet and sauté in the remaining bacon fat until the onions are limp and golden but not brown. Stir frequently. Season the onions with a bit of salt and pepper. Remove from heat and cool. Beat the eggs and sour cream together until the mixture is smooth. Spread half of the crumbled bacon in the bottom of the pie crust and sprinkle with some chives if desired. Spread the cooled onions over the crust, pour the egg and cream mixture over all, and sprinkle with remaining bacon, caraway seeds, and some chives. Bake in a preheated 350° F. oven for about 40 minutes until the filling is set and the shell is lightly browned. Serve warm or at room temperature.

 ## German Country Breakfast Skillet

Makes 6 servings

This breakfast is a savory combination of potatoes, meat, and eggs that's especially fine on a leisurely frosty morning. Big, fresh biscuits, a pot of homemade preserves, and sliced fruit make mouthwatering companions.

4	thick slices of smoked bacon
1½	pounds (675 g) boiled potatoes, sliced
4	thick slices of smoked bacon
1	onion, diced
	Salt and freshly ground pepper to taste
¼	teaspoon (1.5 ml) dried dill weed
8	eggs, well beaten
6	smoked pork loin chops ½ inch (12 mm) thick (precooked and warm), or 6 slices smoked ham (precooked and warm)

Fry bacon in a large, heavy skillet until it is crisp and brown. Drain on paper toweling, crumble, and set aside. Add sliced potatoes and onions to the hot fat in the skillet and brown. Lift and turn with a spatula, gently so as not to break the potatoes. Sprinkle with salt, pepper, and dill weed. Pour beaten eggs over all and cover skillet. Turn heat down to low and cook, undisturbed, for about 5 minutes. Lay pork chops or ham slices over all and set skillet in a preheated 350° oven until the eggs are solid, but not dry. Serve immediately.

🌺 Greek Fried Cheese

Makes 4 servings

If you like to cook and entertain your guests at the same time, this dish is a flaming delight. It must be prepared one serving at a time and, since it cooks quickly, it makes a nice "standing" first course. Gather everyone in the kitchen and set out a mini-buffet—Greek calamata olives, cherry tomatoes, lemon, crusty bread, and a hearty wine. Casual but spectacular.

For lunch, Greek fried cheese is nice with a salad of romaine, tomatoes, and bermuda onion rings. Offer some crusty bread, olives, perhaps a glass of wine.

It's essential that the cheese be kept as cold as possible right up to the very last second. Remember to cook it quickly or you'll have a panful of melted cheese.

Kefalotyri and Casseri are hard cheeses that are available in most cheese shops, Middle Eastern, Greek, and Italian grocery stores, and even in some supermarkets. If you can't find either cheese, try a good imported Parmesan. Be sure to cut the cheese in uniform pieces that are the same thickness throughout for even cooking.

The following recipe can easily be divided or multiplied, simply allow about 4 ounces (112 g) of cheese per serving.

  1   pound (450 g) Kefalotyri or Casseri cheese, cut into uniform 4 ounce (112 g) slices
       Ice water with ice cubes
  ½   cup (125 ml) all-purpose flour (approximate)

¼   pound (60 ml) butter (approximate)
2   lemons, cut in half
    Cognac

Put the cheese in a bowl, cover with ice water and ice cubes, and refrigerate for at least an hour until the cheese is very cold. Keep each piece cold until the very last second before cooking. Remove one cheese slice from the water and pat it dry. Flour it lightly on both sides and shake off the excess. Add it immediately to a skillet in which you have 2 to 3 tablespoons (30 to 45 ml) of sizzling butter. Add the cheese and fry very quickly on both sides. Sprinkle with juice from half a lemon and a few drops of cognac. Ignite and serve as soon as the flames die down. Repeat for remaining servings.

Greek Vegetable Omelet

Makes 4 servings

Greeks add just about every kind of vegetable to omelets. Using the basic procedure for preparing this fast, light meal, you might want to introduce some of your own seasonal selections.

3   tablespoons (45 ml) good olive oil
½   onion, chopped
1   green bell pepper, scrubbed, stemmed, and seeded, then cut in ¼ inch (6 mm) strips
1   teaspoon (5 ml) minced fresh sweet basil
¼   cup (60 ml) minced fresh parsley
2   medium boiling potatoes, cooked until tender, then sliced in ¼ inch (6 mm) rounds
6   eggs, well beaten
3   tablespoons (45 ml) grated Kefalotyri or Parmesan cheese
    Freshly ground black pepper
    Sliced ripe tomatoes

In a large skillet or omelet pan, heat the oil. Sauté the onion and pepper until they are soft and golden but not brown. Add the basil and parsley and stir just to heat through. Lay the potato slices in the skillet, distributing the onion, peppers, and herbs throughout. When the potatoes are heated through, pour the beaten eggs over all. Sprinkle with grated cheese and set the skillet, uncovered, in a preheated 350°° F. oven until the eggs are set—about 20 minutes. Top with a couple of grindings of black pepper and garnish with sliced tomatoes. Serve with warm bread, olives, and wine for an easy but elegant brunch.

 HUNGARIAN PALACSINTA

Basic Palacsinta

Makes about 30 pancakes

BATTER

3	cups (750 ml) sifted all-purpose flour
1	teaspoon (5 ml) salt
5	tablespoons (75 ml) sugar (dessert recipes only)
6	large eggs
1½	cups (375 ml) milk
1	teaspoon (5 ml) vanilla (dessert recipes only)
1½	cups (375 ml) plain club soda, just opened (approximate)
	Butter or corn oil for frying

Sift flour and salt together into a large mixing bowl. If you are making dessert *palacsinta*, mix in the sugar. Combine eggs and milk and beat well. Add to the flour a little at a time, beating well after each addition using either a wooden spoon or an electric mixer. Add melted butter gradually and continue to beat until batter is smooth. If you are making dessert palacsinta, beat in vanilla. At this point it is good to cover and refrigerate the batter for at least a few hours—overnight if possible. Just before cooking, gradually stir in the club soda until the batter is thin as light cream. Melt about 1 teaspoon (5 ml) of butter in a small frying pan or crepe pan. If you want to use corn oil, wipe the interior of the pan with a paper towel that is saturated with the oil. Heat the pan just until the butter stops foaming, or until the oil begins to smoke. Pour about 3 tablespoons (45 ml) of batter into the pan and tilt the pan so the batter coats it evenly. Cook until the pancake is lightly browned on one side then turn it over and brown lightly on the other side. Stack one on top of the other and keep warm until all the batter is used. Fill and bake as directed in the following recipes.

🌼 Palacsinta with Ham Filling

This version is especially good for lunch or a light supper. Offer a tomato and cucumber salad, warm poppyseed rolls with butter, and a freshly baked Cherry Strudel (*see* index) for dessert.

- ½ pound (225 g) mushrooms, cleaned and finely chopped
- 3 or 4 scallions, finely chopped
- ½ pound (225 g) cooked smoked ham, finely chopped
- 2 eggs
- 2 cups (500 ml) sour cream
  Pinch of salt (none if ham is salty)
  White pepper to taste
  Basic Palacsinta (made without sugar and vanilla)
    (*see* index)
  Butter
- 1 cup (250 ml) grated mild cheese (jack, brick, etc.)

Sauté mushrooms and scallions in the butter until they are soft. Add ham and sauté just to heat through and mix flavors. Remove from heat and cool. Mix in the eggs, blending well, and then add 1 cup (250 ml) of the sour cream and blend well. Season to taste. Spoon some of the filling on each palacsinta and roll up like a crêpe. Place side by side in a buttered baking dish. Bake for 20 minutes at 350° F. until the filling is heated through and set. Spoon the remaining 1 cup (250 ml) of sour cream over the palacsinta and sprinkle the grated cheese over all. Return to the oven until the sour cream is bubbly and the cheese is melted. Serve warm.

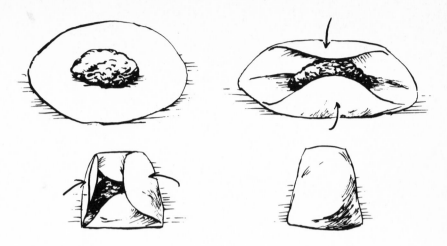

Palacsinta with Pot Cheese Filling

This creamy filling is shaded with herbs and is especially good for brunch, a light supper, or as a side dish with meats or poultry.

1   pound (450 g) pot or ricotta cheese
3   eggs, well beaten
¼   teaspoon (1.5 ml) salt
    Dash of white pepper
2   teaspoons (10 ml) dried crushed dill weed
    Pinch of crushed marjoram
    Basic Palacsinta (made without sugar and vanilla)
      (*see* index)
    Milk
16   ounces (500 ml) container sour cream

Put pot cheese through a food mill or whip ricotta in a food processor or electric mixer. Beat in eggs, salt, pepper, dill weed, and marjoram. Spoon some filling on a pancake and roll it into a tube (like a stuffed crepe). Place the rolls side-by-side in a buttered baking dish. Mix some milk into the sour cream to thin it just a bit and pour over the stuffed palacsinta. Bake at 325° F. for about 20 minutes or just until heated through. Serve warm.

❧ Palacsinta Filled with Preserves

Using warm, freshly made Basic Palacsinta (*see* index), spread each with a layer of your favorite fruit preserves and sprinkle with powdered sugar and chopped walnuts (chopped filberts or hazelnuts are good, too). Fold in fourths and eat them out of hand while they are still warm.

❧ Palacsinta with Sweet Pot Cheese Filling

This is a splendid warm dessert that can be assembled in advance and baked while dinner is on the table.

     1   pound (450 g) pot or ricotta cheese
     ½   cup (125 ml) sugar
     1   teaspoon (1.5 ml) cinnamon
     1   teaspoon (5 ml) vanilla
     1   egg, well beaten
     ½   cup (125 ml) soft seedless raisins (do not use raisins if
            using preserves)
          Basic Palacsinta (*see* index)
     ½   cup (125 ml) chopped walnuts
          Powdered sugar
          Assorted fruit preserves (apricot seems to be the
            favorite but any berry is delicious—or try fresh fruit,
            like peaches, and brandy)

Put pot cheese through a food mill or whip ricotta in a food processor or electric mixer. Add the sugar, cinnamon, vanilla, egg, and mix well. Fold in raisins. Spoon some of the filling into each dessert palacsinta. Roll up like a crepe and place side-by-side in a single layer in a buttered baking dish. Bake in a 325° F. oven for 20 minutes. Serve warm, sprinkled with walnuts and powdered sugar, and pass preserves at the table to spoon over the palacsinta.

VARIATION

Spread each dessert palacsinta with a thin layer of fruit preserves first, then spoon in the sweet pot cheese mixture. Roll and bake as under Sweet Pot Cheese Filling and serve warm, sprinkled with powdered sugar and walnuts.

 # Sausage, Mushroom, and Spinach Frittata

Makes 6 to 8 servings

Frittatas are lovely for brunches or light suppers. The variations are limitless—as are the accompaniments. Often frittatas are slow-cooked in a skillet on the range top, but here's a version that's done in the oven to allow the cook plenty of time to enjoy the guests.

½   to ¾ pound (225 to 340 g) spicy Italian sausage,
        removed from casing
2   tablespoons (30 ml) butter
2   cloves of garlic, peeled and minced
1   small onion, chopped
½   pound (225 g) fresh mushrooms, cleaned and sliced
1   bunch fresh, tender spinach leaves, washed and
        drained, or use 1 10 ounce (280 g) package frozen
        spinach leaves, thawed and squeezed very dry
6   eggs, well beaten
¼   cup (60 ml) chopped fresh sweet basil or 2 to 3
        tablespoons (30 to 45 ml) crushed dried basil
    Pinch of crushed dried oregano leaves
½   teaspoon (3 ml) crushed rosemary
    Salt and freshly ground pepper to taste
1   cup (250 ml) freshly grated imported Parmesan cheese
1   cup (250 ml) shredded mozzarella cheese

Crumble sausage into a skillet and brown slowly. Remove from the pan with a slotted spoon and drain well on layers of paper toweling. Set aside. Discard rendered fat. Melt the 2 tablespoons (30 ml) of butter in a clean skillet until it sizzles. Add garlic, onion, and mushrooms and sauté until soft and lightly colored. Add spinach. If using fresh leaves, arrange them evenly over the top of the vegetables, cover tightly, turn the heat down, and steam until the spinach is tender, using only the moisture that is clinging to the leaves. If you use frozen spinach, add it to the other vegetables in the skillet, stir and sauté just to heat through. When the spinach is ready, stir the sausage back into the skillet and combine well. Simmer for just a couple of minutes, remove from heat, and set aside. In a large mixing bowl, combine the eggs, herbs, and half the grated Parmesan cheese. Mix well. Add the sausage and vegetables and blend. Pour into a buttered 10 inch (250 mm) pie plate, cover with the mozzarella cheese, and sprinkle with the remaining Parmesan cheese. Bake in a preheated 350° F. oven until the eggs are set—about 30 minutes. Serve with hot, crusty rolls, sliced tomatoes seasoned with basil, black pepper, and a drizzle of olive oil, and strong coffee.

VARIATIONS

Here are some ideas for substitutions or additions for your own frittatas:

1. 4 or 5 small, fresh zucchini, cleaned and thinly sliced then sautéed until barely tender

2. 1 green or red bell pepper, seeded, chopped, and sautéed until tender

3. 2 fresh tomatoes, peeled, seeded, and chopped, then sautéed with onions, garlic, and mushrooms

4. 1 package frozen tiny peas, thawed then added to the mixture just before baking

5. ½ cup (125 ml) sliced black olives

6. Thin slices of pepperoni or salami, sautéed and drained

7. 2 cups (500 ml) cooked, diced potatoes

 Tomato and Zucchini Frittata

Makes 4 to 6 servings

4   tablespoons (60 ml) good olive oil
3   small, tender zucchini, scrubbed and thinly sliced

6   eggs, well beaten
2   firm but ripe tomatoes, cut in wedges
    Salt and pepper
3   tablespoons (45 ml) grated Parmesan cheese
½   teaspoon (3 ml) crushed dried sweet basil

Heat the olive oil in a large skillet and fry the zucchini slices until they are crisp and browned. Pour the eggs over all, cover, and cook gently until the eggs are nearly set. Arrange the tomato wedges over the top, sprinkle with salt, pepper, cheese, and basil. Slide under a hot broiler for a couple of minutes until the tomatoes are heated through. Cut in wedges and serve immediately with black olives and chunks of crusty French or sourdough bread.

Mozzarella Marinara

Makes 4 to 6 servings

This is a favorite recipe of vivacious Cindy Leonetti, a gifted actress and writer, and a superb Italian cook. Free-spirited and fun-loving as well, Cindy weaves her culinary magic in the galley of a yacht anchored in the harbor at San Pedro, California.

Of all her recipes I've coveted, from her own spinach gnocchi to her special dark, rich chocolate cake, *mozzarella marinara* is truly a treasure.

A fabulous lunch or first course, this marvelous marriage of crisply fried cheese and classic tomato sauce should be served with plenty of crusty French bread, some black olives, and a good dry red wine.

1   pound (450 g) mozzarella cheese
1   egg, well beaten
    All-purpose flour for breading
¾   cup (180 ml) fine bread crumbs
2   tablespoons (30 ml) finely grated Parmesan cheese
    Vegetable oil for frying
    Marinara sauce (recipe follows)
    Drained anchovy fillets (1 per serving)

Slice the cheese into pieces 3 inches × 2 inches × ½ inch (75 mm × 50 mm × 12 mm). Dip into the egg, then into the flour, then back into the egg, then roll in the bread crumbs mixed with the Parmesan cheese. Place in one layer on a baking sheet and refrigerate for at least 30 minutes. The cheese must be very cold before you begin to fry it. In the meantime, make the sauce. Heat ½ inch (12 mm) of oil in a large skillet until it is very hot. Add as many of the breaded cheese slices as will comfortably fit in the skillet and brown quickly on both sides. Place on heated serving plates, top with marinara sauce and an anchovy fillet, and serve immediately.

MARINARA SAUCE

¼	cup (60 ml) good olive oil
1	clove of garlic, peeled and minced
1	tablespoon (15 ml) fresh minced parsley
1	teaspoon (5 ml) dried sweet basil, or about 1 tablespoon (15 ml) minced fresh sweet basil
¼	teaspoon (1.5 ml) crushed dried oregano
2	cups (500 ml) chopped, peeled, and seeded fresh tomatoes or drained canned tomatoes
	Salt to taste
	Pepper to taste

Heat the oil in a saucepan. Add the garlic and parsley and cook, stirring often until the garlic is lightly browned. Add basil, oregano, and tomatoes plus the salt and pepper and simmer slowly, uncovered, for about 30 minutes.

❦ BLINTZES

Blintzes are simply the Jewish version of French crêpes. They are usually served for breakfast or brunch with big dollops of sour cream. Sometimes (depending on the filling) they are accompanied by cinnamon sugar, applesauce, and/or assorted fruit preserves. When frozen, they will keep for months, so it's sensible to make big batches at a time and have them on hand.

🌸 Basic Blintzes

Makes about 2 dozen blintzes

> 2   cups (500 ml) milk
> 4   large eggs
> 2   cups (500 ml) sifted all-purpose flour
> ½   teaspoon (3 ml) salt
>   Butter and oil for frying

Beat the milk and eggs together in a large mixing bowl. Sift the flour and salt together. Add the flour a little at a time to the milk-egg mixture, beating continually. Beat until smooth. Using a 6 inch (150 mm) seasoned crêpe pan or nonstick skillet, heat about 1 tablespoon (15 ml) of vegetable oil and about ½ teaspoon (3 ml) of butter. Tilt the pan in all directions to coat it completely. When the oil is quite hot, pour about 2 tablespoons (30 ml) of the batter into the skillet and rotate it immediately in all directions to cover the bottom of the pan with a thin layer of batter. When the batter is set on the top and lightly browned on the bottom (it must not have any liquid spots) turn the blintze out of the pan onto a kitchen towel, uncooked side down. Continue this process until all the batter is used, adding oil and butter to the skillet when needed and adjusting the heat under the pan to keep it moderately hot. Stir the batter occasionally as you go along. After all the "crêpes" are made, you can begin to fill them. Place 2 heaping tablespoons (30 ml) of filling in the middle of each crêpe on the browned side. Fold in the top and bottom and roll up the blintze. (See Hungarian Palacsinta recipes for an illustration of folding technique.) If you would like to freeze the blintzes for later use, at this point wrap each one in foil and flash freeze (lay them in your freezer until they are just solid). Then put all of the blintzes in a heavy plastic bag, tie securely, and store in your freezer. As you want to use the blintzes, remove as many as you need from your freezer. Either bake them on a greased cookie sheet at 375° F. for about 20 minutes, or fry them in butter until they are golden brown on all sides and heated through. If you are serving the blintzes freshly made, place them seam side down in a skillet with about 3 tablespoons (45 ml) of sizzling butter. Fry over moderate heat on all sides until they are golden brown. Serve immediately.

❀ Traditional Cheese Filling for Blintzes

Makes about 2 dozen blintzes

4	ounces (112 g) cream cheese
1	pound (450 g) pot or farmer cheese
1	egg yolk, beaten
¼	cup (60 ml) sugar, or to taste
½	teaspoon (3 ml) vanilla extract (optional)

Soften the cream cheese at room temperature. Beat the pot cheese, cream cheese, and egg yolk together until smooth. Add the sugar and vanilla and continue to beat until all ingredients are well blended and creamy. Refrigerate until you are ready to use.

❀ Blueberry Filling for Blintzes

Makes about 2 dozen blintzes

2	tablespoons (30 ml) butter
½	cup (125 ml) sugar, or to taste
¼	teaspoon (1.5 ml) cinnamon
1	teaspoon (5 ml) finely grated lemon zest (no white)
20	ounces (560 g) frozen blueberries

In a heavy saucepan, melt the butter. Add the sugar and stir until it melts. Add the cinnamon and lemon zest and when the mixture just begins to bubble, add the frozen blueberries. Stir gently until the berries are separated and heated through. Remove from heat and allow to cool. Use as directed.

❀ Lox, Eggs, and Onions

Makes 4 servings

Lox, eggs, and onions are my husband's specialty. On those Sunday mornings when Larry is cooking, I set the table and wait for what seems like an eternity for this glorious blend of flavors to reach its pinnacle.

Larry has endless patience with the onions, which is the key to the delicate flavor of this dish. One burned piece of onions spoils the luscious flavor.

Around our lox, eggs, and onions we serve an assortment of fresh bagels lathered with whipped cream cheese, perhaps some smoked whitefish, baked salmon or barbecued cod, occasionally, thickly sliced bermuda onions and beefsteak tomatoes—and always, fresh, strong coffee. You wanna talk heaven?

3 tablespoons (45 ml) butter
1 medium-sized onion, cut into ¾ inch (18 mm) chunks
3 or 4 ounces (84 to 112 g) lox, cut into small pieces
6 large fresh eggs, lightly beaten

Melt 2 tablespoons (30 ml) of the butter in a large skillet. Add the onions. Since the onion chunks are pretty large, the layers will cling together until they begin to cook through. Keep stirring them with a wooden spoon until all the layers have separated and are coated with the butter. Keep the heat down very low—the onions must cook *slowly* (at least 30 minutes); you don't want them to brown too quickly or they will burn. When the onions are limp, soft, and light brown, add the lox, stirring gently until the lox begins to lighten in color. Melt the remaining tablespoon (15 ml) of butter into the skillet and then pour in the beaten eggs into the skillet. Stir gently to distribute the lox and onions evenly. Cook over medium to low heat until the eggs have just set. Do not overcook them or they will stick to the bottom of the skillet and dry out. They should be moist and very fluffy. Serve immediately.

Pancake-Style Matzo Brie

Makes 4 to 6 servings

Popular around the Jewish Passover holiday, *matzo brie* is simply an egg-and-crumbled-matzo mixture seasoned with a bit of onion.

It's fried gently like a pancake-style omelet. *Brie* means to scald, which is done quickly to the matzos so they won't get soggy.

Most often, this dish is brought to the breakfast table in one big round piece, then cut in wedges and served. It can be topped with a sprinkling of cinnamon sugar or with honey or syrup drizzled over each serving.

½	small onion, finely chopped
	Butter for frying
4	eggs
½	teaspoon (1.5 ml) salt
4	matzos
	Boiling water
2	tablespoons (30 ml) butter

Fry the onion in a small skillet until it is limp and golden brown. Set aside. Beat the eggs and salt together and set aside. Place the matzos in a large colander and quickly pour boiling water over them. Drain well. Coarsely break the crackers into the beaten egg along with the onion and mix well. Heat about 2 tablespoons (30 ml) of butter in a large skillet (preferably with a nonstick coating). When the foam subsides, pour the egg mixture into the pan and turn the heat down. When the pancake is golden brown on the bottom, use a large spatula and turn it over carefully. When the bottom is golden, slide out onto a warm, round serving plate and serve immediately.

 # Pasta, Noodles, & Dumplings

Watching silently from the steps to her downstairs kitchen, I observed Mrs. Taccalone rolling and cutting long ribbons of silken pasta with the speed and precision of a Swiss watchmaker.

I was only 5 years old at the time, but I couldn't have been more astounded as our sweet old neighbor manipulated the dough between her gnarled hands better than a prestidigitator.

Whenever I make pasta today, I think of Mrs. Taccalone. Sometimes I imagine that I, too, am working magic with a mound of dough. Rolling and turning, rolling and turning. Faster and faster. I honestly don't know what I like best—the rolling or the eating.

Certainly nothing compares with handmade pasta and noodles. The look, the texture, the flavor, the feel . . . it's all so glorious.

I've often wondered who the genius was who figured out how to turn flour and water paste into one of the world's great masterpieces. It must have been a sweet Italian mother, rolling and stretching a little food by sheer love, to feed a big family. Somebody just like Mrs. Taccalone.

✿ German Potato Dumplings

There are different varieties of German potato dumplings. Some are more pungent with cinnamon and nutmeg, some are sweet, and others have a crispy, buttery crouton lodged in the center. You can serve them plain, with butter and parsley or, when they are done, you can fry them in butter until they are browned on the outside, then serve them sprinkled with buttered crumbs or accompanied by applesauce.

Certainly, potato dumplings deserve a reserved seat at your next sauerbraten dinner.

2   pounds (900 g) red-skinned potatoes, boiled in
     jackets until tender
2   eggs, well beaten
½   cup (125 ml) flour
½   cup (125 ml) regular farina
     Salt to taste
     Dash of ground nutmeg
     Pinch or two of sugar
¼   cup (60 ml) butter, melted (approximate)
     Fresh minced parsley

Pull the skin off the cooled potatoes and discard. Rice the potatoes in a food mill and spread them out on a piece of waxed paper to dry a little. Place the potatoes in a large mixing bowl and, beating with a wooden spoon, add the eggs, flour, farina, salt, nutmeg, and sugar. Taste and correct seasoning and add a bit more flour if necessary, keeping in mind that the more flour you add, the heavier the dumplings will be. Roll into dumplings the size of ping-pong balls. Using a slotted spoon, lower the dumplings into 6 quarts (6000 ml) of salted, rapidly boiling water. Bring back to a boil immediately, then lower the heat to medium and cook for about 20 minutes until the dumplings float to the surface. Remove with a slotted spoon, roll in the melted butter, sprinkle with parsley, and serve hot.

❧ Spaetzle Dumplings

Makes 6 to 8 servings

Serve these tasty German dumplings as you would potatoes, with most any hearty meat or fowl entree.

    8   eggs
    1   teaspoon (5 ml) salt
    ⅛   teaspoon (.5 ml) white pepper
        Dash of ground nutmeg
    1   to 1½ cups (250 to 375 ml) all-purpose flour
        Boiling salted water or light stock

Break eggs into a mixing bowl, add salt, pepper, and nutmeg, and beat well. Stir in flour gradually until you have a thick batter, just stiff enough to hold its shape on a spoon. Drop by teaspoons into a kettle of rapidly boiling seasoned water or stock and simmer for about 10 minutes or until the dumplings are puffed and tender. Scoop out with a large slotted spoon, drain, and serve immediately with butter and a sprinkling of chopped fresh parsley.

❧ Greek Macaroni and Meat Casserole

PASTITSIO (PAH-*STEET*-SEE-OH)
Makes 6 to 8 servings

The Hellenic version of lasagne—lean meat simmered in red wine and fragrant spices is sandwiched between layers of tender macaroni, all laced with a rich cream sauce and grated cheese.

Make this casserole ahead of time and reheat it for the best flavor. It is a superb buffet dish and, cut into squares, it is easy for guests to help themselves.

Serve a basket of crispy crusted bread, a fresh tossed salad with oil and vinegar dressing, and a carafe of Greek or Italian red table wine.

MEAT FILLING

2   large onions, finely chopped
1   clove of garlic, finely chopped
2   to 3 tablespoons (30 to 45 ml) butter or olive oil
2   pounds (900 g) lean ground beef or lamb, or a
       combination of the two
3   ounces (84 g) canned tomato paste
1   cup (250 ml) dry, full-bodied red wine
¼   teaspoon (1.5 ml) grated orange zest (no white)
1   teaspoon (1.5 ml) ground nutmeg
1   teaspoon (5 ml) ground cinnamon
1   teaspoon (5 ml) ground allspice
     Salt and pepper to taste
2   eggs, well beaten
1½   cups (375 ml) grated Kefalotyri cheese, or substitute
       Parmesan or Casseri
¼   cup (60 ml) fine bread crumbs

In a large skillet, sauté onions and garlic in butter until they are barely soft. Crumble meat into the pan and stir-fry until it has lost all its pinkness. Tilt the skillet and spoon off all the fat. Stir in the tomato paste, wine, and spices. Bring to a simmer and cook, uncovered, until all of the juices have been absorbed, about 45 minutes. Stir occasionally to prevent sticking. Remove the mixture from the heat and when it is thoroughly cool, stir in the eggs, grated cheese, and bread crumbs.

MACARONI

1   pound (450 g) elbow macaroni or ziti
2   to 3 tablespoons (30 to 45 ml) of butter

Cook the macaroni according to package directions until it is tender, but still has some "bite." Drain it thoroughly and toss with the butter. Cover and set aside while you prepare the cream sauce.

CREAM SAUCE

8   tablespoons (120 ml) butter
7   tablespoons (105 ml) flour

1   quart (1000 ml) warm milk
     Salt and white pepper to taste
4   egg yolks
1½   cups (375 ml) grated Kefalotyri cheese, or substitute
     Parmesan or Casseri

In a large, heavy saucepan, melt 8 tablespoons (120 ml) of butter. Gradually stir in the flour and cook, stirring, over medium heat until the roux has lost its floury taste. Do not let it brown. Gradually pour in the warm milk, stirring continually. Bring the sauce to a bubble and simmer until it becomes as thick as heavy cream. Stir often to prevent sticking or scorching. Remove from the heat. Add salt and pepper. Stir some of the hot sauce into the beaten yolks to warm them. Whisk the yolks into the sauce. When the sauce has cooled, stir in the grated cheese.

TOPPING
½   cup (125 ml) fine bread crumbs
     Grated nutmeg
     Additional butter

TO ASSEMBLE
Generously butter a baking dish about 15 inches × 10 inches × 3 inches (375 mm × 250 mm × 75 mm) and sprinkle a few bread crumbs on the bottom. Spread half of the macaroni on the bottom. Cover with the meat filling. Pour about half of the cream sauce over the meat, then add the remaining macaroni in an even layer. Pour the last of the sauce over all and sprinkle the top of the casserole with about ½ cup (125 ml) fine bread crumbs, some ground nutmeg, and dots of butter. Bake in a 350° F. oven for about 1 hour, until the casserole is set and the top is golden brown. Let it stand undisturbed for at least 15 minutes. Cut into square serving pieces.

TO FREEZE
Cover the cooled *pastitsio* with aluminum foil and freeze. Reheat the dish in a 350° F. oven, covered tightly, for about 1¾ hours or until the middle is piping hot.

❧ Hungarian Csipetke Noodles

Csipetke (che-*pet*-kee) noodles (sometimes called pinched noodles) are a common addition to many Hungarian soups and stews. They are usually cooked separately in boiling salted water and added to the bubbling main dish when they are tender.

1   cup (250 ml) sifted all-purpose flour
    Dash of salt
1   large egg
    Few drops cold water
    Additional flour

Sift the flour into a shallow mixing bowl. Mix in salt. Make a well in the center of the flour and break the egg into the well. Using your hands, gradually mix the flour into the egg until the dough is smooth and firm. Sprinkle a few drops of cold water as you go if the dough is unmanageable. Knead the dough by hand or with dough hooks until it is satiny smooth. Cover the dough with a damp kitchen towel and let it rest for about 30 minutes. Roll the dough out on a floured surface until it's about 1/8 inch (3 mm) thick. If you have a pasta machine this chore can be made a bit easier. Simply roll the dough through the machine as you would any other noodle until you have reached the desired thickness. Pinch off pieces of the dough between your thumb and forefinger and roll into pieces about the size of a pinto bean. Lay them in a single layer on a lightly floured cookie sheet until all the dough has been used, then drop them into a large kettle of rapidly boiling salted water and cook until tender (12 to 15 minutes). Drain and rinse. Add to soup, simmer momentarily, and serve hot.

ALTERNATE METHOD
Drop the uncooked csipetke into the simmering soup about 15 minutes before soup is done. Simmer until tender.

🌸 Hungarian Dumplings
GALUSKA

Galuska (ga-loosh-kah) are to Hungarian cooking what rice is to Mexican cooking. So many Hungarian dishes demand these egg dumplings that the art of making fine galuska is a prerequisite to good Hungarian home cooking.

    3   cups (750 ml) sifted all-purpose flour
    1   teaspoon (5 ml) salt
    3   large eggs at room temperature
        Cold water

Sift the flour into a shallow mixing bowl. Mix in the salt. Make a well in the center and add the eggs. Beat the flour into the eggs using a wooden spoon. You'll have to add a little cold water as you go to keep the dough manageable. Of course, if you have an electric mixer with dough hooks, by all means use it. The dough must be worked until the surface blisters. Cover with a damp kitchen towel and let it rest for about an hour. Turn the dough out onto a damp cloth and cut off pieces about the thickness of your little finger and about ½ inch (12 mm) long. Place them in a single layer on a lightly floured cookie sheet until you have a good batch, then drop them into lots of rapidly boiling salted water and cook them just until they rise to the surface. Skim them off with a large strainer, drain well, and put them into a warm, deep casserole, adding a little butter each time and tossing to coat. Repeat until all of the dough is gone. Keep galuska warm until ready to serve.

🌸 Homemade Pasta
Makes about 1 pound (450 g)

    4   cups (1000 ml) flour (semolina or all-purpose)
    3   large eggs

1   teaspoon (5 ml) salt
Cold water as needed

Mound the flour on a wooden work surface. Make a well in the center of the mound. Break the eggs into the well. Add the salt to the eggs. Lightly beat the eggs with a fork, incorporating a little flour. Using your hands, begin to mix the flour into the eggs gradually, until you have a firm dough, but not dry or stiff. Add some cold water, a drop at a time, as you mix if necessary to make the dough manageable. If the dough is too soft, it will tear and stick when you roll it. Wash your hands and clean the board well and dust it lightly with more flour. Knead the dough on the lightly floured board for 10 to 12 minutes until it is smooth and elastic. Sprinkle the board with a bit more flour if necessary from time to time to keep the dough from sticking. Keep in mind, however, that the less flour you add, the better your pasta will be. Divide the dough into four equal parts. Wrap three of them in plastic wrap to prevent them from drying out. Proceed with one of the following methods for rolling out the dough.

ROLLING PIN METHOD

Use a long heavy wooden rolling pin that has been lightly seasoned with olive oil and flour. To season, scrub the rolling pin and dry it well. Using your fingertips, rub a thin layer of olive oil into the wood and, when it is absorbed, rub the pin with a light coating of flour. You should do this every time you use your rolling pin until it will absorb no more oil. Do not overload the wood with oil—the merest amount will do.

Dust a large, clean wooden work surface with a small amount of flour. Place one portion of the dough on the board and flatten it slightly with your hands. Begin to roll it out evenly in all directions, turning it scant quarter turns continually to keep its round shape. Try to keep it as perfectly circular as possible. Add flour if necessary to keep the dough from sticking to the board or the rolling pin. Here are a few things to remember as you work:

1. Don't add too much flour.

2. Work quickly because the pasta will eventually dry out and become brittle.

3. Don't press the dough *down* with the rolling pin. Instead, roll it *out* away from you gently and swiftly in all directions.

When the dough reaches a thickness of about ⅛ inch (3 mm), begin a stretching action with your rolling pin. To accomplish this, roll one top edge of the dough up and around the rolling pin. Roll the pin in a quick back and forth motion with the palms of your hands resting on the top of the pin. As you roll and stretch the dough outward, stretch it from side to side on the pin by moving your hands in close together and then out toward the ends of the rolling pin. Do this evenly on all sides of the dough until the dough is thin enough to see through. Remember to work quickly, before the dough becomes too dry to stretch.

If you are making stuffed pasta, use the dough at this point according to the filling recipe. Otherwise, roll the dough over the pin, then roll it out onto a large clean kitchen cloth. Drape it over the back of a kitchen chair and let it dry until it looks leathery on the surface—for about 25 minutes, but watch it carefully as the temperature of the room, drafts, and humidity all affect its dryness. You must cut the dough while it is still pliable. In the meantime, proceed in the above manner using the remaining dough.

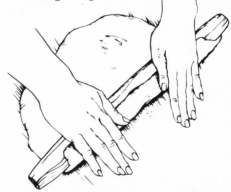

Roll the dried but pliable dough over the rolling pin again and transfer to the work surface. Dust the surface of the dough *very lightly* with flour and fold the dough over and over into a flat roll about 3 to 4 inches (75 to 100 mm) wide. Using a large, sharp knife, cut the dough into strips in the width you desire. Unroll the pasta onto a clean kitchen towel and dry a few more minutes before cooking.

When all the noodles are made, transport them in the towel to a large pot of rapidly boiling salted water, not fewer than 6 quarts (6000 ml), and add all at once. Stir gently and boil for a few minutes until the pasta is *al dente*. Homemade pasta cooks much faster than commercial varieties, so watch it carefully and don't overcook it. Drain in a colander and serve with sauce or butter and grated cheese. Serve as hot as you possibly can. For this reason, I suggest keeping the serving plates nice and hot.

PASTA MACHINE METHOD

These are basic instructions for the manual, crank-handled type of imported pasta machine. If you are buying a new or different kind of machine, try to get complete instructions and/or a demonstration with it.

Separate the pasta dough into four equal parts. Wrap three tightly in plastic wrap and set aside. Flatten one portion with your fingers and dust it lightly on both sides with flour.

Set the machine at its widest setting and crank the dough through the machine. Dust the pasta with flour and fold it in thirds. Seam side first, roll it through the machine again. Continue this process, dusting lightly with flour, rolling in thirds, and cranking through the machine until the dough is smooth and satiny. Begin to roll the dough through the machine at gradually narrower settings. When the dough becomes too large to handle easily, cut it into thirds. Cover two pieces with plastic wrap to prevent them from drying out.

Continue to roll the dough thinner and thinner until you have reached the thinnest setting (or the one you desire) on the machine. Roll the dough through the cutters at the desired width (or roll and cut as in the rolling pin method above), catching the strips over your forearms. Transfer to a clean kitchen cloth to dry or hang over the rods of a collapsible wooden clothes drying rack. Proceed in this manner until all of the dough is used. Cook as directed above.

HOW TO STORE HOMEMADE NOODLES

Lay the pasta out on a clean, floured kitchen towel or hang over the rods of a collapsible clothes drying rack. When dry and hard, pack them very carefully into plastic bags or large glass containers with tight-fitting lids. If you prefer to freeze the noodles, dry them partially to the point where they will no longer stick together, then pack them loosely in plastic bags and tie securely. They will keep frozen for a couple of months.

Homemade Spinach Pasta

Makes about 1 pound (450 g)

Spinach, or green, pasta has just a slight variation in taste and the dough itself is usually a bit softer. This colored noodle looks especially pretty in layers, as demonstrated in the recipe for Spinach Lasagne with Pine Nuts and Fresh Tomatoes (*see* index).

    1   cup (250 ml) cooked, puréed spinach, squeezed
            dry (approximate)
    3   large eggs
    1   teaspoon (5 ml) salt
    4   cups (1000 ml) all-purpose or semolina flour

Proceed as for Homemade Pasta (*see* index). Add the spinach to the egg and salt "well" with one hand as you mix the flour into the well with your other hand. Mix in spinach and flour gradually until you have a firm dough. Complete and cook in exactly the same manner as for regular pasta. See the recipes in this book that call for spinach pasta.

🌺 Pasta with Spring Vegetables, Herbs, and Cream

PASTA PRIMAVERA
Makes 6 to 8 servings

This memorable medley of tender egg pasta, fresh vegetables, nuts, herbs, cream, and cheese must be cooked at the last possible moment before serving. In spite of this final flurry, *pasta primavera* is the most successful pasta dish I have ever served.

Offer it as a first course, followed by tangy *Turkey Scaloppine with Lemon** and either *Fresh Watermelon Ice** or *Cafe Ricotta** for dessert.

3	small, fresh zucchini, scrubbed and sliced diagonally into ¼ inch (6 mm) slices
2	cups (500 ml) tiny sweet peas, freshly shelled
8	to 12 spears of fresh asparagus, sliced diagonally into 1½ inch (37 mm) lengths
¼	cup (60 ml) olive oil or sweet butter
½	cup (125 ml) shelled pine nuts
4	or 5 cloves of garlic, finely chopped
½	pound (225 g) fresh white mushrooms, cleaned and sliced
¼	cup (60 ml) fresh minced parsley
¼	cup (60 ml) fresh minced sweet basil leaves or 3 to 4 tablespoons (45 to 60 ml) dried basil
½	teaspoon (3 ml) crushed dried rosemary
16	firm cherry tomatoes or small ripe Italian plum tomatoes, cut in half lengthwise
1	cup (250 ml) heavy cream
1	tablespoon (15 ml) sweet butter
½	pound (225 g) freshly grated imported Parmesan cheese
1	pound (450 g) homemade or imported No. 8 spaghetti Salt and freshly ground pepper to taste

*See index.

Steam the zucchini, peas, and asparagus separately until each is nearly tender. Rinse them immediately with cold water to stop the cooking process. Drain and set aside, covered with plastic wrap. In a large skillet, heat the olive oil. Sauté the pine nuts quickly until they are golden brown. Watch them carefully, because they can burn easily. Transfer the nuts with a slotted spoon to a paper towel to drain. Add the garlic, mushrooms, parsley, basil, and rosemary to the skillet and simmer until the mushrooms are tender. Add the zucchini, peas, asparagus, and the tomatoes and toss gently just until they are heated through. Stir in the pine nuts and remove from the heat, but keep warm. In a very large saucepan, heat the cream to a boil. Add the butter and stir to melt. Add about half of the cheese and stir until the mixture thickens.

Meanwhile, cook the spaghetti in plenty of rapidly boiling salted water until it is *al dente*. Homemade pasta cooks much faster than does the commercially produced, so try to time your noodles to be done at the same time you finish the sauce.

The object is to keep the vegetables as fresh and unwilted as possible, and yet bring the whole dish to the table piping hot. Therefore, carry out the next steps as quickly as possible.

Drain the spaghetti. Add the spaghetti to the cream sauce and toss to coat. Pour all ingredients from the skillet into the spaghetti and toss again very gently. Place the spaghetti on a large, heated serving platter, add a few grindings of salt (if needed), and freshly ground black pepper. Sprinkle with some of the remaining cheese and whisk the platter off to the table. Pass the extra cheese at the table. *Pasta primavera* must be served immediately.

Fresh Vegetable Spaghetti Sauce

Makes about 2½ quarts (2500 ml)

A thick, fresh-tasting sauce that's chock full of vegetables and herbs.

¼ cup (60 ml) olive oil
2   large onions, chopped

5   or 6 cloves of garlic, peeled and chopped (or to taste)
¾   pound (340 g) fresh white mushrooms, cleaned and sliced
1   large green bell pepper, stemmed, seeded, and cut in 1 inch (25 mm) chunks
5   pounds (2250 g) fresh ripe tomatoes, peeled, seeded, and chopped, or 28 ounces (784 g) canned chopped Italian plum tomatoes with juice
2   to 3 tablespoons (30 to 45 ml) tomato paste
¼   cup (60 ml) dry red wine
¾   cup (180 ml) fresh sweet basil leaves or about 3 to 4 tablespoons (45 to 60 ml) dried basil
2   or 3 teaspoons (10 to 15 ml) crushed dried oregano
½   teaspoon (3 ml) crushed dried rosemary
1   teaspoon (5 ml) sugar
     Salt and freshly ground pepper to taste
4   small fresh zucchini, well scrubbed, trimmed, and thinly sliced [about ¼ inch (6 mm) thick]

Heat the olive oil in a large saucepan and add the chopped onions. Sauté a couple of minutes until they begin to soften. Stir in the chopped garlic and cook another 2 minutes, then add the mushrooms. Cover and simmer for about 4 minutes, then add the bell pepper. Cover and simmer until the vegetables are nearly tender—do not fully cook. Add the tomatoes, tomato paste, red wine, herbs, sugar, salt, and pepper. Bring to a good simmer. Add the zucchini and simmer uncovered until the zucchini is tender. Do not overcook. Serve hot over *al dente* spaghetti. Sprinkle with lots of freshly grated Parmesan cheese.

FRESH TOMATO SAUCE
Cook as directed above, omitting the mushrooms, bell pepper, and zucchini. Add more chopped tomatoes, adjusting the seasoning accordingly, if you wish to make a bigger batch. Simmer until all the ingredients taste well balanced, about 30 minutes. Fresh tomato sauce freezes nicely either in a large airtight container or in an ice cube tray (to make smaller, easier-to-use portions). If you use an ice cube tray, let the sauce freeze solid, then wrap each cube in either plastic wrap or foil, and store all in a large, sealed plastic bag.

✿ Cheese-Stuffed Ravioli with Walnut Pesto

Makes 6 to 8 servings

These tender pillows depend upon fresh sweet basil for the proper flavor. Basil is easy to grow in a sunny window sill, and a few seeds will yield an abundance of long-lasting leaves.

FILLING
½ pound (225 g) ricotta cheese
8 ounces (225 g) cream cheese, at room temperature
⅓ cup (85 ml) finely grated Parmesan cheese
2 egg yolks, well beaten
1 teaspoon (5 ml) grated lemon zest (no white)
3 to 4 tablespoons (45 to 60 ml) minced fresh
   sweet basil leaves
Salt and white pepper to taste
Dash of ground nutmeg

Combine the three cheeses in a mixing bowl and cream together with a wooden spoon. Beat in the egg yolks. Add lemon zest and spices to taste. Cover and refrigerate while you prepare the pasta.

PASTA
1 pound (450 g) Homemade (plain) or Spinach Pasta
   (*see* index)

Follow recipe for the pasta. Roll out into two rectangular pieces, the same size and shape. Place spoons of the filling about 2 inches (50 mm) apart all over one of the pasta sheets. Brush the other sheet of pasta lightly with water and place it, moist side down, over the filling. Press the dough together all around each of the mounds of filling with your finger. Using a zigzag pastry roller, cut the ravioli apart into little square pillows with filling well sealed inside each one. Place the ravioli on a large, clean kitchen towel and dry for a couple of hours. Meanwhile, make the pesto sauce.

WALNUT PESTO
½ cup (125 ml) shelled chopped walnuts
4 or 5 cloves of garlic, peeled and bruised

½   teaspoon (3 ml) salt
2   cups (500 ml) fresh sweet basil leaves
⅓   cup (85 ml) olive oil
⅓   cup (85 ml) grated Parmesan cheese
⅓   cup (85 ml) grated Romano cheese
¼   pound (112 g) butter, softened

In a blender at high speed, pulverize the nuts, garlic, salt, and basil. You'll have to stop the motor and scrape down the jar with a spatula a few times to process the ingredients evenly. When the mixture is a thick paste, begin to add the olive oil a drop at a time, while the blender is running, until the sauce is thick and creamy. Transfer to a mixing bowl and beat in the cheese with a wooden spoon. Add the butter and beat until smooth. Refrigerate in a tightly covered container until ready to use.

TO SERVE
Drop the ravioli into 6 quarts (6000 ml) of rapidly boiling salted water and cook until they are tender. Watch them carefully and test to ensure they're properly cooked. They should be *al dente*. Drain in a colander. Place the ravioli back into the hot kettle and add the pesto sauce. Toss gently to coat all the pieces. Spoon onto warm serving plates and eat immediately. Pass extra Parmesan cheese at the table if you wish.

Spinach Lasagne with Pine Nuts and Fresh Tomatoes
Makes 10 to 12 servings

This colorful casserole is rich with cheeses, meats, and pine nuts, and can be made with either a creamy white sauce or a more traditional marinara sauce.

Ripe, red tomatoes add a refreshing splash of both color and flavor to this unique version of the Italian classic. Uncomplicated accompaniments are called for—crusty bread, a crisp salad and wine, and then for dessert perhaps an assortment of Fresh Fruit Ices (*see* index).

1	pound (450 g) Homemade Spinach Pasta (*see* index) cut into 3 inch × 6 to 8 inch (75 mm × 150 to 200 mm) strips
2	tablespoons (30 ml) butter or oil
1	large onion, peeled and diced
3	or 4 large cloves of garlic, peeled and finely chopped
¾	pound (340 g) fresh white mushrooms, cleaned and sliced
2	to 2½ pounds (900 to 1125 g) lean ground meat (a combination of veal, pork, and beef is most flavorful)
½	cup (125 g) shelled pine nuts
½	cup (125 g) dry white wine
4½	ounces (126 g) canned tomato paste
¼	cup (60 ml) minced parsley
1	teaspoon (5 ml) crushed dried rosemary
1	teaspoon (5 ml) crushed dried thyme
½	cup (125 ml) minced fresh sweet basil leaves Sprinkling of ground nutmeg
2	eggs
½	pound (225 g) cooked, chopped spinach, squeezed dry
1½	cups (375 ml) grated Parmesan cheese (approximate) Salt and pepper to taste
4	to 5 large, ripe tomatoes, peeled, seeded, and chopped
1½	pounds (675 g) ricotta cheese Cream Sauce or Marinara Sauce (*see* index)
1½	to 2 cups (375 to 500 ml) shredded mozzarella cheese

Follow the recipe for making the noodles and, while they dry slightly on a clean kitchen towel, proceed with the filling as follows.

Heat the butter in a large skillet. Add the onion, garlic, and mushrooms and sauté, stirring often until they are soft. Crumble the meat into the pan and stir-fry until the pinkness is gone. Add the pine nuts and cook a few minutes longer. Remove from the heat and spoon off most of the excess fat. Return to the stove and add wine and tomato paste. Stir until well blended over medium heat. Add the herbs and nutmeg, and turn down the heat. Simmer slowly for about 30 minutes or until most of the liquids are absorbed. Set aside to cool.

When completely cool, break eggs into mixture, add dry spinach plus about ½ cup (125 ml) grated Parmesan, and mix well. Set meat mixture aside while you prepare the sauce of your choice. While the sauce is cooking bring a large kettle of salted water to a rapid boil. Add the fresh noodles and cook just until barely tender. Drain well and then submerge the noodles in a kettle of clean, cool water to keep them separated. Drain as you need them.

TO ASSEMBLE

Spoon a little of the sauce to cover the bottom of a 16 inch × 10 inch × 3 inch (400 mm × 250 mm × 75 mm) baking dish. Place one layer of noodles on the bottom overlapping the edges to cover completely. Spread half of the meat mixture on the noodles. Spoon some of the sauce over, spread out half of the fresh tomatoes, dot with one third of the ricotta, and sprinkle with some Parmesan. Repeat this layering once more, then top the casserole with the remaining noodles and sauce. Dot with ricotta, and sprinkle with the remaining Parmesan and all of the mozzarella. Bake at 350° F. for about 1 hour or until the top is slightly browned. Let stand undisturbed for about 15 minutes before cutting. Serve warm.

TO FREEZE

Cool then wrap tightly with aluminum foil. Can be kept frozen for up to 3 months. Place frozen lasagne in a 325° F. oven for about 1½ hours. Turn heat up to 350° F., uncover, and continue to bake until hot throughout and bubbly on top.

🌸 POLENTA

This Italian version of corn meal mush is a home-cooked staple that can be served a variety of ways.

With cubes of soft cheese and butter melted into the simmering corn meal, polenta becomes a hearty, hot pudding of sorts, to be eaten all by itself.

Crisply fried slices of *polenta* topped with butter and cheese often accompany a meal, like bread and butter.

In a more elegant manner, fried slices of polenta are ladled with a slow cooked thick beef sauce laced with Marsala and herbs.

Imported polenta meal can be obtained at most Italian grocery stores. However, coarse-ground yellow corn meal works just fine.

Plain cooked polenta, like corn meal mush, can be cooked ahead and refrigerated for several days before using.

Basic Polenta

Makes 4 to 6 servings

6½	cups (1625 ml) water
1	teaspoon (5 ml) salt
2	cups (500 ml) coarse-ground yellow corn meal or polenta
3	or 4 tablespoons (45 to 60 ml) butter

Bring the water and salt to a boil in a large, heavy kettle. Pour in the corn meal very, very slowly, stirring constantly. You should be able to see the individual grains of the meal, or you're pouring too fast. A slow pour prevents the mixture from being lumpy. Simmer gently, stirring almost continually for around 30 minutes. The polenta is done when it pulls away from the pan.

Polenta with Melted Butter and Cheese

1	recipe Basic Polenta (preceding recipe)
2	cups (500 ml) Fontina or Bel Paese cheese, cubed
¼	pound (112 g) butter, cubed
	Freshly grated Parmesan cheese

When the corn meal is nearly done, begin stirring in lumps of cheese and butter alternately until all are used. Spoon into bowls and serve immediately topped with some grated cheese.

❧ Fried Polenta

    1   recipe Basic Polenta (preceding recipe)

Pour the hot cooked polenta into a buttered loaf pan and cool. Turn out onto a board and cut with a taughtly stretched string into ½ inch (12 mm) slices. Brush slices lightly with butter. Fry in sizzling butter for several minutes on each side, until crisp and lightly browned. Serve hot with more butter and grated cheese.

❧ Fried Polenta with Simmered Beef Sauce

    1   recipe Simmered Beef Sauce
    1   recipe Fried Polenta (preceding recipe)
         Freshly grated Parmesan cheese

SIMMERED BEEF SAUCE
    3   tablespoons (45 ml) butter
    1   onion, finely chopped
    1   carrot, scraped and finely chopped
    1   large stalk of celery, finely chopped
    ½   cup (125 ml) fresh minced parsley
    ⅛   teaspoon (.5 ml) crushed dried rosemary
    2   cloves of garlic, peeled and finely chopped
    ½   pound (225 g) mushrooms, cleaned and chopped
    1   pound (450 g) lean beef (round or chuck),
            diced (not ground)
    ½   cup (125 ml) dry Marsala or red wine
    1⅓   cups (335 ml) strong beef stock, boiling
         Salt and black pepper to taste
         Grated rind from ½ lemon

In the bottom of a small Dutch oven, melt the butter and add the onion, carrot, celery, parsley, rosemary, garlic, and mushrooms. Simmer several minutes, stirring frequently until the vegetables are soft, but not brown. Add the diced meat to the pan and stir until it has lost all pinkness. Add the Marsala, boiling stock, salt, pepper, and lemon rind and bring the sauce to a good simmer. Cover tightly and place in a 275° F. oven for about 4 to 5 hours. The meat should be broken down and the sauce very thick. Serve hot.

TO SERVE
Place slices of fried polenta on heated plates and ladle some of the meat sauce over them. Sprinkle with grated cheese and pass extra cheese at the table.

🌺 Potato Noodles

GNOCCHI (NYAW-KEE)
Makes 4 servings

I have found that the very lightest potato gnocchi are made with baked—not boiled—potatoes. White Rose potatoes seem to work best of all.

If you have a microwave oven in which to bake the spuds, by all means do so. They will bake nicely enough in a regular oven, but of course it will take longer.

Potato gnocchi can be served as a first course or as a main event, and all they really need is plenty of butter and grated cheese.

Cook just before serving them although, uncooked, they will keep for a couple of hours.

2   pounds (900 g) White Rose potatoes
    Sifted all-purpose flour
    Butter
    Freshly grated Parmesan cheese

Prick the potatoes all over with a fork to let as much steam escape during baking as possible. Bake either in a microwave or in a regular oven until the potatoes are tender throughout. Remove the potatoes from the oven and cut them open to cool. When they are completely cool, scrape out all of the meat and discard the shells. Force the potatoes through a food mill and spread out on a sheet of waxed paper to dry for about 45 minutes to an hour. Gather the potatoes into a ball and begin to add sifted flour a little at a time. Mix well after each addition. Stop adding flour as soon as you have a nonsticky dough. Remember, the more flour you add, the heavier the gnocchi will be. When you have a cohesive, manageable dough, use lightly floured hands to break off pieces of dough about the size of an egg. Roll out into ropes about the diameter of your index finger. Cut into lengths of ¾ inch (18 mm). Place each piece on a fork and make an indentation in the center of the dough with the tip of your index finger. The ridges caused by pressing the dough against the fork, plus the indentation from your finger will hold the butter and cheese better once they are cooked. Lay the gnocchi on a lightly floured baking sheet until they are all finished. Cover with a clean kitchen towel and set aside until you are ready to serve them. Bring 6 quarts (6000 ml) of salted water to a rapid boil. Drop the gnocchi into the water and boil for about 10 seconds until they float to the surface. Skim them off with a slotted spoon, drain momentarily, and place in a heated casserole. Toss with lots of butter and grated cheese. Serve immediately. Pass extra cheese at the table.

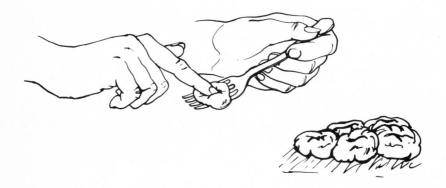

Groats with Bow-Tie Noodles
Kasha Varnishkas
Makes 6 servings

This is novelist Genevieve Davis' favorite recipe for this typically Jewish side dish. The groats can be cooked one day ahead and reheated. But don't cook or add the bow-tie noodles until just before serving. This dish is pleasantly tasty, but not highly seasoned.

    1   egg slightly beaten
    1   cup (250 ml) medium grind groats (kasha)
    2   cups (500 ml) boiling chicken stock
    2   tablespoons (30 ml) butter
        Salt and pepper to taste
   12   ounce package bow-tie noodles

    Stir the beaten egg into the groats and mix well. Put this mixture in a dry skillet and stir over a high flame for 2 or 3 minutes until each grain is separate. Add the boiling chicken stock, butter, salt, and pepper. Cover the skillet tightly, turn the heat down, and simmer for 15 to 20 minutes until the moisture is absorbed. Cook the bow-tie noodles according to the directions on the package until they are *al dente*. Just before serving, gently toss the cooked bow-ties with the groats. Add more butter, salt, and pepper if desired and serve immediately.

Knishes

Makes 6 dinner-sized pastries or about 2 dozen appetizers

    These Jewish filled pastries (k-*nish*-es) can be made in big dinner-sized patties or little bites for snacking. Either way they boast tender, tissue-thin dough, layered with seasoned meats and potatoes, then browned to perfection in a hot oven. They keep nicely when made in advance and can go from freezer to stomach in short order.

    2½   cups (625 ml) all-purpose flour
     ½   teaspoon (3 ml) salt
      3   eggs, separated
      2   tablespoons (30 ml) vegetable oil
     ¾   cup (180 ml) warm water (110° F.)
          Additional oil and flour
          Filling

Sift the flour and salt together into a mixing bowl. Make a well in the center. Add whites from two eggs, 2 tablespoons (30 ml) of oil and about half the warm water. Stir with a wooden spoon, then mix with your hands, adding more water as needed to make a smooth, pliable dough. Turn the dough out onto a lightly floured board and knead a few times. Brush the dough with a good coating of oil and cover it with a warm mixing bowl (large enough not to touch the dough). Let the dough rest for about 1 hour. Roll the dough out on a well floured board until it is thin as possible [less than ⅛ inch (3 mm)]. Brush the dough with a little oil and let it rest a few more minutes. Spoon the filling out along one edge of the dough. Beginning with that side, roll the dough over and over itself pinwheel fashion, with the filling rolled up inside the center. Cut into six equal pieces. Pinch the ends closed and flatten the *knishes* into thick patties. Brush all the tops with the remaining egg white beaten with a little water. Place on a well greased cookie sheet in a preheated 350° F. oven for about 25 minutes. Remove from the oven, brush tops with beaten egg yolks, and return to the oven for another 10 to 15 minutes until they are richly browned. Serve hot.

KNISH APPETIZERS

If you want to serve the knishes with cocktails instead of dinner, divide the filling in half and spread each half in a row along opposite edges of the rolled out dough. Roll each filled end pinwheel fashion toward the middle. Cut the rolls apart down the middle with a sharp knife. Then cut each long roll into pieces about 1¼ inches (31 mm) long. Gently pinch ends closed and brush tops with egg white. Bake on a well greased cookie sheet for about 15 minutes at 375° F. Remove from oven and brush tops with beaten egg yolk. Return to oven and bake an additional 10 minutes or until tops are brown.

Serve hot, or cool, wrap in foil, and freeze for later use. To reheat frozen knishes, place them frozen onto a greased cookie sheet and bake at 375° F. for about 20 minutes. Place foil over the tops if they are becoming too brown before the centers are hot.

LIVER FILLING

Use recipe for Chopped Liver (*see* index). I recommend using broiled beef liver stuffing for these knishes. Grind all ingredients for the chopped liver coarsely.

POTATO FILLING

2 cups (500 ml) mashed potatoes
2 onions, diced
¼ cup (60 ml) melted butter or rendered chicken fat
1 large egg, beaten
  Salt to taste
  White pepper to taste

Mash the potatoes until they are completely smooth. Sauté the onions in 2 tablespoons (30 ml) of the butter until they are soft and golden. Add these to the potatoes along with the remaining melted butter, egg, salt, and pepper. Beat until fluffy.

Kreplach

Which came first—the Jewish *kreplach* (*krep*-lokh) or the Chinese wonton?

A Chinese delegate to the U.N. sat savoring a steaming bowl of chicken soup with kreplach in one of New York's lower East Side eateries.

Contemplating one of the plump, glistening kreplach on his spoon he marveled, "Funny, it doesn't look Jewish."

BASIC EGG NOODLES

2 cups (500 ml) all-purpose flour
2 large eggs
½ teaspoon (3 ml) salt

Make a well in the center of the flour and add the eggs and salt. Mix with your hands until the dough is cohesive. Turn out onto a lightly floured board and knead until the dough is elastic and satiny. Roll out the dough to a thickness of ⅛ inch (3 mm) or less. You'll have to lean on the pin and stretch a bit as you go to overcome the dough's elasticity. Cut the dough into 3 inch (75 mm) squares. Try to visualize an imaginary diagonal line from corner to corner on each noodle square. Place the filling on one half, and fold the other half over to form a plump triangle. Moisten the edges with a little water to seal (make sure no filling gets on the edges, or the noodle will come undone and lose its filling as it cooks). Press the edges lightly with the tines of a fork. Drop the stuffed kreplach into rapidly boiling stock or soup and cook them until they rise to the surface and are tender. Serve hot.

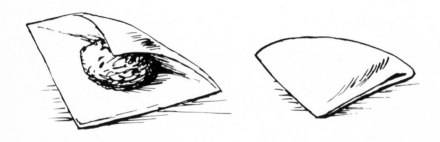

LIVER FILLING

Use the recipe for Chopped Liver (*see* index). I recommend using broiled beef liver for this recipe. Grind all ingredients coarsely as directed.

Matzo Balls

The making of a light, delicate matzo ball can be fairly elusive when you're a beginner.

I first made matzo balls to take to a friend's Passover Seder some years ago. My husband and I weren't married then, and I wanted so to impress him with my culinary wizardry. Foolish of me. Those matzo balls were so heavy they lay on the bottom of the kettle like mortally wounded battleships.

In a panic, I whipped up another batch following a different recipe. The new dumplings were light as little clouds. I arrived at the Seder in the nick of time, and eventually I got my man. Which proves you should never underestimate the power of a matzo ball.

3	eggs, separated
1	cup (250 ml) matzo meal
3	tablespoons (45 ml) rendered chicken fat
½	teaspoon (3 ml) salt
2	teaspoons (10 ml) finely minced parsley
¾	cup (180 ml) hot broth or soup

Separate the eggs cold, being especially careful not to get any yolk into the whites. Put the whites into a clean mixing bowl (not plastic). In another mixing bowl, combine the matzo meal, chicken fat, and egg yolks. Add the salt and parsley and mix well. Pour the hot broth over this, and blend thoroughly. Using an electric mixer with clean beaters, beat the egg whites at high speed until big bubbles form. Add a pinch of salt and continue beating until they are foamy and white and stand in soft peaks (don't let them get dry and glossy). Gently fold the whites into the matzo-egg mixture. Using wet hands, form the mixture into balls about the size of golf balls. Drop into a kettle of boiling chicken soup. Put a lid on the pot and cook for about 30 minutes. Put a serving of the matzo balls into a shallow soup plate and ladle the hot soup over.

Dairy Noodle Pudding

Makes 12 servings

With fresh eggs, sweet creamery butter, smooth rich cream cheese, and oodles of sour cream, Mimi Marks of Fairlawn, New Jersey creates this delectable dish.

Dairy noodle pudding is an age-old Jewish favorite, and Mimi's version is the ultimate. You can make it a few hours ahead and reheat it before serving. It should be served warm.

Offer it plain as a luscious side dish with dinner, or serve it for dessert with fruit compote or berry preserves or thick sweet cream spooned over each serving.

1	pound (450 g) medium width egg noodles
½	pound (225 g) butter, melted
8	ounces (225 g) cream cheese, at room temperature
½	pound (225 g) butter, melted
1	pint (500 ml) sour cream
5	eggs, separated
1¼	cups (310 ml) sugar
¼	cup (60 ml) dry bread crumbs
	Butter

Cook the noodles according to package directions and drain completely. Add melted butter to the noodles and toss to coat the noodles thoroughly. In a blender, place the cream cheese, sour cream, and egg yolks and blend until smooth. Pour this mixture into the noodles and mix well. Beat the egg whites with the sugar until they are stiff and glossy. Gently fold into the noodles. Pour into a large glass baking dish that has been well buttered. Melt a bit more butter [a tablespoon (15 ml) or so] in a small skillet and add the bread crumbs. When they have browned, sprinkle over the top of the noodles. Place on the middle shelf of a preheated 350° F. oven and bake for 1 hour until the top is lightly browned.

Stuffed Noodle Dumplings
PIEROGI, PIROGEN, PELMENY, AND VARENIKI
Makes enough for about 50 dumplings

To Poles they're *pierogi*. To Jews they're *pirogen*. To Russians they're *pelmeny* and *vareniki*. And to just about everyone, they're incredibly delicious.

Thin, tender rounds of fine homemade noodle dough are wrapped around fillings of meat, mushrooms, buttery potatoes, savory cabbage, rich creamed cheese, or fruits. These dumplings are served as main dishes, side dishes, additions to soups and stews, and sometimes for dessert.

Stuffed noodle dumplings are either boiled, fried in butter, or baked in sour cream. Their accompaniments include melted butter, buttered bread crumbs, sour cream, slivered scallions, sugar, spices, and assorted preserves, depending, of course, on the filling.

Pierogi, pirogen, and pelmeny are all made with the same dough. However, their fillings can be decidedly different. As for vareniki, the dough is fundamentally the same, but melted butter is used instead of oil, and milk replaces the water.

All of these dumplings can be frozen with great success.

DOUGH
- 3 large eggs
- 2 tablespoons (30 ml) corn oil (use melted butter for vareniki)
- 1 tablespoon (15 ml) salt
- 1 cup (250 ml) warm water (for vareniki, use milk)
- 4 to 5 cups (1000 to 1250 ml) sifted all-purpose flour
  Additional oil and flour
  Desired filling
  Egg white

In a large mixing bowl, beat the eggs until they are frothy. Add 2 tablespoons (30 ml) of oil, the salt and water, and beat thoroughly. Gradually mix in enough flour to form a stiff dough. Turn the dough out onto a floured surface and knead until the dough becomes smooth and elastic. This should take about 20 to 25 minutes. Rub the dough lightly with oil, cover it with a large, heavy mixing bowl (big enough not to touch it), and set aside to rest about an hour.

Meanwhile, make the filling of your choice.

Turn the dough out onto a lightly floured surface and knead several times. Divide the dough in two. Cover one half with the bowl and set it aside. Roll the other half out on the floured surface to scarcely ⅛ inch (3 mm) thick. Cut the dough into 3 inch (75 mm)

rounds.* Put a heaping spoonful of filling on each circle. Be careful
not to get filling on the edges of the dough as this prevents the edges
from sealing and all of the filling will be lost when the dumplings are
boiled. Brush all around the edges with a little egg white and fold the
dough in half to make half circles. Press the edges together with your
fingers to seal the filling inside. Place the dumplings on a large baking
sheet and cover with a kitchen towel while you repeat this procedure
with the remaining dough and filling. Drop the dumplings into a large
kettle of rapidly boiling salted water. Boil for about 10 minutes or until they float to the top. Remove with a slotted spoon and drain well.
Keep warm until serving.

FROZEN DUMPLINGS

After they have been boiled, cool dumplings thoroughly and
drain well. Place the dumplings on a baking sheet (not touching each
other) and put them in the freezer to flash freeze. When they are hard,
put them into heavy plastic bags and tie securely. They will keep for
up to 3 months and sometimes longer. Drop frozen dumplings directly
into boiling water a few at a time, and cook until they are hot
throughout. Drain and serve warm.

*Pirogen are usually much bigger, so cut the dough according to the size
dumpling you want. They expand a little during cooking.

FRIED DUMPLINGS

Melt enough butter to cover the bottom of a large skillet about ¼ inch (6 mm). Sauté the boiled, well drained dumplings until they are a crisp, light golden brown on both sides. Serve hot.

BAKED DUMPLINGS

Place the boiled well drained dumplings in a buttered, shallow baking dish. Cover them with sour cream. Dot with butter and fine bread crumbs or finely grated cheese (depending on the filling). Bake at 350° F. for 25 minutes or until the top is lightly browned.

Cheese Filling for Stuffed Noodle Dumplings

Fills about 50 pierogi, pirogen, pelmeny, or vareniki

- 2 pounds (900 g) pot cheese, crumbled
- 2 egg yolks, beaten until light in color
- ¼ pound (112 g) butter, melted
- ¼ cup (60 ml) sugar

Mash the crumbled pot cheese in a large mixing bowl. Add the beaten egg yolks and beat until the mixture is fairly smooth and well mixed. Drizzle in the melted butter a little at a time, beating constantly. Add the sugar and beat well. Use as directed. Serve hot and sprinkle with toasted, buttered bread crumbs, melted butter, sour cream, cinnamon and sugar, applesauce, or assorted fruit preserves.

Potato Filling for Stuffed Noodle Dumplings

Fills about 50 pierogi, pirogen, or pelmeny

- 4 large potatoes, peeled and quartered
- 2 tablespoons (30 ml) sour cream
- 2 onions, chopped
- ¼ pound (112 g) butter

2 to 3 teaspoons (10 to 15 ml) dill weed (optional
    for pelmeny only)
   Salt to taste

Boil the potatoes in salted water until they are tender. Drain them well and mash them with 2 tablespoons (30 ml) of sour cream. In a large, heavy skillet, sauté the onions in the butter until they are limp and golden (not brown). Stir often to prevent scorching. Add the mashed potatoes to the pan, sauté, and mix until the potatoes are heated through and the mixture is well blended. Add the seasonings and remove from heat. Use as directed. Serve with lots of melted butter and thick sour cream. Potato pierogi are sometimes sprinkled with buttered, browned bread crumbs.

Cabbage Filling for Stuffed Noodle Dumplings

Fills about 50 pierogi or pelmeny

1   pound (450 g) lean ground pork
½   small head of white cabbage, finely shredded
1   onion, finely chopped
    Chopped garlic or dill weed to taste (optional)
    Salt and pepper to taste

Combine all ingredients together in a mixing bowl and blend well. Use as directed in Stuffed Noodle Dumplings recipe. Serve hot with butter, sour cream, and fresh scallions.

Mushroom Filling for Stuffed Noodle Dumplings

Fills about 50 pierogi or pelmeny

2   ounces (56 g) dried mushrooms, soaked until soft and
       plump, then drained
1   large onion, finely chopped
3   to 4 tablespoons (45 to 60 ml) butter

2   cups (500 ml) cooked long grain rice
     Salt and pepper to taste
2   to 3 teaspoons (10 to 15 ml) dried dill (optional)

Sauté the mushrooms and onions in the butter until the onions are soft and limp but not brown. Add the rice, salt, pepper, and dill weed if desired. Cook a couple of minutes and then remove from heat. Use as directed. Serve hot with lots of thick sour cream and butter.

🌸 Meat Filling for Stuffed Noodle Dumplings

Fills about 50 pierogi or pelmeny

½   pound (225 g) lean ground beef
½   pound (225 g) lean ground pork
2   large onions, finely chopped
1   clove of garlic, minced
2   or 3 teaspoons (10 to 15 ml) dried dill weed
1   egg
     Salt and pepper to taste

Combine all ingredients in a mixing bowl and blend well. Use as directed. Serve hot with sour cream and butter and garnish with shredded fresh scallions.

🌸 Fruit Filling for Stuffed Noodle Dumplings

Fills about 50 pierogi, pirogen, or vareniki

Apples, blueberries, raspberries, cherries, apricots, boysenberries, gooseberries, and peaches are just some of the fruits you can use. Prepare them as you would for pie filling—paring, peeling, coring, and slicing if necessary. Apples, for instance, should be peeled, cored, sliced, and cooked until tender. On the other hand, berries need only be washed and drained. Simply prepare your fruit accordingly.

3   cups (750 ml) of fresh or frozen unsweetened
        fruit or berries
    Sugar to taste
    Sour cream

Place the prepared fruit in a deep bowl and add sugar to taste. Mix the fruit and sugar and allow it to stand at room temperature for about 2 hours. Use as directed. Serve with either sour cream or sweet cream or melted butter.

 Russian Filled Turnovers

PIROZHKI
Makes 10 to 15 individual pies

These popular little pies are most often served as an appetizer, hot from the oven. On occasion, they accompany bowls of homemade soup.

Pirozhki filled with mushrooms or ground beef should be served warm. But the fish-filled turnovers are equally good cold and are a refreshing summer luncheon treat.

I have found that poached, drained fillet of sole or salmon make the most delicious fish fillings. Of course, you can add herbs of your choice—parsley, marjoram, thyme, etc.—to any of the fillings for variation.

Wrapped in foil and then newspaper, pirozhki travel well and make an excellent out-of-hand picnic.

PASTRY
1   recipe for Flaky Pie Crust (*see* index)*
1   egg, well beaten with a little water, for wash

FILLING
2   tablespoons (30 ml) butter
1   large onion, finely chopped

*When you make the crust for pirozhki, you may use butter as a substitute for half the shortening called for in the recipe. Freeze the butter first, and cut it into pea-sized pieces.

2   scallions, finely chopped
¾   pound (340 g) very lean ground beef, cooked white
      fish or salmon, or mushrooms, finely chopped
1   teaspoon (5 ml) dried dill weed
     Salt and pepper to taste
1   egg, well beaten
2   to 3 tablespoons (30 to 45 ml) sour cream
     Dash of nutmeg (optional)

Make the pastry and refrigerate it, wrapped tightly in plastic, while you make the filling.

Melt the butter in a large skillet and sauté the chopped onion until it is soft and limp but not brown. Add the scallions and ground beef (crumbled well), or the fish, or mushrooms. Stir often and cook over a medium flame until the meat has lost its pinkness. In the case of the fish, it should be just heated through. The mushrooms should cook until they are soft. Add the dried dill weed and cook an additional minute or two. Remove from the heat and cool. Add the salt, pepper, egg, sour cream, and nutmeg. Blend well. On a lightly floured board, roll the chilled pastry out into one large rectangle, a scant ⅛ inch (3 mm) thick. Using a small sharp knife, cut the pastry into 4 inch to 5 inch (100 mm to 125 mm) squares. Mentally divide the squares in half diagonally. Place a large spoonful of filling just below the center line on one half of the pastry. Fold the pastry over corner-to-corner, to make a plumply stuffed triangle. Seal the edges with a fork, being careful not to puncture through to the filling. Reroll the scraps. Cut as many squares as you possibly can. Any small scraps can be cut into decorative shapes (leaves, flowers, fish, etc.) to decorate the tops of the pirozhki. Place the turnovers on a large baking sheet, leaving some space between each. Brush the tops with the egg and water wash. Bake in a 400° F. oven for about 25 minutes until the pies are golden brown. Cool slightly before serving.

Main Dishes

While a number of recipes from other sections in this book can also be served as the main dish, the foods presented in this chapter are set apart by the predominance of meats, fish, and poultry.

In the ethnic home most of these dishes are considered to be special enough for company and the most celebrated occasions.

There are grills, barbecues, slow simmered casseroles, pot roasts, deep dish pies, and much more. Though most are substantial enough to be served "*a cappella*," serving suggestions are offered for all of the trimmings.

Basque Marinated Lamb

Makes 4 to 6 servings

Refer to the recipe for the Greek Lamb Kebobs* for procedure on cutting the leg of lamb. Here, the marinating technique is the same, using the same amount of meat, but omitting the vegetables and substituting a different marinade. Basque lamb can be cut into cubes, or left in one butterflied piece to be charcoaled like a large steak.

Serve with a kettle of Garbanzos with Chorizo,* a loaf of fresh Basque Sheepherder's Bread,* and a raw vegetable platter, including thinly sliced cucumbers, tomatoes, onions, green bell peppers, and black olives with an oil and vinegar dressing. Dessert should be no

*See index.

more than a basket of sweet ripe fruit and perhaps a wedge of Spanish Cream Sherry Cake.*

4   to 6 pound (1800 to 2700 g) leg of lamb [will yield 2 to 3 pounds (900 to 1350 g) of meat]
2   cups (500 ml) dry red Spanish wine
½   cup (125 ml) good olive oil
4   cloves of garlic, peeled and chopped
1   large yellow onion, minced
1   large bay leaf, crumbled
1   teaspoon (5 ml) oregano, crumbled
     Coarse ground black pepper to taste
     Salt to taste

Bone and trim the lamb as directed in the recipe for Greek Lamb Kebobs. Leave the meat whole and butterfly it, or cut it in cubes. Combine wine, oil, garlic, onion, bay leaf, oregano, and pepper. Pour over meat in a deep glass bowl, cover, and refrigerate from 8 to 24 hours, turning occasionally. Salt the meat to taste just before cooking. Broil over charcoal embers until the meat is pink in the middle. Turn frequently to ensure even cooking, and baste with the marinade if you wish.

🌺 Cuban Pork Roast
Makes 6 to 8 servings

With this delightfully piquant roast, offer Black Beans and Rice (*see* index), a salad of papayas, bananas, and pineapple with chile-flavored oil and lime juice dressing, plus a batch of freshly baked Pumpkin Bread (*see* index) with butter.

3   to 4 pound (1350 to 1800 g) boneless top loin pork roast
⅓   cup (85 ml) fresh orange juice with 2 tablespoons (30 ml) fresh lime juice (strained)
2   teaspoons (10 ml) oil

*See index.

4   cloves of garlic, peeled and minced
1   tablespoon (15 ml) dried oregano leaves
    Salt and freshly ground pepper to taste
2   tablespoons (30 ml) butter or oil
2   large onions, coarsely chopped
2   stalks celery, chopped

Wipe the roast with a damp, clean kitchen towel. Marinate the meat for at least an hour in the juice. Using a mortar and pestle, make a pulp out of the oil, garlic, oregano, and salt and pepper. Drain the pork, reserving the marinade. Rub the paste all over the roast. Place the chopped onions and the celery in the bottom of a roasting pan and sprinkle lightly with salt and pepper. Place the roast on the vegetables and pour the reserved marinade into the roaster, not over the meat. Place the roaster in a 325° F. oven and cook, uncovered, basting often with the pan juices until the meat reaches an internal temperature of 170° F. (well done) and is nicely browned, about 3 hours. If the pan becomes dry, add either orange or lime juice. Let the meat rest on a carving board for 15 minutes before cutting it. Meanwhile, pour the pan juices into a blender and whirl to pureé the vegetables into a smooth sauce. Spoon fat off the top and discard. Slice the pork into ½ inch (12 mm) thick rounds and arrange on a heated serving platter. Spoon the sauce over the meat. This roast may be served either hot or cold.

VARIATION
Scrub and quarter yams or sweet potatoes and add them to the roaster after 1 hour of cooking time. Baste the meat and potatoes until they are tender.

🌺 Cuban Pot Roast

Makes 6 to 8 servings

For fabulous, tangy flavor, let the meat marinate at least 12 hours.

4	to 5 pound (1800 to 2250 g) beef chuck roast
¼	cup (60 ml) fresh lemon or lime juice, strained
3	cloves of garlic, finely chopped
2	teaspoons (10 ml) sugar
2	tablespoons (30 ml) red wine vinegar
¼	cup (60 ml) dry red wine
1	bay leaf
1	onion, finely minced
1	teaspoon (5 ml) crumbled oregano
½	teaspoon (3 ml) crumbled marjoram
	Salt and freshly ground pepper to taste
	Flour
4	tablespoons (60 ml) oil
1	large onion, thinly sliced
1	large green pepper, seeded, stemmed, and sliced in ¼ inch (6 mm) strips
1	red pepper, seeded, stemmed, and sliced in ¼ inch (6 mm) strips
2	carrots diced
2	cups (500 ml) canned or fresh tomatoes, chopped, with juice

Using a very sharp knife, score the roast on each side about ¼ inch (6 mm) deep. In a saucepan, combine juice, garlic, sugar, wine vinegar, red wine, bay leaf, minced onion, oregano, and marjoram and bring to a boil. Pour boiling marinade over roast, cover tightly and refrigerate for several hours, turning the roast over several times to marinate evenly in the spices. Drain the meat, reserving the marinade. Strain the marinade, saving both vegetables and juice. Pat the meat dry with a paper towel and season on both sides with salt and freshly ground pepper. Dust the meat lightly with flour and shake off the excess. In a heavy Dutch oven just large enough to hold the meat, heat the oil until it ripples. Add the meat and brown quickly on both sides. When it has reached a deep, rich color, transfer to a plate. Brown the sliced onion, green pepper, red pepper, and carrots in the remaining fat, stirring often. Add vegetables and spices from the marinade and simmer for a few minutes. Place the roast back in the pan and add the tomatoes, some salt, and freshly ground pepper. Add the reserved marinade, cover, and simmer over very low heat for about 2½ to 3 hours, until the meat is tender. Add a little wine, water, or stock if the pot becomes too dry. Slice thin and arrange on a heated serving platter. Spoon the pan juices over the meat. Serve with black beans and rice, a dry red wine, and crusty bread and butter.

Jamaican Fried Chicken

Makes 6 to 8 servings

Serve this fried chicken with fluffy white rice and a salad of papaya, oranges, and bananas with fresh lime juice.

2	2½ to 3 pound (1125 to 1350 g) fryers, cut in eighths
¼	cup (60 ml) dark Jamaican rum
3	tablespoons (45 ml) peanut oil
¼	cup (60 ml) dark soy sauce
1	egg white
2	¼ inch (6 mm) slices fresh ginger, minced
	Flour for breading
	Peanut oil for frying
	Shortening

Wipe the chicken pieces with a clean damp towel and place them in a deep, glass mixing bowl. Combine the rum, peanut oil, soy sauce, egg white, and ginger and pour over the chicken. Cover loosely and marinate for about 2 hours, turning pieces once or twice. Drain each chicken piece momentarily. Roll in flour and shake off excess. Fry in about 1 inch (25 mm) hot oil with a little shortening added, until the chicken is tender and nicely brown on all sides.

🌺 Jamaican "Pickled" Fish

ESCOVITCH

Makes 6 to 8 servings

This fish isn't pickled in the sense that it's put up in jars
. . . it gets its title from the spicy, vinegar-accented sauce that smothers
the tender fresh fillets.

4	pounds (1800 g) firm-fleshed whitefish fillets
	Salt and white pepper to taste
	All-purpose flour
	Butter or vegetable oil for frying
¾	cup (180 ml) olive oil
2	onions, peeled and thinly sliced
1	large red pepper, seeded, stemmed, and cut in thin strips
	Pinch of ground mace
1	bay leaf
	Fresh ground pepper
3	¼ inch (6 mm) slices fresh ginger, peeled and finely chopped
	Salt to taste
½	cup (125 ml) malt vinegar

Cut fish into serving size pieces and pat dry with a paper towel.
Salt and pepper on each side and flour each piece, shaking off excess.
Heat butter and/or vegetable oil in a large skillet and add a few pieces
of the fish. Brown lightly on both sides, cooking the fish through.
Transfer to a shallow serving dish and set aside. Repeat with the remaining fish. Heat the olive oil in a saucepan. Add the onions and
pepper and fry, stirring often, until the vegetables are lightly brown.
Add mace, bay leaf, pepper, ginger, and a bit of salt and continue to
cook for about 1 minute. Add vinegar and bring to a boil. Simmer for
10 minutes. Remove bay leaf and pour hot sauce over fish. Serve hot
as an entree or cold as a first course with hot sauce or hot peppers if
desired.

🌺 Spicy Sauerbraten with Buttered Potato Dumplings

Makes 6 to 8 servings

A *sauerbraten* platter is simply spectacular on a frosty night. And what an enticing aroma fills the house! It is hearty, so a light appetizer (if any) is recommended. Red Cabbage with Apples* is the perfect side dish and you can add either German Potato Dumplings* or German Potato Pancakes* or some of both!

Dessert should be light but not bland. I recommend warm Cherry Strudel* and coffee.

MARINADE

4	pound (1800 g) rump roast
2	cups (500 ml) red wine vinegar
2	cups (500 ml) red wine
10	to 12 whole peppercorns
2	large bay leaves
10	whole cloves
1	onion, chopped
2	stalks of celery with tops, chopped
2	carrots, scraped and chopped
5	to 6 fresh juniper berries (optional)
½	teaspoon (3 ml) allspice

Wipe the roast with paper toweling and tie it with kitchen twine so it will keep its shape. Place in a deep crock or casserole, one that holds the meat with little side room to spare, so the marinade will come up as high as possible. A 2 gallon (8 l) earthenware crock is ideal for sauerbraten. Bring the wine vinegar, wine, spices, and chopped vegetables to a boil in a saucepan, and simmer for a few minutes. Pour the hot marinade over the roast. Cool, cover, and refrigerate for at least 48 hours. Turn the roast at least twice a day so that the meat marinates evenly.

*See index.

TO COOK

2   tablespoons (30 ml) shortening
Flour
Salt and pepper to taste
1   cup (250 ml) chopped carrots
1   cup (250 ml) chopped celery
1   large onion, peeled and thinly sliced
1   large garlic clove, peeled and stuck with a
    toothpick

Remove the meat from the marinade and pat dry. Strain the marinade pressing out all of the juice from the vegetables and spices. Discard the pulp and reserve the liquid. Melt the shortening in a large Dutch oven until it is quite hot. Dust the meat lightly with some flour and brown on all sides in the hot fat, until the meat is a deep, rich, even color. Remove the meat from the pan and set aside. Add the chopped carrots, celery, and sliced onion to the hot fat and sauté, stirring frequently until they are soft and lightly browned. Dust the vegetables with a little flour and stir until the flour begins to brown. Pour the marinade liquid into the Dutch oven and bring it to a boil. Add the meat and garlic plus some salt and pepper and cover. Reduce heat and cook slowly and gently for about 2 to 2½ hours until the meat is very tender. You may also put the meat into a preheated 350° F. oven if you wish, for the same cooking time.

GRAVY

¼   cup (60 ml) apple jelly
1   cup (250 ml) crumbled gingersnaps
½   cup (125 ml) sour cream (optional)

Transfer the meat to a warm platter, cover, and keep warm while you make the gravy and prepare to serve dinner. Strain the pan juices into a large measuring cup and skim off the fat. Return the remaining juices to the Dutch oven and bring them to a boil. Reduce liquid until you have about 2 cups (500 ml) left. Add the apple jelly and gingersnap crumbs and stir to dissolve. Simmer until smooth. If desired, stir some of the hot gravy into the sour cream to warm it, then whisk the mixture into the hot gravy. Remove from heat immediately.

TO SERVE

Slice the roast into thick slices [½ inch (12 mm) or so] and set them, overlapping, down the center of a warm serving platter or wooden serving board. Surround with either potato dumplings or German potato pancakes, ladle a bit of the gravy over the meat, and serve immediately. Pass the remaining gravy at the table to spoon over the meat and the dumplings. Offer a hearty red wine or ice cold beer.

 ## Spareribs with Apple and Prune Stuffing

Makes 6 to 8 servings

A well seasoned stuffing laden with sweet fruits and savory vegetables is sandwiched between racks of sizzling pork ribs finished with a sprinkling of sage. To complete this handsome feast, add German Potato Pancakes,* homemade Applesauce,* and a warm fruit Strudel* or fragrant Gingerbread.*

> 6   to 8 pounds (2700 to 3600 g) pork spareribs cut in
>   two pieces [buy 1 pound (450 g) per person]
> ⅓   cup (85 ml) flour
> 2   tablespoons (30 ml) dry mustard
> ¼   teaspoon (1.5 ml) sage
>   Salt and pepper to taste
>   Apple and prune stuffing (recipe follows)
>   Paprika

Plunge the spareribs (one piece at a time) into a kettle of boiling water. When the water returns to a boil, time for 4 minutes. Remove, drain, and pat dry with a paper towel. Mix flour, spices, salt, and pepper together and coat the ribs on both sides. Lay one rack of ribs concave side up and fill with stuffing. Lay the other piece over the filled rack concave side down, and tie the ribs together securely with kitchen twine. Sprinkle the top with some additional paprika. Place on a rack in a large roaster, in a preheated 375° F. oven and bake uncovered for 2 to 2½ hours or until the meat is tender when pierced with a fork. Baste often with melted butter or drippings from the bot-

*See index.

tom of the roaster. Remove from the roaster and cut away string. Cut the ribs apart. Fill the center of a large serving board with the stuffing, surround with the ribs.

APPLE AND PRUNE STUFFING

2   to 3 tablespoons (30 to 45 ml) butter or
      vegetable oil
2   large onions, peeled and chopped
3   large tart apples, peeled, cored, and chopped
1   cup (250 ml) celery, including tops, finely chopped
1   clove of garlic, minced
1   pound (450 g) pork sausage
2   cups (500 ml) cooked, mashed yams
½   pound (225 g) pitted prunes, soaked, drained,
      and chopped
1   cup (250 ml) dried bread cubes
      Juice from ½ lemon, strained
2   tablespoons (30 ml) brown sugar
1   teaspoon (5 ml) dried crushed thyme
1   tablespoon (15 ml) sweet Hungarian paprika
¼   teaspoon (1.5 ml) each of sage and marjoram
      Salt and pepper to taste
      Chicken stock or water

In a large, heavy skillet, melt the butter until it sizzles. Add onions, apples, and celery and sauté until they are limp and golden, stirring often. Add garlic and crumble the sausage into the pan. Cook, stirring occasionally, until the sausage has lost all of its color. Remove from heat. In a deep, large mixing bowl, combine yams, prunes, bread cubes, and the ingredients in the skillet. Mix well. Add lemon juice, brown sugar, and spices and blend thoroughly. Taste for seasoning and add salt and pepper to taste. Moisten with a little stock if necessary.

Greek Chicken Oregano

Makes 8 servings

This is truly family fare, and it couldn't be more simple. Double or triple the recipe easily for parties—everyone seems to love it!

Serve it with any number of side dishes—from a simple dressed salad to an elaborate Spanakopita (*see* index). Add bread, wine, and Baklava (*see* index) to make it memorable.

16   chicken thighs with skin
     Salt and pepper
 2   large garlic cloves, peeled and split in half
     Juice of 2 lemons
¼   cup (60 ml) imported olive oil
 3   to 4 tablespoons (45 to 60 ml) dried crumbled oregano

Rinse the chicken under cold, running water and remove any pin feathers from the skin. Drain and pat dry on paper toweling. Sprinkle lightly with salt and pepper. Combine the remaining ingredients in a deep bowl. Place the chicken pieces in the marinade and coat all of the pieces well. Cover tightly and refrigerate for 1 to 2 hours. Drain the thighs, reserving the marinade. Broil the chicken, basting continually with the remaining marinade until the pieces are tender and the skin is crisp. Sprinkle with more lemon juice before serving. This chicken is also delicious cooked over charcoal. Turn and baste it often with the remaining marinade until it is tender and crispy. Serve on a large platter garnished with chunks of lemon and sprigs of fresh mint.

 Greek Deep Dish Chicken Pie

KOTOPETA (KO-*TO*-PEA-TAH)
Makes 15 servings

Multilayers of thin, buttery brown Phyllo Dough (*see* index) form the crispy crust of this creamy chicken-filled pie, richly flavored with eggs, cream, a dash of nutmeg, and grated imported Kefalotyri cheese.

The phyllo dough and Kefalotyri cheese can be purchased at most Greek, Italian, and Middle Eastern grocery stores. You might even like to try making your own phyllo.

Since this pie is rather time consuming, it makes sense to construct it in stages. Cook the filling and chill overnight, then assemble and bake the *kotopeta* the following day.

Deep dish chicken pie is a handsome buffet dish and tastes best slightly warm. For a luncheon or late night supper, I like to accompany it with herbed green beans and mushrooms, tart fresh cranberry-orange relish, chilled white wine, and a frozen fresh lemon mousse for dessert.

Kotopeta, when tightly wrapped, will freeze beautifully.

FILLING

8 to 8½ pounds (3600 to 3825 g) chicken thighs and breasts
1 teaspoon (5 ml) salt
4 medium onions, peeled and thinly sliced

Rinse the chicken under cold running water and place in a very large kettle with lid. Barely cover with cold water, bring to a slow simmer, and skim off all foam that rises to the surface. Add salt and thinly sliced onions, cover, and simmer gently until pieces are tender—about 40 to 50 minutes. Remove chicken pieces with tongs and set aside to cool. Bring stock and onions to a rapid boil and cook uncovered to reduce stock to about 3 cups (1500 ml). Watch the stock carefully as it approaches the 3 cup (1500 ml) level and stir frequently to prevent the onions from sticking or scorching. Pour the broth in a glass container, cover, and refrigerate. When thoroughly chilled, discard the hard fat on the surface. Skin and bone the chicken. Remove all fat and sinew. Tear or cut meat into bite-sized pieces, cover, and refrigerate. Construct Greek deep dish chicken pie about 3½ hours before serving.

TO ASSEMBLE

½ cup (125 ml) warm milk
½ cup (125 ml) warm heavy cream

1   pound (450 g) commercial or homemade phyllo
    dough
¾   pound unsalted butter melted in the top of a
    double boiler over hot water
5   eggs at room temperature
4   tablespoons (60 ml) Kefalotyri cheese, finely grated
    White pepper to taste
    Salt to taste
¼   teaspoon (1.5 ml) ground nutmeg

Put the refrigerated chicken stock in a large, heavy saucepan and heat over a low flame. Add the chicken meat and heat through. Combine milk and cream and add to the chicken. Cook and stir over medium heat until the mixture begins to bubble. Stir and remove from heat. Let stand to cool. On a large work surface, organize a 17 inch × 11 inch × 2½ inch (425 mm × 275 mm × 62 mm) baking pan, the melted butter kept warm over the hot water in a double boiler, and a large pastry brush. Lay the sheets of phyllo dough out flat on a piece of plastic wrap. Cover completely with more plastic wrap and lay a damp kitchen towel overall to help keep the dough moist and pliable. Brush the pan generously, bottom, sides, and corners, with melted butter. Brush the top of the first phyllo sheet with butter. Lay it into the pan, butter side up, completely covering one corner and part of the pan's bottom and allowing the edges to hang over the sides a couple of inches (50 mm). Butter a second sheet in the same manner and overlap the first sheet covering a different corner of the pan, allowing the edges to hang over the sides. Continue in this manner

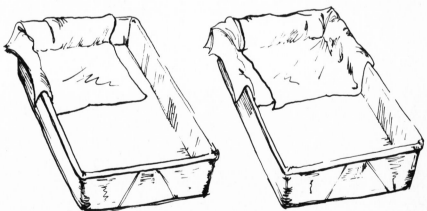

alternating sides and corners of the pan until you have layered 8 sheets of phyllo on the bottom of the pan. Recover the stack of phyllo with plastic wrap and the damp towel after each sheet is removed. The filling should now be cool. Add the eggs, grated cheese, salt, pepper, and nutmeg and mix well. Pour this mixture into the phyllo-lined baking pan and spread out evenly. Cover filling with remaining phyllo, painting each sheet's top with butter like the bottom layers. Overlap the phyllo and extend over the edges of the pan until all the dough is used up. Roll overhanging dough up and over to make a neat roll around the inside edge of the pan. Paint with remaining butter. Using the tip of a small sharp knife, score the top couple of layers only of the dough into serving-sized pieces. Don't cut through to the filling. This will make the pie easier to cut and serve after it is baked. Cut through most of the edge roll to indicate serving pieces. Flick a few drops of water on top of the pie to keep the crust from curling. Place in a preheated 350° F. oven for 1 hour until the pie is a deep golden brown. If it starts to brown too quickly, place a piece of foil over the top. Allow the pie to cool and set at least 30 minutes before cutting. To serve, cut along lines with a very sharp knife. Completely slice through all of the layers. Remove each piece carefully with a flexible spatula. Once it is baked, this pie can be reheated, but the crust will never again be as crispy.

TO FREEZE

To freeze a baked cooled pie, cover tightly with layers of foil and freeze. Place in a preheated 325° F. oven, uncovered, and bake for about 1½ hours until the filling is hot throughout.

To freeze an unbaked pie, cover with layers of foil and freeze. Place directly in a preheated 350° F. oven for 1½ hours. Reduce oven heat to 325° F. and continue to bake for another hour until the crust is deep golden and the filling thoroughly hot. Serve as suggested above.

 Greek Deep Dish Cheese and Spinach Pie

Sᴘᴀɴᴀᴋᴏᴘɪᴛᴀ (SPAHN-AH-ᴋᴏ-PEA-TAH)
Makes 24 servings

Follow all of the directions for assembling the *Greek Deep Dish*

Chicken Pie (preceding recipe), but substitute the traditional filling of cheese and spinach.

Like the chicken pie, *spanakopita* tastes best either slightly warm or at room temperature.

This cheese and spinach pie is most often served as a side dish with roast lamb or chicken, a big tossed salad with oil and vinegar, and a good, country wine.

Casseri cheese can be purchased at Greek, Italian, and Middle Eastern groceries and specialty cheese shops.

30	ounces (840 g) packaged frozen chopped spinach, thawed, drained, and squeezed dry
¼	cup (60 ml) olive oil
1	large onion, finely chopped
3	or 4 scallions, chopped, including green tops
1	pound (450 g) Feta cheese, crumbled
¾	pound (340 g) farmer cheese or pot cheese
¼	cup (60 ml) grated Casseri or Parmesan cheese
	Few drops fresh lemon juice
3	or 4 sprigs fresh mint leaves, finely chopped, or ½ to 1 teaspoon (3 to 5 ml) dried dill weed
¼	cup (60 ml) minced fresh parsley
	3 eggs
	Pepper to taste
	Salt (take care—the cheese is very salty)
½	pound (225 g) unsalted butter
1	pound (450 g) homemade or commercial Phyllo Dough (*see* index)

Place the spinach in a large mixing bowl. Heat the oil in a skillet and sauté the onions until they begin to soften. Add the scallions and cook until all are soft and limp, but not browned. Add the onions to the spinach along with the cheeses, lemon juice, mint or dill, and parsley. Break the eggs directly into the bowl and mix with your hands to blend well. If the mixture seems dry (depending on the moisture in the cheese) you may add another egg. The filling should be moist, but not loose. Salt and pepper to taste. Using the butter and phyllo dough as directed in the recipe for Greek Deep Dish Chicken Pie, assemble and bake the pie. Let it set, undisturbed, for at least 15 minutes before cutting. Freeze according to Greek Deep Dish Chicken Pie directions.

🌺 Larry's Lamb Chops Avgolemono
Makes 4 to 6 servings

A few years ago, my husband, Larry, was asked to share a favorite recipe with the "Guys and Galleys" column of the Los Angeles Times. This tangy Greek recipe is the one they liked best . . . and understandably. It's perfect family-style fare. It's simple and quick to prepare, unusual, and very tasty. The sauce deserves a good loaf of bread for dunking. Add a crisp lettuce and onion salad with oil and herb dressing and some wine or a cold beer.

1   pound (450 g) small new potatoes in their jackets
2   tablespoons (30 ml) olive oil
6   shoulder lamb chops
3   small stalks of celery, diced
1   large onion, diced
1   cup (250 ml) meat or chicken stock
1   egg
    Juice of 1 lemon
1   tablespoon (15 ml) cornstarch

Boil the potatoes until they are tender, drain, set aside, and keep warm. In a large, heavy skillet, heat the oil. Brown the lamb chops quickly on both sides. Remove from the skillet, and set aside. Sauté the celery and onions in the remaining fat until they are soft and translucent but not brown. Lay the lamb chops over all and pour the stock into the skillet. Simmer covered for about 20 minutes. Remove from the heat and keep covered while you make the sauce. Beat the egg until it is frothy. Beat in the lemon juice and cornstarch. Transfer chops to a heated serving platter and surround with the potatoes. Quickly bring the skillet juices back to a boil. Add a spoonful of the hot juice to the egg-lemon mixture to warm it, then whisk the eggs into the pan juices. Remove from heat immediately. Pour the sauce over the lamb and potatoes and serve hot.

🌸 Greek Marinated Lamb Kebobs

SOUVLAKIA
Makes 4 to 6 servings

Kebobs are a welcome summer treat and an easy way to feed a crowd. You can double or triple this recipe easily, but you may have to increase the proportions of herbs to get a rich, full flavor.

I buy a whole leg of lamb and bone it myself, but you could have your butcher do this. Out of that leg, I usually get one rolled or butterflied roast plus enough meat for a big *souvlakia*, and, of course, the bone for soup. Trim the souvlakia meat carefully, leave very little fat, and remove as much sinew as possible.

The marinade tenderizes the meat and gives the vegetables a distinct flavor. If you like softer vegetables, adjust the precooking time accordingly. A good souvlakia offers pink charcoaled meat and tender (not soft) vegetables.

Good accompaniments for this casual dinner are crusty bread, saffron-laced rice pilafi, black Greek olives, dry red wine, and anything from fruit to pastry for dessert.

Souvlakia is tempting eaten out of hand inside the pocket of warm, freshly baked *Pita Bread* (*see* index). Watch over the broiling skewers continually for best results. Souvlakia cooks quickly.

1	small leg of lamb—approximately 3 to 4 pounds (1350 to 1800 g)—will yield 2 to 3 pounds boned (900 to 1350 g) of meat
1	cup (250 ml) good olive oil
	Juice of 2 lemons, strained
½	cup (125 ml) dry, hearty red wine
3	cloves of garlic, peeled and slivered
	Salt and pepper to taste
3	tablespoons (45 ml) crumbled dried oregano
2	bay leaves, crumbled
2	or 3 tablespoons (30 to 45 ml) chopped fresh basil or 1 to 2 tablespoons (15 to 30 ml) dried basil
	Pinch of dried or fresh thyme
	Pinch of crushed rosemary

 1   pound (450 g) fresh white mushrooms, cleaned
       and sprinkled with the juice of 1 lemon
 2   large yellow onions, peeled and cut into quarters
 3   large green bell peppers, scrubbed, seeded, and
       cut into 1½ inch (37 mm) chunks
12   to 18 firm cherry or Italian plum style tomatoes,
       washed and left whole (allow 3 per serving)

Remove the fat from the lamb, along with the sinew. Cut it into 2 inch (50 mm) chunks like large stew meat. Combine the olive oil, juice from two lemons, red wine, slivered garlic, salt, pepper, oregano, bay leaves, basil, thyme, and rosemary in a large stainless steel kettle and bring them to a boil. Drop the mushrooms into the boiling marinade and cook, stirring to coat for about 1 minute. Drop the onions and green pepper into the marinade, stir just to coat, and cook for about 1 minute then remove the kettle from the fire. Let it stand uncovered until it cools. Add the meat chunks and stir to coat everything. Add the tomatoes and mix again. Cover tightly and refrigerate from 6 to 24 hours. The longer you marinate, the better the flavor. Thread the ingredients alternately on metal shish-kebob skewers. Sprinkle the completed skewers with a bit of salt and pepper if you wish and place them on a charcoal grill when the coals have burned to white. Grill on all sides, turning frequently and basting with some of the reserved marinade until the meat is brown on the outside and slightly pink in the middle. Slip the meat and vegetables off the skewers using a fork, and slide them onto individual plates. Serve immediately.

Greek Roast Leg of Lamb
Makes 6 to 8 servings

Greeks roast a fine leg of lamb in many different fashions. Some are wrapped in thick layers of aluminum foil and slow-roasted. Others are wrapped in layers of clean cheesecloth and basted frequently with dry red wine. On very special occasions, a leg of lamb is spit-broiled over hot coals, or wrapped in several thicknesses of foil and buried in a pit of glowing charcoal. The following recipe represents the simplest method—and in my estimation, one of the tastiest.

Allow yourself plenty of time for slow roasting, and careful basting. The results are worth the effort.

Roast lamb is best rare or a pink medium rare. Rely on a good meat thermometer to register the internal temperature, and remember not to let the thermometer touch the bone. After it's cooked about 15 minutes per pound (450 g), keep a watchful eye on it.

The quantity of garlic in this recipe is variable, according to your own taste. Likewise, depending on the strength of your herbs, their proportions can be regulated to taste.

Serve roast leg of lamb in ¼ inch to ⅜ inch (6 mm to 9 mm) slices accompanied by pan juices, Stuffed Grape Leaves,* Orange and Olive Salad,* perhaps the roasted vegetables (see variation), a good red wine, fresh bread with sweet butter, and Ravanie* or a fresh fruit platter for dessert.

1	whole leg of spring lamb, bone in [6 to 8 pounds, (2700 to 3600 g)]
6	to 8 cloves of garlic, peeled
¼	cup (60 ml) select quality olive oil
1	teaspoon (5 ml) dried oregano
½	teaspoon (3 ml) dried rosemary
½	teaspoon (3 ml) dried marjoram
	Salt and coarsely ground black pepper
1	onion, chopped
1	carrot, chopped
1	cup (250 ml) chopped celery
1	bay leaf
½	cup (125 ml) good dry red wine
1	cup (250 ml) hearty Lamb Stock*

Remove the layer of fat from the underside of the lamb and cut off the lower shank portion if it is still attached. If the fell has a strong aroma, remove it as well. You should leave just a mere coating of fat on the top side of the lamb. Discard the fat. Place the scraps and lower shank bone in the bottom of a large roaster. Make several small slits

*See index.

all over the lamb with the tip of a very small, sharp knife. Insert a clove of garlic in each slit. Rub the entire outside of the lamb with a cut piece of garlic and the olive oil. Using a mortar and pestle, crush all of the dried herbs together, except the bay leaf. Rub them all over the surface of the lamb with your hands. Salt and pepper to taste, patting the herbs and spices into the meat with your hands. Place the roast fat side down on a rack in the roaster containing the lamb trimmings. Add the chopped vegetables and bay leaf to the bottom of the roaster. Roast uncovered at about 325° F. to reduce the shrinkage until the internal temperature of the meat registers rare (130° F.) or medium rare (140° F.) on a reliable meat thermometer. After the surface of the meat has begun to brown, add the red wine to the bottom of the roaster, and baste the lamb about every 20 minutes. Remove the lamb from the oven and let it rest on a carving platter for about 15 minutes. In the meantime, strain the pan juices and skim off the fat. Add the lamb stock to the bottom of the pan and return all of the pan juices. Bring to a rapid boil stirring up any browned bits. Carve the lamb and arrange on a warm serving platter. Pass the juices at the table to be spooned over each serving.

VARIATION

Place the roast directly on the bed of chopped vegetables instead of a rack. Substitute a good dry white wine for the red. During the last hour of cooking, add 4 white rose potatoes, scrubbed and quartered; 2 large onions, peeled and quartered; and 16 to 20 baby carrots, trimmed and scraped. Baste them often with the pan juices and add a few more herbs if desired. The vegetables should be very tender.

 Greek Meat and Eggplant Casserole

MOUSSAKA (MOOS-AH-KAH)
Makes 15 servings

Moussaka is a smart choice for buffet entertaining. It can be made several hours ahead, it reheats well, and tastes good either warm or at room temperature. Cut into squares, it is easy to serve.

If your time is budgeted, prepare this Mediterranean melange in stages. Make the meat filling one day, then cook the eggplant, assemble, and bake the casserole on the following day.

Surround this substantial main course with pungent Calamata olives and a tossed green salad laced with oil, fresh lemon, and herbs. A basket of bread and a jug of robust red wine are suitably earthy companions. For dessert, my choice would be a platter of slightly chilled fresh and dried fruits, a dish of roasted almonds, a plate of Baklava (*see* index), and strong coffee.

2	pounds (900 g) lean ground beef or lamb, or a combination of both
2	medium-sized onions, peeled and finely chopped
2	cloves of garlic, peeled and minced
6	ounces (168 g) canned tomato paste
½	cup (125 ml) dry white wine
1	teaspoon (5 ml) ground cinnamon
¼	cup (60 ml) minced fresh parsley
	Salt and pepper
1	cup (250 ml) grated Kefalotyri or Casseri cheese, or substitute Parmesan
1	cup (250 ml) dry fine bread crumbs
2	eggs, at room temperature, well beaten
1	recipe Fried Eggplant (*see* index)
	Cream Sauce Topping (below)

In a large, heavy skillet, crumble the ground meat and cook, stirring, until it loses most of its pinkness. Add the chopped onion and garlic and sauté until the meat is well done and the onions are soft and limp. Spoon off all fat. Stir in the tomato paste, wine, cinnamon, parsley, plus a little salt and pepper and simmer slowly until all of the liquid has been absorbed, about 35 minutes. Remove the skillet from the heat and cool completely. Stir in the half of the cheese and bread crumbs plus the eggs and adjust the seasoning. Set aside while you prepare the eggplant. Scatter about 2 tablespoons (30 ml) of the remaining bread crumbs over the bottom of a 16 inch × 13 inch × 3 inch (400 mm × 325 mm × 75 mm) baking pan. Place one layer of the fried eggplant on the bottom. Spread about half the meat mixture over the eggplant. Add another layer of eggplant, then the rest of the meat, and finally the remaining eggplant. Pour the cream sauce over all. Sprinkle with the last of the grated cheese and bread crumbs. Bake in a preheated 350° F. oven for about 1 hour or until the casserole is golden brown on top. Remove from the oven and let stand undisturbed for about 30 minutes before cutting. Serve warm or at room temperature.

CREAM SAUCE TOPPING
  6 tablespoons (90 ml) sweet butter
  7 to 8 tablespoons (105 to 120 ml) all-purpose flour
  4 cups (1000 ml) warm milk
  2 egg yolks, well beaten
     Salt and white pepper to taste

Melt the butter in a large saucepan. Stir in the flour gradually until the mixture is smooth. Cook, stirring continuously, over low heat for 1 to 2 minutes—just until the floury taste is gone, but don't let it brown. Add the warm milk gradually, constantly stirring until the sauce is smooth. Cook and stir over medium heat until the sauce begins to bubble slowly, and eventually becomes thick. Add a bit of the sauce to the beaten egg yolks to warm them. Then quickly whisk the yolks into the sauce and remove from the heat immediately.Add salt and white pepper to taste. The sauce must be used as soon as possible.

Hungarian Sour Cabbage Rolls
TOLTOTT KAPOSZTA
Makes 15 to 18 rolls (serves 6 to 8)

Various versions of this wonderful dish are found in many ethnic cuisines, including Jewish, Rumanian, and Polish. This recipe combines the typically Transylvanian flavors—smokey and sour—in a truly magnificent make-ahead dish.

Serve with some freshly baked black bread, soft, sweet butter, some creamy mashed potatoes, and a chilled fruity white wine.

  1 large, firm head of white cabbage
  1 slice of rye bread
  2 tablespoons (30 ml) salt

STUFFING

½ cup (125 ml) long grain white rice
1¼ pounds (562 g) ground pork
2 onions, finely chopped
2 eggs
6 thick slices smoked bacon
Pinch of crushed dried marjoram
3 cloves of garlic, minced
1 teaspoon (5 ml) dill
Paprika to taste
Salt and pepper to taste
2 cups (500 ml) beef stock or sauerkraut juice
(or a mixture of both)
½ pound (225 g) smoked sausage
6 to 8 smoked pork chops
3 tablespoons (45 ml) butter
3 tablespoons (45 ml) flour
16 ounce (450 g) container sour cream, at room
temperature
Chopped fresh dill
Paprika

Rinse the cabbage under cold water and remove any bruised outer leaves. Cut out most of the core. Lay the slice of rye bread at the bottom of a 2 gallon (8 l) pottery crock and place the cabbage on the bread. Mix the 2 tablespoons (30 ml) of salt with about 2 quarts (2000 l) of cold water and pour over the cabbage. Add water if necessary to cover. Place a heavy dish on the cabbage to keep it submerged. Cover the crock with two or three layers of kitchen towels and set the crock in a cool spot for about 1 week. Drain cabbage by inverting it in a colander and allowing it to stand for several minutes. Place the cabbage in a deep pan or bowl and pour boiling water over it to cover. Let it stand in the boiling water until it cools. Separate the leaves carefully and spread them out on a towel in a single layer. When the leaves at the core are reached (too small and tough for cabbage rolls) shred them to the consistency of sauerkraut and set aside.

TO MAKE THE STUFFING

Parboil the rice in salted water for 8 to 10 minutes, drain, and cool. Combine the ground pork, onions, eggs, rice, 2 slices of the bacon which have been diced, marjoram, 1 clove of the garlic, dill, paprika, salt, and pepper to your taste. Mix with your hands until all ingredients are well blended. Count the cabbage leaves and divide the stuffing accordingly. Place the stuffing in the middle of the leaf, fold the base up and over the stuffing, then fold the sides in and continue to roll. Place each cabbage roll seam side down until all are ready.

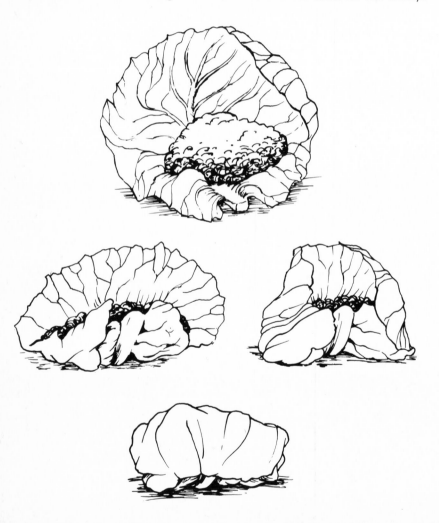

Place the remaining 4 strips of bacon in a layer in the bottom of a large heavy kettle or casserole. Arrange the shredded cabbage over the bacon, then place the cabbage rolls, seam side down, over all. Cover with meat stock or sauerkraut juice (if you like the tartness) or a mixture of both. Add the remaining 2 cloves of garlic to the pot. Bring pot to a boil, reduce heat, cover, and simmer slowly for about 1½ hours. Slice the sausage into ½ inch (12 mm) thick rounds and tuck them in among the cabbage rolls. Lay the smoked pork chops over all and continue to simmer, covered, for another ½ hour. Remove from heat, keep covered, and allow the kettle to cool completely. For maximum flavor, the cabbage rolls should be refrigerated overnight at this point. Reheat very slowly over low heat until pot bubbles gently.

TO SERVE

Melt the 3 tablespoons (45 ml) of butter in a heavy saucepan and gradually add the flour to make a roux. Stir and cook for about 2 to 3 minutes until the mixture just begins to color. Add the juices from the cabbage rolls and continue to cook and stir until mixture thickens. Add some of this sauce to the sour cream and stir back into the sauce. Pour the sauce over the cabbage rolls. Dust with finely chopped fresh dill weed and a bit of paprika. Serve right out of the kettle.

Chicken Paprikash

Makes 6 servings

At the very heart of this classic stew is the sweet, peppery paprika, so use the very finest.

Containers labeled simply "paprika" probably contain a spice with no discernible flavor. However, the variety labeled "sweet Hungarian paprika" (available in many specialty stores) should be quite flavorful and exude a peppery aroma just right for a really delicious, authentic *paprikash*.

    3   tablespoons (45 ml) olive oil
    2   broiler/fryer chickens, cut into 8 pieces each [about 5
        pounds (2250 g) in all]

Salt and pepper to taste

2 medium-sized onions, finely chopped

2 to 3 tablespoons (30 to 45 ml) sweet Hungarian paprika

2 cloves of garlic, minced

½ pound (225 g) fresh mushrooms, cleaned and thickly sliced

2 green bell peppers, seeded and cut into 1 inch (25 mm) chunks

1 bay leaf

1 cup (250 ml) canned plum tomatoes, drained (reserve liquid)

1 cup (250 ml) water (or tomato liquid or chicken stock)

¼ cup (60 ml) instant blending flour

1 cup (250 ml) sour cream at room temperature

Chopped fresh parsley

Galuska or Spaetzle (*see* index)

Heat the olive oil in a large heavy skillet. Rinse the chicken pieces under cold running water and pat dry. Salt lightly and add a few pieces at a time to the hot oil. Do not brown, just turn evenly in the oil until the chicken skin turns yellow. Transfer pieces to a large flame-proof casserole until all chicken has been cooked. Tip the skillet and spoon off all but 3 tablespoons (45 ml) of fat. Add onions to the fat in the skillet, and sauté until limp and golden. Add paprika, garlic, mushrooms, green pepper, and bay leaf and sauté stirring often for about 2 minutes. Add tomatoes and 1 cup (250 ml) of liquid and bring to a simmer. Pour the sauce over the chicken in the casserole. Bring to a gentle simmer. Cover loosely and cook for about an hour or until the chicken is tender when pierced with a fork. Using a large slotted spoon, transfer the chicken pieces to a warm serving dish. Remove the bay leaf and discard. Bring the sauce to a boil. Add a ladleful of hot sauce to the flour, stirring to dissolve the flour. Add this to the sour cream along with another couple of spoonfuls of the hot sauce to warm the sour cream. Slowly pour the sour cream mixture into the boiling sauce, stirring continuously until the sauce is well- blended. Adjust seasonings. Pour some of the sauce over the chicken and Galuska or Spaetzle and pass remaining sauce at the table. Garnish with fresh chopped parsley.

🥀 Transylvanian Sauerkraut Casserole

Makes 6 to 8 servings

This splendid casserole needs nothing more than some crusty black or brown bread with sweet butter, perhaps boiled new potatoes in their jackets and, for dessert, a slice of warm Apple Strudel (*see index*).

¼ pound (112 g) smoked bacon, diced

1   medium onion, chopped

¼ pound (112 g) smoked sausage cut into 1 inch (25 mm) chunks

¼ pound (112 g) smoked ham, cut in ½ inch (12 mm) cubes

1   pound (450 g) lean ground pork

2   tablespoons (30 ml) sweet Hungarian paprika

2   cloves of garlic, minced

2   teaspoons (10 ml) crushed caraway seeds

2   large red-skinned potatoes, washed and sliced into ¼ inch (6 mm) thick slices (you may peel them, if you wish)

2   pound (900 g) jar sauerkraut, drained and squeezed dry

16 ounces (450 g) sour cream
    Dash of salt (go easy because the meats are salty)
    Several grindings of black pepper
    Additional paprika

Put diced bacon in a cold, heavy skillet and set over medium flame until bacon fat begins to render. Sauté until bacon is just lightly brown and remove the bacon from the skillet with a slotted spoon and set aside. Add the onion to the hot bacon fat and sauté until limp. Add the sausage, ham, and ground pork, and sauté until the sausage and pork have lost all pinkness. Remove from heat. Spoon off as much fat as possible. Return to heat. Add paprika, garlic, and caraway. Sauté for 2 to 3 minutes, being careful not to let anything burn. Remove from heat. In a deep baking dish, place one layer of potato slices, a layer of half the drained sauerkraut, then half of the meat mixture. Place a few dollops of sour cream over the meat and repeat the layers with the remaining ingredients. Top with a layer of sour cream and sprinkle generously with sweet Hungarian paprika. Bake in a 350° F. oven for about 1 hour or until the sides shrink away from the pan. Cool for about 15 minutes before serving.

🍀 Irish Corned Beef and Cabbage
Makes 6 to 8 servings

Corned beef brisket is widely available in most supermarkets and butcher shops. It is practically impossible to give an accurate timetable for cooking the meat, because corned beef varies. Just start it several hours before you intend to serve it and simmer it very slowly until tender.

Some corned beef needs to be soaked in cold water overnight to rid it of excess salt. Ask your butcher or read the label. Corned beef that is cooked way ahead of schedule can stand immersed in its stock for a few hours without any problem. However, the vegetables are best when cooked just before serving.

If you especially like the flavor of dill, add a few fresh sprigs as the vegetables cook.

      3   to 4 pounds (1350 to 1800 g) lean corned beef
      4   cloves of garlic, peeled
      8   to 10 whole peppercorns
      2   tablespoons (30 ml) pickling spice
      2   tablespoons (30 ml) dill weed
      1   large onion, coarsely chopped
      1   large, firm head white cabbage
      6   to 8 smallish red potatoes, scrubbed and cut in half
      2   large onions, peeled and quartered

Place the corned beef in a large kettle and cover with cold water. Bring to a boil over medium heat, skimming the surface of all foam. Add the garlic, peppercorns, pickling spice, dill weed, and coarsely chopped onion to the kettle and simmer for 3 or more hours, or until the meat is fork-tender. Transfer the meat to a warm platter and cover tightly with foil to keep warm. Strain the stock, discarding spices and vegetables. Skim fat from the stock and return it to the kettle. If the stock tastes too salty, dilute it with water. Bring to a rolling boil. Add potatoes and onions and simmer for about 15 minutes. Meanwhile, discard the outer leaves of the cabbage and cut it in six to eight wedges. Trim off most of the core, but leave some so the leaves won't fall apart. Lay the cabbage on top of the other vegetables and continue to simmer for 15 to 20 minutes, until the vegetables are tender. Slice the corned beef across the grain into thin slices. Lift the vegetables from the kettle with a large slotted spoon and arrange them on the platter surrounding the meat. Ladle some of the hot stock over all and dot the vegetables with butter. Serve with good rye bread, a pot of brown mustard, coarse salt and pepper, and icy mugs of beer. Leftovers are great in sandwiches and will keep for several days if wrapped tightly in foil and refrigerated. Leftover vegetables can be added to a kettle of homemade soup.

 ## Irish Smoked Fish and Rice with Saffron
KEDGEREE
Makes 4 servings

This dish of Indian origin found its way into British homes in the eighteenth century. Primarily it was served as a breakfast dish.

Today its character and ingredients have changed somewhat but the idea remains intact: a spicy one-dish meal of rice, onions, and smoked fish drizzled with fresh lemon juice and served with plenty of good chutney.

4	tablespoons (60 ml) butter
1	large onion, peeled and finely chopped
1	teaspoon (5 ml) grated lemon zest (no white)
⅛	teaspoon (.5 ml) allspice
⅛	teaspoon (.5 ml) cayenne pepper
¼	teaspoon (1.5 ml) curry powder
⅛	teaspoon (.5 ml) powdered saffron
1	small bay leaf

1   cup (250 ml) long grain white rice
2   cups (500 ml) boiling chicken stock
    Salt and freshly ground pepper to taste
1   pound (450 g) cooked smoked haddock, broken into
     pieces
    Fresh lemon juice

In a large saucepan, heat butter until it sizzles. Add onion and fry over fairly low heat, stirring constantly until the onion becomes limp and soft, but not brown. Stir in lemon zest, spices, and bay leaf and simmer another minute. Pour in the rice and stir with the spices until the rice is lightly colored. Pour in the boiling chicken stock and simmer, covered, for about 20 minutes, or until the rice is tender. Gently fold in the pieces of haddock and, if there is too much liquid in the rice mix, keep over a low flame, uncovered, until the *kedgeree* becomes dry. Squeeze lemon juice to taste over all, and serve hot. Accompany with chutney.

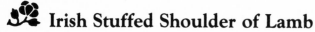 Irish Stuffed Shoulder of Lamb
Makes 6 to 8 servings

This Irish lamb makes a particularly flavorful "Sunday" dinner. Potatoes and onions are roasted in the pan juices, and in addition, you might offer some broiled herbed tomatoes and a bowl of sweet Irish Peas (*see* index).

3½   pound (1575 g) boneless lamb shoulder
1   cup (250 ml) cooked white rice
¼   cup (60 ml) seedless white raisins
2   tablespoons (30 ml) finely grated orange zest
    (no white)
1   clove of garlic, minced
1   tablespoon (15 ml) finely minced onion
¼   teaspoon (1.5 ml) crushed marjoram
¼   teaspoon (1.5 ml) crushed rosemary
6   tablespoons (90 ml) melted butter

> Salt and pepper
>
> ¼ cup (60 ml) flour
> 4 medium white rose potatoes, peeled and quartered
> 2 onions, quartered
>   Rosemary
> ¼ cup (60 ml) sweet sherry
> 1 jigger brandy
>   Meat stock as needed

Lay the lamb shoulder out flat and pound it with a flat wooden mallet to even its thickness. Sprinkle lightly with salt and pepper. Combine rice, raisins, orange zest, garlic, minced onion, herbs, and 3 tablespoons (45 ml) of the butter to make a stuffing. Spread evenly over the lamb, leaving a margin on all sides. Starting at the narrowest end, roll the lamb up jelly-roll style. Tie securely with clean kitchen twine. Lightly salt and pepper the lamb roll, then roll in the flour to evenly coat, and shake off the excess. In a Dutch oven or flame-proof casserole large enough to accommodate the lamb, heat the remaining butter until it sizzles. Brown lamb quickly on all sides. Remove it from the pan temporarily. Add the quartered potatoes, onions, a sprinkling of salt and pepper, and a pinch of crushed rosemary. Lay the stuffed lamb over the vegetables and pour in the liquor. Cover and set in a 325° F. oven for 1½ to 2 hours, basting often, and adding a little meat stock if necessary to keep the pan juicy. The vegetables should be soft and the meat nicely done. Transfer roast to a carving board and let stand for about 10 minutes before cutting. Slice crosswise into ¾ inch (18 mm) thick pieces. Arrange on a heated serving platter and surround with potatoes and onions from the pan. Spoon pan juices over all.

Pot Roast Pork with Wine Vinegar and Herbs

Makes 6 to 8 servings

The fine flavor of pork braised in wine vinegar is a good example of how sophisticatedly simple Italian home cooking can be. Serve with pasta, rice, or fried vegetables.

3   pound (1350 g) boneless pork loin roast, trimmed of
     most fat
    Salt and freshly ground black pepper to taste
1   clove of garlic, split in half
3   tablespoons (45 ml) olive oil
1   onion, peeled and sliced
1   bay leaf
1   teaspoon (5 ml) crushed dried rosemary
¾   cup (180 ml) red wine vinegar

Season the pork with salt and pepper and rub with the cut side of a piece of garlic. Heat the oil in a Dutch oven just large enough to hold the meat. Brown the pork on all sides. Add the sliced onion to the pan and stir it around with a wooden spoon until it browns. Add the garlic and herbs and pour in the vinegar. Cover the pan tightly and turn down the heat to a low simmer. Cook very slowly for about 3 hours. Add a little water or red wine if the liquid cooks down. Transfer the meat to a cutting board and let it rest for about 10 minutes. Slice crosswise into pieces about ½ inch (12 mm) thick. Arrange them on a heated platter and spoon some of the pan juices over the meat.

 Turkey Scaloppine with Fresh Lemon
Serves 6 to 8

Like veal, this is a wonderfully light course to serve after pasta. It must be cooked at the last possible minute and brought to the table crisp and hot. I've served it many times, but one particular incident always comes to mind.

We were entertaining a couple who pride themselves on their culinary expertise and educated palates.

We had just finished our Pasta Primavera (*see* index) and were starting on the Turkey Scaloppine (*see* index) when one of these gourmets gushed, "Oh my! This veal is delicious!" And her husband chimed in, "What a treat! I haven't had veal like this in such a long time!" (How right he was!)

At that point, it would have been tactless to tell them it was turkey, so I smiled and said nothing.

That would have been the end of the story, but a few weeks later she called to find out where I had bought my veal. When I explained that it had been turkey breasts and not veal, she coolly quipped, "Well, if you don't want to tell me your source, why don't you just come right out and say so!"

3   pounds (1350 g) skinless, boneless turkey breasts (buy only fresh, young turkey)
2   cups (500 ml) milk
2   eggs
2   cups (500 ml) all-purpose flour
1   cup (250 ml) fine bread crumbs
     Salt and white pepper to taste
¼   pound (112 g) butter
     Corn oil for frying
2   large ripe lemons
1   bunch Italian parsley, washed and drained

Partially freeze the turkey breast to make it easier to slice. Use an electric knife or a very sharp chef's knife to slice the breast crosswise into ⅜ inch (9 mm) thick rounds. Pound the meat with a flat kitchen mallet to a little over ¼ inch (6 mm) thick. In a deep mixing bowl, beat together the milk and eggs. Submerge the turkey, coating all pieces well. Cover and refrigerate for a couple of hours. Mix the flour and bread crumbs together on a piece of waxed paper. In a large skillet, heat 2 tablespoons (30 ml) of butter and about ¼ cup (60 ml) of oil. Drain only the amount of turkey that will fit in the pan in one batch. Coat the pieces on both sides with flour and shake off the excess. Coat with crumbs, sprinkle lightly with salt and pepper. Fry in hot butter and oil until golden on both sides, turning once. Do not overcook or the pieces will become dry. Transfer the turkey to a heated serving platter draining them momentarily as you lift them from the pan. Keep warm, uncovered, in a 150° F. to 200° F. oven. Keep bits of burned coating out of the pan by straining the oil periodically. Add butter and oil between batches and heat sufficiently before adding more turkey. Never add oil while the turkey is in the skillet. When all the turkey has been cooked in this manner, squeeze the juice of 1½ lemons over the slices, taking care not to let seeds or pulp fall on the meat. Slice the remaining ½ lemon into thin rounds to garnish the platter. Accent with sprigs of fresh parsley and serve immediately.

Veal and Peppers
Makes 4 to 6 servings

Molly Custrini, one of New Jersey's finest Italian cooks, offers this recipe for her favorite and simplest stew.

Be sure to use veal shoulder for best results, and vary the garlic and herbs according to your own taste.

Molly serves veal and peppers with pasta or rice and a side of mushrooms fried in butter with garlic and herbs.

2   pounds (900 g) boneless veal shoulder, cut in 1½ inch (37 mm) cubes
¼   cup (60 ml) olive oil
3   to 4 tablespoons (45 to 60 ml) butter
2   to 3 cloves of garlic, peeled and finely chopped
¼   cup (60 ml) fresh parsley, finely minced
2   tablespoons (30 ml) all-purpose flour
3   large green bell peppers, seeded, stemmed, and cut in 1 inch (25 mm) strips
½   cup (125 ml) dry white wine
1   cup (250 ml) canned Italian tomatoes, drained and chopped
½   teaspoon (3 ml) dried, crushed rosemary
½   teaspoon (3 ml) dried, crushed sweet basil
    Pinch of ground sage
    Salt and pepper to taste

Heat the olive oil and butter in a heavy Dutch oven. Brown the veal cubes on all sides. Add the garlic and parsley. Simmer slowly until they wilt, tending them often with a wooden spoon. Sprinkle with flour and stir until the mixture thickens. Add the green peppers, wine, tomatoes, and seasonings and simmer very slowly, uncovered, until the meat is quite tender.

Italian Veal and Sausage Loaf
Serves 8 to 10

A wonderful make-ahead meat loaf laced with cheese, herbs, peas, and pine nuts.

It can be made hours (or weeks) ahead. Because it can be served at room temperature, it's an appropriate choice for a buffet or picnic.

Serve with crusty bread, fresh pasta, a tossed salad with oil and vinegar, and a white wine.

¾   cup (180 ml) freshly grated Parmesan cheese
1   cup (250 ml) soft bread crumbs
10   ounce (280 g) package frozen chopped spinach, thawed and squeezed dry
1   pound (450 g) very lean ground beef
1   pound (450 g) sweet Italian sausage (casings removed) or ground pork
1   pound (450 g) ground veal
1   medium-sized yellow onion, minced
¼   cup (60 ml) fresh basil leaves, chopped and packed, or 2 tablespoons (30 ml) dried basil
1   teaspoon (5 ml) fresh thyme leaves or ½ teaspoon (3 ml) dried thyme
½   teaspoon (3 ml) ground nutmeg
¼   cup (60 ml) milk
2   cups (500 ml) shelled sweet peas (fresh or frozen and thawed)
½   cup (125 ml) shelled pine nuts or coarsely chopped walnut meats

Combine all ingredients except peas and nuts in a large mixing bowl, and work with your hands until the ingredients are well blended. Do not overmix. Fold in the peas and nuts and divide the mixture in half. Shape gently into two long narrow loaves. Do not pack the meat. Place the loaves side-by-side in a 15 inch (375 mm) glass baking dish. Bake in a 350° F. oven for 1½ hours, basting with pan juices frequently. Cool the loaves in the baking dish, continuing to baste until the loaves are room temperature. Serve slightly warm, or at room temperature, or wrap tightly in foil and freeze. These meat loaves freeze extremely well. To thaw, keep them wrapped in foil and place in a slow (140° F. to 175° F.) oven until they are warmed through. Keep tightly wrapped until serving.

 Braised Brisket of Beef
Makes 8 servings

A succulent brisket of beef is simple to make. Start with a rather lean, choice piece of meat. Simmer it ever so slowly until it is tender and moist. Then slice it thinly across the grain.

This humble, but divine pot roast is elevated to holiday status for the Jewish Passover Seder dinner. Sharing the menu might be Chicken Soup with Matzo Balls,* Charoses,* Gefilte Fish* with horseradish, stewed carrot and prune Tzimmes,* crisp Potato Kugel,* fresh broccoli with lemon and butter, and, finally, freshly baked Sponge Cake* with strawberries and thick sweet cream.

Serve thinly sliced leftover brisket on buttered rye bread with a good mustard and thick slices of sweet onion.

> 5 to 6 pound (2250 to 2700 g) whole boneless
>   beef brisket
> 2 tablespoons (30 ml) shortening
>   Salt to taste
>   Coarse ground pepper
> 3 large onions, peeled and thinly sliced
> 2 small bay leaves
> 2 cloves of garlic, peeled and stuck with a toothpick
> 2 cups (500 ml) boiling water

* *See* index.

Slice off any large pieces of fat from the beef and pat it dry with a paper towel. It's good to leave a very thin layer of fat on one side. Melt the shortening in a heavy 5 quart (5000 ml) kettle or Dutch oven. Salt and pepper the beef on both sides and brown it in the hot fat. This will take several minutes on each side to achieve a rich deep brown color. When the meat is deeply browned, add the sliced onions to the pan and stir them around the meat in the hot fat until they become limp and pick up some of the brown color. Add the bay leaves, garlic, and boiling water to the kettle. Cover with a tight-fitting lid and turn the flame down to low. Simmer on the stove top for 2½ to 3 hours, adding a little boiling water when necessary, until the brisket is very tender. Remove the brisket from the kettle and place it on a warm platter. Skim the excess fat from the pan juices and remove the bay leaves and garlic. Slice the brisket across the grain into slices about ⅜ inch (9 mm) thick. Spoon some of the pan gravy over the meat and pass the rest at the table.

⚜ Stuffed Breast of Veal

Makes 4 servings

This succulent dish is the specialty of Genevieve Davis, the celebrated novelist, who is an accomplished and creative cook as well. She's an expert on medieval cookery and loves to serve big batches of elegant peasant fare.

For her stuffed breast of veal, Genevieve uses a Magnalite roaster that's "years old," because it "makes its own juice." Also, the painstakingly slow roasting pays off with reduced shrinkage. She bastes the meat persistently to achieve plump, tender, and richly flavored results.

MEAT
5   to 6 pound (2250 to 2700 g) veal breast with bones, at room temperature
Chunk of fresh lemon
1   or 2 large garlic cloves, peeled and cut
Freshly ground pepper to taste

Sweet Hungarian paprika
Onion powder

STUFFING
- 2   tablespoons (30 ml) butter
- 1   onion, peeled and chopped
- 1   cup (250 ml) diced celery, including tops
- 2   cloves of garlic, peeled and minced
- ¾   pound (340 g) fresh mushrooms, cleaned and sliced
- 1½ cups (375 ml) cubed good bread, toasted in the oven on a cookie sheet until dry and lightly browned
- 1   carrot, scraped, trimmed, and grated
- 4   tablespoons (60 ml) melted butter
  Chicken stock to moisten
- ½   teaspoon (3 ml) thyme, pinch of rosemary, and sage to taste, all ground together with a mortar and pestle
  Salt and fresh pepper to taste

FOR THE ROASTER
- 2   tablespoons (30 ml) butter
- 2   carrots, scraped, trimmed, and diced
- ½   onion, chopped
- 2   celery stalks, diced
  Chicken stock
  Splash of good, dry sherry

Select good white veal and have the butcher cut a pocket in the breast between the bones and the meat. Wipe the breast completely with a damp, clean kitchen towel. Rub the meat all over, inside and out, with the cut side of the lemon chunk and garlic. Sprinkle with pepper, including the inside of the pocket. Let the veal come to room temperature while you make the stuffing. Melt the 2 tablespoons (30 ml) of butter in a large skillet. Add the chopped onion and celery and sauté until they begin to soften. Add the garlic and mushrooms and cook over moderately low heat, stirring frequently, until all of the vegetables are soft and cooked through. In a large mixing bowl, combine the toasted bread cubes, sautéed vegetables, the grated raw carrot, and 4 tablespoons (60 ml) of melted butter. Add just enough chicken stock to make a moist—not mushy—stuffing. Season to taste with the herbs, salt, and pepper. Lay the stuffing inside the pocket of the veal. Secure with skewers or tie with string to keep the stuffing in while it roasts. At the rib end, you may fold or crimp a piece of aluminum foil around the meat to hold the stuffing in place. Prepare the ingredients for the roaster. Sauté the chopped vegetables in the butter until they are crisp-tender. Lay them on the bottom of a roaster large enough to hold the veal without crowding it. Pour about ½ inch (12 mm) of chicken stock into the bottom of the pan and add some sherry if you wish. Rub a coating of paprika and garlic powder all over the veal and place it on the bed of vegetables in the roaster. Roast, covered, at 250° F. for 4 to 5 hours, basting frequently. Uncover for the last half hour to brown the veal. The meat should be very tender and full of juice, and deeply brown on top and bottom. If you wish to brown it even more, slip it under the broiler for a final turn.

TO SERVE

Transfer the veal to a large carving platter and let it rest for at least 15 minutes before cutting. Slice through the meat and stuffing between bones for each portion. Serving pieces should look like a ring of thin veal encasing moist stuffing. Strain the pan juices and skim off the fat. Pass the juice at the table, to be spooned over each serving.

 ## Braised Chicken with Sauerkraut

Makes 4 servings

Variations of this dish exist in many Eastern European homes. This one is predominantly Polish—and uncommonly tasty.

    1   large frying chicken, cut in eighths
    2   tablespoons (30 ml) oil for browning
    2   pounds (900 g) of sauerkraut
    8   small new potatoes, parboiled with jackets
    1   teaspoon (5 ml) caraway seeds
    2   cups (500 ml) sour cream

In a heavy skillet, heat the oil and brown the chicken until each piece is nicely colored on both sides. Place the chicken in a 3 quart (3000 ml) casserole along with the potatoes and the sauerkraut. Sprinkle with the caraway seeds. Cover and bake at 350° F. for ½ hour. Uncover and bake an additional 30 minutes. Serve with big dollops of sour cream. A good complement is warm, crusty black bread and butter.

VARIATION

1. For an extra-special treat, omit the new potatoes and serve with homemade Pierogi with potato filling (*see* index).

2. Sauté 1 pound fresh, cleaned mushrooms in the skillet drippings until just cooked through. Add to the casserole and bake as directed.

Polish-Style Pork Loin Roasted in Beer
Makes 6 to 8 servings

Slow roasting in beer keeps this loin of pork meltingly tender and juicy. It's one of those recipes that guests always ask for.

3	to 4 pound (1350 to 1800 g) pork loin roast
2	tablespoons (30 ml) flour
1	tablespoon (15 ml) dry mustard
1	teaspoon (5 ml) sage
	Salt and pepper to taste
24	ounces (744 ml) beer
6	medium-sized yellow onions
12	soaked prunes, pitted
12	small carrots, peeled
3	medium-sized white rose potatoes with jackets, quartered

Trim excess fat from the roast leaving just a thin layer on the top. Mix the flour, mustard, sage, and about 1 teaspoon (5 ml) of salt together on a large piece of wax paper. Roll the roast in the flour mixture until it is evenly coated. Put the roast into a deep covered roaster.

Sprinkle with a bit more salt and pepper to taste. Pour the beer into the roaster (not directly on the roast). Cover and roast for 2 hours at 300° F. basting often. Meanwhile, prepare the vegetables. Peel the onions and slice off the ends. Push the centers out of each onion and stuff with pitted prunes that have been soaked in warm water for an hour (one or two prunes per onion depending on their size). After the pork has roasted for 2 hours, add the vegetables to the pan and baste with the juices. Continue to cook uncovered for another 1½ hours, basting often. Cook until the internal temperature of the pork reaches 160° F. to 165° F., it's brown and tender, and the vegetables are fork-soft. Allow the roast to rest on a heated platter for about 10 minutes before carving. Using a slotted spoon, transfer the vegetables to a warm serving dish. Skim the fat off the pan juices and pass the juice at the table to accompany the meat and vegetables.

🌺 Polish Hunter's Stew

Makes 8 to 10 servings

It's called hunter's stew because it used to contain all the different varieties of wild game from the day's hunt.

It does taste best with assorted meats, sausages, and poultry, and if you have good leftover smoked ham or other nice meats, use them as well. However, I don't subscribe to the notion that a hunter's stew should be a catch-all to clean out the refrigerator. It should be carefully orchestrated.

If you like a thick sauce, make a brown roux with equal parts of butter and flour and add it to the simmering kettle about 30 minutes before the stew is done.

Serve right out of the kettle and have freshly baked Black Bread (*see* index), butter, and cold beer on hand. For dessert, a homemade Cherry Strudel (*see* index) couldn't hurt.

2   or 3 thick slices salt pork, diced
2   pounds (900 g) lean meat cut in 1 inch (25 mm) cubes
      (use any combination of beef, pork, lamb, veal,
      smoked ham, or venison)

½   cup (125 ml) flour
    Salt and pepper to taste
2   tablespoons (30 ml) sweet Hungarian paprika
2   tablespoons (30 ml) butter
1   large tart apple, peeled, cored, and chopped
2   medium onions, thinly sliced
1   clove of garlic, minced
½   pound (225 g) fresh mushrooms, cleaned and sliced
2   pounds (900 g) sauerkraut, well drained
2   tablespoons (30 ml) minced parsley
1   teaspoon (5 ml) caraway seeds
1   pound (450 g) kielbasa (Polish) sausage, cut in 1 inch
    (25 mm) chunks
½   cup (125 ml) dry white wine
    Meat stock or water
8   to 10 new potatoes in their jackets, boiled until tender
    and drained

In a heavy 8 quart (8000 ml) kettle, render the fat from the salt pork over medium heat. When the salt pork browns, remove it from the fat with a slotted spoon. Dredge the raw meat cubes in the flour seasoned with salt, pepper, and the paprika. Brown cubes on all sides in hot fat. Do this in batches so as not to crowd the pieces. When the meat cubes are brown, remove them from the kettle with a slotted spoon and set aside. Add some butter if necessary to the remaining fat in the kettle and sauté the apple and onion until they are limp and golden. Add the garlic and mushrooms and sauté another 3 or 4 minutes. Add the sauerkraut, parsley, and caraway seeds. Simmer for several minutes. Return the browned meat cubes to the kettle along with the kielbasa pieces and the white wine. Stir gently with a large wooden spoon to intersperse all ingredients. Cover tightly and lower heat to a slow simmer. Cook for 2 to 2½ hours until all the meat is tender. Shake the pot gently to prevent anything from sticking to the bottom. Add a little water or stock if needed and adjust the seasoning. The stew should be thick, but not dry. About 20 minutes before the stew is done, add the precooked boiled potatoes to heat them. Serve hot.

✿ Danish Boiled Beef with Sweet and Sour Horseradish Sauce

Makes 6 to 8 servings

Serve this flavorful meat with boiled new potatoes in their jackets tossed with sweet butter, parsley, and dill, some steamed fresh green beans, and a mug of ice-cold beer.

4	pound (1800 g) lean beef brisket
10	to 12 whole black peppercorns
5	carrots, scraped and halved
2	large onions, peeled and quartered
4	or 5 celery stalks, including tops
2	leeks, cleaned, soaked in several changes of cold water, and halved
	Salt to taste
2	tablespoons (30 ml) butter
2	teaspoons (10 ml) white or apple cider vinegar
3	to 4 tablespoons (45 to 60 ml) brown sugar
½	cup (125 ml) soaked raisins or currants, finely chopped
½	teaspoon (3 ml) Dijon mustard
2	teaspoons (10 ml) grated horseradish (not creamed)
½	pint (250 ml) sour cream (optional)
	Coarse salt

Wipe the meat with a damp, clean cloth. Place in a large soup or stock pot and cover with cold water. Bring to a boil over medium heat, skimming the surface constantly with a wire mesh strainer until no more foam rises to the top. Add the peppercorns, vegetables, and salt to the kettle, cover, and simmer very slowly for about 3 hours until the meat is quite tender. Transfer the meat to a warm serving platter and cover to keep warm while you prepare the sauce. Strain the stock through a large wire sieve reserving both the stock and the vegetables. Pick out all or most of the peppercorns from the vegetables. Purée the vegetables in a blender or food processor and set aside. In a small saucepan, melt the butter and add the vinegar, brown sugar, and raisins. Bring to a slow boil and cook over moderately low heat for about 3 minutes. Add the mustard, horseradish, and about 1½ cups (375 ml) of the reserved stock (save the remaining stock for another use). Bring to a rapid boil and cook for about 1 to 2 minutes, stirring often. Remove from the heat and taste for seasoning. You may whisk in some sour cream at this point if you want a creamy sauce. Slice the brisket crosswise into thin slices. Spoon some of the sauce over the center of the meat. Pass the remaining sauce and coarse salt at the table.

Swedish Sailor's Beef

Makes 6 to 8 servings

Serve this casserole with Marinated Tomatoes (*see* index) on butter lettuce, a good, heavy bread, and icy *aquavit* with cold beer chasers.

2	pounds (900 g) bottom round steak, sliced only ¼ inch (6 mm) thick
	Flour, salt, and pepper
	Butter for frying
8	large potatoes, peeled and sliced
5	onions, peeled and sliced
¼	cup (60 ml) minced fresh parsley
2½	cups (625 ml) strong beef broth
1	cup (250 ml) beer

Flour the beef slices on both sides and shake off the excess flour. Salt and pepper each slice lightly. Heat about 3 tablespoons (45 ml) of butter in a skillet and brown the beef on both sides. In a large baking dish [16 inch × 10 inch × 3 inch (400 mm × 250 mm × 75 mm)] place half of the meat on the bottom. Add a layer of about half the potatoes and then half the onions. Sprinkle with salt and pepper and about half the parsley. Repeat these layers with the remaining ingredients. Pour the broth and the beer over all. Cover with aluminum foil and bake in a 250° F. oven for 3 to 4 hours until the meat and potatoes are very tender. Let stand about 15 minutes before serving.

Norwegian Skillet Chicken with Lemon and Fruit

Makes 4 servings

Tangy and sweet, this one-skillet chicken dish should be made with the plumpest, softest dried fruits and the freshest almonds obtainable. Note: All of one type of fruit may be used. A delicious example would be chicken with dried apricots. Also, filberts may be substituted for almonds.

It reheats beautifully, so you can successfully make it in advance. The recipe also doubles easily.

Serve with plain rice or buttered noodles and homemade whole-wheat rolls with sweet butter.

3	tablespoons (45 ml) butter
½	cup (125 ml) chopped almonds
2½	to 3 pounds (1125 to 1350 g) frying chicken, cut in eighths
	Salt and pepper to taste
	Vegetable oil or butter for frying
½	teaspoon (3 ml) crumbled dried thyme
1	ripe lemon, scrubbed and thinly sliced, with seeds removed
2	cups (500 ml) soft dried mixed fruit (pears, pitted prunes, apricots, apples, or peaches)

Melt 3 tablespoons (45 ml) of butter in a large skillet (one that can be used for serving) and sauté the nuts until they have a toasted flavor. Remove them from the skillet and set aside. Wipe the chicken pieces with a clean damp cloth and pick out any pin feathers from the skin. Salt and pepper the pieces lightly on both sides. Add another tablespoon (15 ml) of butter or vegetable oil to the fat in the skillet and add the chicken pieces when the oil is hot. Brown the chicken well on all sides, but do not cook through. Sprinkle with crumbled thyme and arrange the lemon slices and dried fruit in the skillet. Cover tightly and reduce heat to a slow simmer. Cook for about 40 minutes until the chicken is tender, spooning accumulated pan juices over all at intervals of about 10 minutes. Sprinkle the nuts over all and serve right from the skillet. Offer thick slices of fresh whole-wheat bread and some noodles tossed with butter and cream.

Swedish Ham in Sherried Cream
Makes 6 to 8 servings

Mellow, aged sherry, premium quality ham, and imported Gouda cheese are combined with fresh cream to create this uncommonly good buffet dish.

Bring it to the table in its baking dish and either keep it hot on a warming tray, or serve it at room temperature.

If you want to serve it for a sit-down dinner, surround it with homemade egg noodles tossed with sweet peas and butter, Marinated Tomatoes* on butter lettuce, and moist spicy Black Bread.* For dessert, Gingered Apple Rings* with almonds and mace are just right.

2	pounds (900 g) baked or boiled ham, cut in ¼ inch (6 mm) slices
1	cup (250 ml) good dry sherry
1½	cups (375 ml) heavy cream
	White pepper to taste
2	cups (500 ml) grated imported Gouda cheese

Arrange the ham slices in a shallow baking dish and cover with the sherry. Cover and marinate from 12 to 24 hours, turning the slices occasionally. Roll up each ham slice and lay them side-by-side in a shallow glass baking dish. Mix 2 or 3 tablespoons (30 or 45 ml) of the remaining sherry into the cream and pour over the ham rolls. Sprinkle lightly with white pepper and cover with the grated cheese. Bake in 350° F. oven until the cheese and cream are bubbly, about 35 minutes.

*See index.

🌸 Pickled Herring

Makes 6 to 8 servings

This makes a simple supper for a few friendly folks. Serve the herring right out of the crock and surround it with a pot of sweet butter, assorted moist breads and knackbrod, a bowl of hot boiled new potatoes in their jackets tossed lightly with butter and minced parsley, a salad of Marinated Tomatoes (*see* index) and crisp butter lettuce, and tiny glasses of iced *aquavit* with mugs of cold, cold beer.

2	dozen small herring
2	lemons, scrubbed, thinly sliced, and seeded
2	sweet white onions, peeled and thinly sliced and separated into rings
2	cloves of garlic, peeled and slivered
½	cup (125 ml) mixed pickling spices
12	whole black peppercorns
2	teaspoons (10 ml) sugar
1	bay leaf
3	cups (750 ml) malt vinegar
1	cup (250 ml) water
2	teaspoons (10 ml) dark mustard

Remove the heads and tails from the fish and discard them. Using the point of a small sharp knife, slit the herring down the back and lay on a flat surface. Gently lift off the top filet of the fish, leaving as many bones attached to the underside and backbone as possible. Use the knife to help pull the meat away from the bones. Starting at the head end and working toward the tail end, use the knife to lift the backbone and its attached bones away from the lower half. The bones and spine should come out in one piece leaving two boneless filets. Discard all bones. Cut the fileted fish in quarters. In a large earthenware crock, place a small layer of fish on the bottom. Then layer in a few lemon slices, a few onion rings, and some garlic slivers. Repeat these layers until all these ingredients are used. In a small saucepan, combine the pickling spices, peppercorns, sugar, bay leaf, vinegar, water, and mustard. Bring to a boil. Simmer for about 1 minute. Remove from heat and cool. Pour over the layers in the crock. Cover tightly and refrigerate for at least 1 week. Serve chilled, right out of the crock.

❧ Norwegian Pork Chops with Caraway Apples

Makes 6 to 8 servings

Sweet apples and pungent caraway seeds give a surprising lilt to this sage-scented pork chop casserole.

I like to serve it with crisp brown home-fried potatoes or buttered noodles, and mustard-glazed baby carrots. Choose a light fruit dessert like the Danish Apricot Dessert (*see* index) or the Swedish Fresh Raspberry Tart (*see* index).

> 8   pork chops, ½ inch to ¾ inch (12 to 18 mm) thick
>   Flour
>   Sage to taste
>   Salt and pepper to taste
>   Vegetable oil for frying
> 8   medium-sized apples, peeled, cored, and sliced in
>   ¼ inch (6 mm) rings
> 2   teaspoons (10 ml) caraway seeds
> ¼   cup (60 ml) apple juice

Dust the pork chops lightly with the flour and shake off any excess. Sprinkle each chop with ground sage, salt, and pepper on both sides. Heat about 3 tablespoons (45 ml) of oil in a large skillet. Brown the chops lightly on both sides and set aside. Butter a large, shallow baking dish and spread half of the apples over the bottom. Sprinkle with salt and pepper if you like, and then add about half the caraway seeds, crushed slightly with the back of a spoon. Lay the pork chops over the apples and top with the remaining apples and caraway seeds. Deglaze the skillet with the apple juice and pour over all. Cover and bake at 350° F. for about 1 hour. Baste occasionally with the pan juices.

Swedish Pork Tenderloin with Orange-Raspberry-Rhubarb Relish

Makes 6 to 8 servings (makes about 2 to 2½ cups
[500 to 625 ml] of relish)

The combination of oranges, raspberries, and fresh tart rhubarb are the perfect complement for a simple sautéed pork tenderloin.

Keep the relish on hand to serve with roast meats and poultry.

MEAT

2½   to 3 pounds (1125 to 1350 g) boneless pork
         tenderloin
       Salt and pepper
½   teaspoon (3 ml) dried marjoram
¼   teaspoon (1.5 ml) dried dill weed
       Flour for dredging
       Butter for frying
2   large onions, sliced ¼ inch (6 mm) thick

Slice the tenderloin crosswise into ½ inch (12 mm) thick rounds. Using a flat-headed mallet, pound the slices out to about a thickness of ⅜ inch (9 mm). Sprinkle both sides of each tenderloin with salt and pepper. Using a mortar and pestle, pulverize the marjoram and dill weed. Dust each piece of pork with some of the herbs, reserving just a bit for the onions. Dredge the filets and set aside, in one layer. In a large skillet, melt about 3 tablespoons (45 ml) of butter. Add the sliced onions, and cook over medium low heat until the onions are a deep golden color, and quite soft. Add the reserved herbs to the onions and stir just to blend. Transfer the onions to a bowl, cover, and keep warm. Melt more butter in the skillet—about ¼ inch to ½ inch (6 mm to 12 mm). Fry the filets in the butter a few at a time over moderately low heat until each piece is brown on both sides and cooked through. Transfer the pork to a heated serving platter, top with the onions and serve immediately accompanied by Orange-Raspberry-Rhubarb Relish.

ORANGE-RASPBERRY-RHUBARB RELISH

1   pound (450 g) fresh rhubarb, washed and cut in
        ½ inch (12 mm) pieces
¾   cup (180 ml) sugar
    Juice of ½ lemon
    Dash of salt
1   pint (500 ml) fresh, ripe raspberries or 10 ounce
        (280 g) package frozen berries, thawed
2   sweet oranges, peeled of rind and white membrane,
        seeded, and coarsely chopped
2   teaspoons (10 ml) finely grated orange zest
    Apple cider vinegar to taste

In a heavy saucepan, combine rhubarb, sugar, lemon juice, and salt. Let stand for about 10 minutes. Stir well and bring to a slow boil. Simmer slowly uncovered until rhubarb is tender and a thick syrup is formed. Drain the rhubarb, reserving the syrup. Combine the raspberries and chopped oranges with just enough of the reserved syrup to moisten them. Set over low heat and cook, stirring carefully until the berries are heated through. Fold the rhubarb back into the raspberry mixture. Add the orange zest and vinegar. Taste for seasoning. Spoon into a sterilized jar, cover tightly, and refrigerate. Serve chilled with braised, fried, grilled, or roasted meats.

Ham Hocks with Black-Eyed Peas

Makes 6 to 8 servings

A minimum of two ham hocks should be used in this stew for the best flavor. But you can add more of them if you're catering to hearty appetites.

1   pound (450 g) dried black-eyed peas, washed and
        picked over
2   large smoked ham hocks
1   onion, peeled and chopped

2   cloves of garlic, chopped
3   or 4 stalks of celery with tops, chopped
    Salt and crushed red pepper to taste
1   teaspoon (5 ml) crumbled thyme
3   tablespoons (45 ml) tomato paste (optional)

Cover the black-eyed peas with water and soak overnight, or bring them to a boil for 2 minutes, remove from heat, and soak for 1 to 2 hours. Place ham hocks in a large, heavy kettle and cover with water. Bring to a boil, skimming the surface of all foam. Add onion, garlic, and celery to the kettle and simmer for about an hour. Drain the peas, reserving the water. Add the peas to the kettle with the ham hocks. Cover and simmer for about an hour or until the peas are very tender, adding some of the soaking water if needed to keep the kettle's contents liquid, but not watery. About 15 minutes before everything is done, add the salt if needed, crushed red pepper, thyme, and, if a red soup is desired, stir in the tomato paste. Serve hot with boiled rice, hot pepper sauce to taste, and Homemade Corn Bread (*see* index) with butter. A mug of cold beer is called for.

Ham Hocks with Greens

Makes 4 to 6 servings

Bake up a big batch of Crisp Corn Bread (*see* index) to serve with this meal-in-a-kettle. Ladle out the *pot likker* to those who want to dunk.

2   large smoked ham hocks
¼   pound (112 g) salt pork
2   cloves of garlic, chopped
2   large onions, chopped
1   teaspoon (5 ml) sugar
    Hot crushed red pepper to taste
2   big bunches of greens (mustard, turnip, or collard),
    well washed

Place the hocks in a large kettle and cover with water. Bring to a boil, skimming the surface of all foam. Turn heat down to a simmer and cook slowly for about 2 hours. Boil the salt pork in water to cover for about 10 minutes, then drain it and pat dry. Cut it into small cubes. Fry in a heavy skillet over fairly low heat until all of the fat has been rendered. Add the garlic and onion and cook just until it begins to wilt. Add the entire contents of the skillet plus the sugar, crushed pepper, and washed greens to the ham hocks. If you like the pot likker stronger, tie the green stems in a bundle with some kitchen twine and throw them into the kettle too. Simmer very slowly for about 35 minutes or until the greens are tender. Discard the bundle of stems. Use a big slotted spoon to transfer the greens to a large, warm serving bowl. Break each ham hock open and pull off some meat. Place in the serving bowl. Ladle some of the pot likker over all and serve hot. Pass plenty of hot corn bread and butter at the table and offer hot pepper sauce as well. Buttered or red rice may be served on the side.

🌺 Jambalaya
Makes 8 to 10 servings

This colorful Creole classic made with sausage, ham, seafood, and rice in a lusty fresh tomato sauce, is the American descendant of Spanish *paella*. The name jambalaya stems from the French provincial version of paella called *jambalaia*.

Since Creole cookery is the combination of Spanish, French, Italian, and Cajun cuisines as interpreted and re-created by Southern Black cooks, *jambalaya* is one of its most exemplary and delicious creations.

If you've got a kettle big enough, this recipe can double and triple easily to put on a big feed.

½   pound (225 g) hot sausage, cut in ½ inch
      (12 mm) pieces
½   pound (225 g) smoked sausage, cut in ½ inch (12 mm)
      pieces
½   pound (225 g) smoked ham, cubed or diced

1 tablespoon (15 ml) rendered bacon fat
1 large onion, finely chopped
1 large green bell pepper, seeded, stemmed, and finely chopped
3 or 4 cloves of garlic, peeled and chopped
1 cup (250 ml) diced celery, including tops
5 large, ripe tomatoes, peeled, seeded, and chopped (drain and reserve liquid)
2 tablespoons (30 ml) tomato paste
5 finely chopped scallions
¼ cup (60 ml) minced fresh parsley
1 tablespoon (15 ml) paprika
1 teaspoon (5 ml) chile powder
1 bay leaf
1½ teaspoons (8 ml) crumbled dried thyme
Salt and crushed red pepper to taste
2 pounds (900 g) medium-sized raw shrimp, peeled and deveined
1 quart (1000 ml) fresh shucked oysters (drain and reserve liquid)
6 cups (1500 ml) hot, cooked white rice

In the bottom of a large, heavy kettle, combine sausages, ham, bacon grease, onion, bell pepper, garlic, and celery and simmer over low heat, covered, until the vegetables are very soft. Stir often to prevent sticking or scorching. Add chopped tomatoes, tomato paste, chopped scallions, parsley, paprika, chile powder, bay leaf, thyme, salt, and crushed red pepper and simmer for about 15 minutes. Stir in shrimp and oysters and simmer for a few minutes until the shrimp turn pink and the oysters curl around the edges. Add the hot cooked rice and mix well. If more liquid is needed to make it moist, add some of the reserved tomato and oyster liquid. Season to taste. Place the jambalaya in an accommodating serving casserole and keep warm in the oven until serving. Dish directly out of the casserole.

🌺 Southern Fried Fish

Makes 6 to 8 servings

After you cook the fish, add more shortening to the skillet and fry up a batch of Hush Puppies (*see* index) to be eaten with plenty of butter. Serve with boiled new potatoes tossed with butter, dill weed, and parsley and a Wilted Lettuce Salad (*see* index).

5   pounds (2250 g) boneless fish fillets with skin (catfish, perch, trout, butterfish, etc.)
2   cups (500 ml) buttermilk
1   egg
    Shortening and peanut oil for frying
    Salt and pepper to taste
1½   to 2 cups (375 to 500 ml) fine white corn meal

Soak the fillets in the buttermilk beaten with the egg. Heat about 1 inch (25 mm) oil with a big spoon of shortening added in a heavy, black skillet until the fat ripples. Drain enough pieces of fish to fit comfortably in the pan at one time. Salt and pepper them on both sides and roll in corn meal. Fry in the hot fat until the outside is crisp and lightly browned and the fish flakes easily. Drain momentarily and place on a heated platter, uncovered, in a warm oven. Fry the remaining fish in this manner. Serve warm with lemon or homemade tartar sauce.

🌺 Red Beans and Rice with Pickled Pork

Makes 6 to 8 servings

Nothing's more mouthwatering than the aroma of simmering beans as they begin to break down in the kettle. Add the smell of sizzling spices and the fragrance of homemade corn bread browning in the oven and you could die from anticipation!

This fabulous stew is rooted in the Deep South—a blissful marriage of Cajun and Tex-Mex cookery. I adore it hot and spicy, but you can tone down the tongue scorchers and still come up with a great taste.

The pickled pork adds depth to the flavor. Since it's hard to get, I offer you this flavorful and easy recipe.

Serve the stew right out of the kettle over deep bowls half-filled with hot rice. Mugs of cold beer and crispy corn bread dripping with butter would be sheer ecstasy.

PICKLED PORK

- ¼ cup (60 ml) mustard seed
- 2 tablespoons (30 ml) celery seed
- 1 small dried, hot chile pepper
- 4 cups (1000 ml) distilled white vinegar
- 2 teaspoons (10 ml) salt
- 10 to 12 whole black peppercorns
- 3 cloves of garlic, peeled and slightly bruised
- 1½ pounds (675 g) boneless pork butt, cut in 2 inch (50 mm) cubes, or 2½ to 3 pounds (1125 to 1350 g) country-style ribs

Combine the mustard seed, celery seed, chile pepper, vinegar, salt, peppercorns, and garlic in a stainless steel saucepan and bring to a full boil. Cook for 3 to 4 minutes. Cool thoroughly. Place pork cubes or ribs in a deep crock or bowl and pour the pickling liquid over all. Stir with a wooden spoon to mix everything well. Cover and refrigerate for about 3 days, stirring occasionally.

RED BEANS

- 1 pound (450 g) red beans
- 1 large onion, peeled and finely chopped
- 3 to 4 tablespoons (45 to 60 ml) bacon drippings
- 2 large onions, peeled and finely chopped
- ¼ cup (60 ml) fresh parsley, finely minced
- 1 large green bell pepper, finely chopped
- 1 cup (250 ml) diced celery
- 2 garlic cloves, minced
- 1 bay leaf
- Salt and pepper to taste

1   pound (450 g) hot sausage (Louisiana hot sausage,
      pepperoni, chorizo, etc.), sliced
     Ground hot chile peppers to taste (optional)
     Tabasco sauce to taste (optional)
¼   to ½ cup (60 to 125 ml) chile powder to taste
      (optional)
6   to 8 servings hot, cooked, white long grain rice

Wash and pick over the beans. Place beans in a deep bowl or kettle. Add 1 chopped onion. Cover with water and let stand overnight. Drain well. Place beans in a large kettle. Cover with water and bring to a slow boil. Simmer, uncovered, over low heat for about 1½ hours. Meanwhile, heat the bacon drippings in a large skillet and add the remaining 2 onions, parsley, green pepper, celery, garlic, and bay leaf. Cook until very soft, stirring often. Add this to the beans along with the pickled pork. Continue to cook over low heat for about 1 more hour. Add the hot sausage, ground chile peppers, Tabasco, and chile powder and simmer another 30 minutes. Watch the beans very carefully from about 2 hours of cooking time, because the liquids will be running low. The beans should be thick and rather mushy, and the meat should be very tender. Season the stew with some of the pickling juice if desired. Serve hot, right out of the kettle. Ladle beans and meat into big soup bowls over hot rice.

Russian Chicken on a Spit with Tart Plum Sauce

Makes 4 servings

This thick fresh plum sauce can be served with other grilled meats. It's especially good with garlic-seasoned, charcoal-broiled lamb.

Because the temperatures of coals and electric rotisseries vary so much, a cooking time is not given in this recipe. The cook must mind the meal continually to achieve the proper results.

I like to serve this chicken with hot noodles tossed with butter, sour cream, and chopped, toasted walnuts plus homemade black bread, and fresh cucumber sticks.

2½   to 3 pound (1125 to 1350 g) broiling chicken
     Salt and pepper to taste
1   large garlic clove, split
4   tablespoons (60 ml) melted butter

Wipe the chicken with a clean, damp towel and remove any pin feathers. Dry the chicken with paper towels. Salt and pepper the inside of the bird. Rub the chicken all over with the cut side of the garlic. Tie the wings close to the body with kitchen twine, and tie the legs together. Skewer the chicken on the spit on an electric or charcoal rotisserie. Broil the chicken evenly on all sides until the skin is crisp and brown and the juices run yellow—1½ to 2 hours. Brush often with melted butter. Remove the chicken from the spit and cool slightly. As soon as you're able to handle it, cut it into serving pieces and spoon a little of the plum sauce over each piece. Pass the rest of the sauce at the table.

TART PLUM SAUCE
½   pound (225 g) pitted sour plums
1   teaspoon (5 ml) fresh lemon juice
½   cup (125 ml) water
½   cup (125 ml) unsweetened pomegranate juice
1   clove of garlic, peeled and minced
4   tablespoons (60 ml) chopped fresh coriander leaves,
     or 2 tablespoons (30 ml) dried dill weed
     Salt and red pepper to taste

Chop the plums and combine with the lemon juice, water, pomegranate juice, and garlic and simmer over low heat until the plums break down. The sauce should be quite thick, so if there is too much liquid in the pan, cook uncovered to reduce the water, watching carefully so the plums do not scorch. Stir in the spices. Bring to a boil and remove from the heat. Cool before using.

Russian Cold Poached Whitefish with Spiced Walnut Sauce

SATSIVI

Makes 6 to 8 first course servings or 4 to 6 main course servings

Fresh, firm whitefish, walnuts, pomegranate juice, and an array of exotic spices make this *satsivi* a rare jewel in the world of fish cookery. With small potatoes boiled in their jackets, a platter of sliced cold cucumbers, sweet onions, and fresh cut garden herbs, plus oven-warm black bread with sweet butter, it's a hot weather feast extraordinaire.

Make this dish in advance and chill it thoroughly before serving.

2	pounds (900 g) whitefish filets or filet of sole, red snapper, cod, etc.
2	bay leaves
5	or 6 whole cloves
2	or 3 whole peppercorns
	Salt
¾	cup (180 ml) unsweetened pomegranate juice or wine vinegar
1	cup (250 ml) finely chopped walnut meats
3	large onions, minced
3	large cloves of garlic, minced
1	teaspoon (5 ml) ground allspice
1	teaspoon (5 ml) ground cinnamon
1	teaspoon (5 ml) ground coriander seed
	White pepper to taste
	Salt to taste

Rinse the filets under cold running water. Place in a fish poacher or deep kettle and barely cover with water. Add the bay leaves, cloves, and peppercorns and salt lightly. Bring to a slow simmer. Cover and cook gently for about 10 minutes, depending on the thickness of the filets, until the fish is cooked through and flakes easily. Carefully transfer the fish to a concave serving platter and let cool while you make the sauce. Strain the fish liquor, reserving the stock. In a large saucepan, combine about 1 cup (250 ml) of the reserved fish stock, pomegranate juice or vinegar, walnuts, onions, garlic, allspice, cinnamon, coriander, and salt and pepper. Bring to a rapid boil and cook for about 25 minutes until all ingredients are melded. Pour the hot sauce over the fish and cool before serving. Garnish with fresh sprigs of coriander.

Russian Braised Lamb Shanks with Vegetables

CHANAKHI
Makes 6 servings

This is a meal in a pot. It needs nothing but a batch of crusty homemade bread, a hearty wine, and perhaps a light fruit dessert. Bring it hot from the oven in its casserole and serve it directly from the pan. Spoon some of the good pan juices over each serving and offer some fresh cracked pepper.

6	meaty lamb shanks
3	tablespoons (45 ml) olive oil or shortening
1	onion, finely chopped
3	cloves of garlic, chopped
	Salt and pepper
½	cup (125 ml) meat stock or dry red wine
4	large potatoes, cut in 2 inch (50 mm) chunks
3	firm medium-sized tomatoes, peeled, seeded, and cut in half
1	large eggplant, washed, stemmed, and cut in 1 inch (25 mm) cubes
2	large onions, thinly sliced
¾	pound (340 g) fresh string beans, cleaned, removed strings

Brown the lamb shanks in hot oil in a very large Dutch oven. When they are deeply colored on all sides, add the chopped onion, garlic, salt, and pepper and stir the onions with a wooden spoon until they are limp and brown. Pour in the meat stock, cover tightly and place in a 325° F. oven for 1½ hours. Add the vegetables to the casserole and enough wine if needed to keep things moist. Salt and pepper the vegetables lightly and baste with the pan juices. Return to the oven and continue to cook at 325° F. for another 1½ hours, or until lamb and vegetables are very tender. Serve hot.

Vegetables & Salads

Within the context of ethnic cookery there is a myriad of imaginative ways in which fresh and dried vegetables, fruits, nuts, legumes, and grains are served. Most often these dishes have been devised as foils for robust, highly seasoned soups, stews, and main dishes.

Each of the recipes in this chapter is important within the framework of an ethnic menu. Elaborately seasoned black beans and rice, for instance, is the needed balance for a peppery Cuban pot roast. Just as the simple tang of a cool, cucumber salad provides refreshment in the midst of a robust Hungarian feast.

There are threads of commonality throughout this diverse collection. There is an unwavering reliance on the freshest and best produce available. What's more, there is a commitment to prepare this produce with care—to enhance, not to mask, the natural flavors.

Basque Garbanzos with Chorizos

Makes 4 to 6 servings

This stew is usually simmered in a black iron kettle using dried garbanzos and homemade *chorizo*, the peppery-flavored garlic pork sausage that so many Basques make themselves. Chorizo can be purchased in many Mexican specialty food shops and is even available in supermarkets occasionally. If you can't get it, substitute hot pepperoni or any garlic-flavored sausage like *kielbasa*.

1   pound (450 g) dried garbanzo beans, washed and
      picked over
    Salt and crushed red pepper to taste
1   bay leaf
¼   cup (60 ml) olive oil
3   cloves of garlic, chopped
1   large onion, minced
1   large green bell pepper, seeded, stemmed, and
      finely chopped
1   pound (450 g) chorizo, cut in ½ inch (12 mm) pieces,
      or substitute kielbasa or 2 sticks of pepperoni
1   tablespoon (15 ml) crumbled oregano
    Dash of nutmeg
1   small can tomato paste

Cover the garbanzos with water and soak overnight. Add 1
teaspoon (5 ml) of salt and the bay leaf to the garbanzos and bring to a
boil, skimming the surface until no more foam arises. Simmer,
covered, for about 2 hours, until the beans are tender. If the beans
seem too watery, leave the lid off during the last half hour of cooking.
In a large, heavy skillet, heat the olive oil and add the garlic, onion,
green pepper, and sausage. Cook very slowly over low heat, stirring
often until all the vegetables are soft. Add the oregano, nutmeg, salt,
peppers, tomato paste, and the contents from the skillet to the beans.
Simmer, uncovered for another 20 minutes. For maximum flavor,
refrigerate overnight. Remove hardened fat from the top of the kettle
and reheat slowly. Remove bay leaf and serve.

Basque Bean Salad

Makes 4 to 6 servings

Make this salad several hours in advance and chill. Let it come
to room temperature before serving.

4   cups (1000 ml) cooked, drained red kidney beans
1   large sweet onion, minced
1   green bell pepper, stemmed, seeded, and diced

¼   cup (60 ml) minced fresh parsley
½   cup (125 ml) olive oil
    Juice of 1 lemon, or to taste
    Salt and crushed red pepper to taste
    Hard-boiled eggs and chopped parsley for garnish

In a deep glass bowl, combine the beans, onion, pepper, and parsley. Blend the olive oil and lemon with a wire whisk or in a blender, until the mixture is thick. Pour the dressing over the beans and toss to coat. Season to taste, cover, and refrigerate from 2 to 12 hours. Garnish salad with egg wedges and a sprinkling of parsley.

Black Beans and Rice
Makes 8 to 10 servings

Black beans are slowly simmered to a soft thick stew and the Piquant Sauce (recipe follows) is added during the final minutes of cooking. Feel free to add more or less vinegar and some hot, crushed red peppers if you like.

Black beans are especially good with pork, and I like to have either homemade Corn Bread (*see* index) or Pumpkin Bread (*see* index) on the side.

1   pound (450 g) black beans, washed and picked over
1   bay leaf
    Salt and pepper
2   cloves of garlic, peeled and finely chopped
1   onion, peeled and finely chopped
½   teaspoon (3 ml) crumbled oregano

Soak the beans overnight in enough water to cover. Add the bay leaf and bring to a boil in the soaking water, skimming the surface if necessary. Add a bit of salt and freshly ground pepper plus the garlic, onion, and oregano. Simmer, covered for about 2 to 3 hours (cooking time varies a great deal depending on the beans) or until the beans are rather mushy. Watch the kettle continually toward the end, stirring and adding a bit of water to keep the beans from scorching or sticking. During the last hour of cooking time, remove the bay leaf and make the sauce.

PIQUANT SAUCE
- ½   cup (125 ml) olive oil
- 1   clove of garlic, minced
- 1   onion, finely chopped
- 1   large green bell pepper, finely chopped
- 4   ounce (112 g) jar fire-roasted pimentos, chopped
- ½   teaspoon (3 ml) crumbled oregano
       Pinch of dried thyme
- 2   to 3 tablespoons (30 to 45 ml) cider vinegar, or
          to taste

Combine all ingredients in a saucepan and simmer very slowly, stirring often, until the vegetables are really soft, but not brown. Stir this mixture into the beans during the last 15 minutes of cooking time.

Have 6 cups (1500 ml) of hot, cooked white rice ready to serve. Ladle beans over the rice and serve hot. Pass crushed red pepper and hot pepper sauce at the table. Leftovers can be successfully frozen in an airtight container.

🌺 Rice Cubano

Makes 6 to 8 servings

- 1   recipe Piquant Sauce (see Black Beans and
          Rice—preceding recipe)
- 6   cups (1500 ml) hot, cooked white rice

Pour the hot sauce over the rice and toss to mix well. Serve hot with entrees of meat or poultry.

🌺 Fried Plantains
PLATANOS FRITOS
Makes 4 servings

Plantains, the banana's not-so-sweet cousins, are available in many major markets. They are never eaten raw, but are cooked and served like a vegetable with meats and poultry.

Don't be put off by the plantain's firmness. It never softens like a banana. One large plantain will usually serve two people. You can easily multiply this recipe.

    2   large, ripe plantains or greenish bananas, peeled and
            split in half lengthwise
    3   tablespoons (45 ml) butter

Heat the butter in a large skillet and when it sizzles, add the plantains, cut side down. Simmer, uncovered, for about 10 minutes until brown, then turn carefully and brown the other side. Serve hot.

🌺 Tropical Fruit Salad with Chile and Lime Dressing
Makes 6 to 8 servings

This fiesta-y montage of fresh fruits is a marvelous complement to many Latin American and Caribbean menus.

Serve it to contrast hot chile-flavored entrees or as cool refreshment with summer barbecues.

    2   large, ripe but firm papayas, peeled, seeded, and
             cut in cubes
    2   large greenish bananas, peeled and sliced
    1½   cups (375 ml) cubed fresh pineapple
    1   large orange, peeled, seeded, white membrane
             removed, and coarsely chopped
    ⅓   cup (85 ml) peanut oil

3   to 4 tablespoons (45 to 60 ml) fresh lime juice
2   tablespoons (30 ml) chile powder
    Salt to taste
    Sugar to taste

Combine fruit in a glass salad bowl. In a blender whirl peanut oil, lime juice, chile powder, salt, and sugar until smooth and thick. Pour immediately over fruit and toss gently. Chill before serving.

VARIATIONS

1. Use any tropical fruits in season like mangoes, avocados, and melons.

2. Add a dash of cayenne pepper to the dressing.

3. Add thinly sliced sweet white onions to the salad.

Heaven and Earth

Makes 6 to 8 servings

Heaven and earth (*Himmel und Erde* in German) is the perfect side dish for assorted smoked meats, sausages, and spareribs. It will keep in a warm oven (200° F.) for at least an hour before serving, so it can be made well in advance.

3   pounds (1350 g) red potatoes, peeled and
       cut in eighths
2   pounds (900 g) pippin apples, peeled, cored, and
       quartered
2   tablespoons (30 ml) cider vinegar
2   tablespoons (30 ml) sugar
    Salt to taste
    Freshly ground black pepper
    Sugar to taste
    Cider vinegar to taste
½   teaspoon (3 ml) nutmeg
4   thick slices smoked bacon

2 large onions, peeled and cut into ⅜ inch (9 mm) thick
slices
Minced fresh parsley

Place the potato pieces and the apple pieces in a large kettle. Barely cover with cold water. Add 2 tablespoons (30 ml) each of vinegar and sugar plus the salt. Bring to a boil, cover, reduce heat and simmer until the potatoes and apples are tender, 25 to 30 minutes. Drain thoroughly and purée. Season with additional salt, pepper, sugar, vinegar and nutmeg, place in a covered serving bowl, and keep warm. In a skillet, brown the bacon on both sides until it is crisp. Drain the bacon on a paper towel, crumble, and set aside. Add the onion slices to the hot fat in the skillet and sauté them (separating them into rings) until they are golden brown. Sprinkle the crumbled bacon over the puréed potatoes and apples and arrange onion rings over all. Sprinkle with parsley and add a few grindings of pepper.

German Potato Pancakes

Makes 6 servings

These crispy potato cakes, at near 5 inches (125 mm) round, are big enough to satisfy a good appetite. For hungrier crowds, the recipe doubles successfully.

Don't forget to make plenty of fresh applesauce beforehand (ready-made just doesn't do these heavenly pancakes justice).

4 thick slices smoked bacon
5 or 6 medium-large potatoes [about 2 pounds (900 g)]
1 large onion, finely grated
2½ tablespoons (37 ml) all-purpose flour
2 eggs, lightly beaten
Salt and pepper to taste
Pinch of grated nutmeg
1½ tablespoons (22 ml) minced fresh parsley
Vegetable oil for frying

Fry the bacon until it is crisp. Drain on paper toweling. Crumble and set aside. Place potatoes in a large bowl of cold water as each is peeled. Grate the potatoes and drain off all excess liquid. Add grated onion, flour, eggs, salt, pepper, nutmeg, parsley, and the bacon and mix well. Heat about 1 inch (25 mm) of vegetable oil in a large skillet. You may want to add a bit of butter to the oil for flavor. Drop the potato mixture into the hot oil by a large spoon or strainer [about ⅓ cup (85 ml) each] draining off excess liquid as you go. Flatten each pancake with a spatula to make 5 inch (125 mm) patties and fry on both sides until crisp and golden brown. Drain on paper towel and keep warm until all the pancakes have been cooked. Serve hot with plenty of Homemade Applesauce (*see* index).

German Red Cabbage with Apples

Makes 8 to 10 servings

Red cabbage and apples can be made well in advance. In fact, it improves with 2 or 3 days of refrigeration. Remember to cover it tightly and reheat it very slowly, stirring occasionally.

The portions of salt, sugar, and vinegar are truly left up to your own palate—adjust according to the dish it's accompanying. For instance, I like it quite tart with roast duckling, but sweet with stuffed spareribs. Adjust the flavor slowly as it cooks—and taste often.

2	pound (900 g) head of firm red cabbage
1¼	cups (310 ml) red wine vinegar
1	teaspoon (5 ml) salt
2	tablespoons (30 ml) sugar
4	tablespoons (60 ml) butter
2	large, firm pippin apples, peeled, cored, and chopped
1	large onion, peeled and thinly sliced
1	small onion, peeled
8	whole cloves
1	small bay leaf
1½	cups (375 ml) boiling water
½	cup (125 ml) sweet red wine

Salt to taste
Sugar to taste
¼ cup (60 ml) malt vinegar
½ cup (125 ml) red currant jelly

Shred the cabbage into a large mixing bowl. Mix the red wine vinegar, 1 teaspoon (5 ml) of salt, and 2 tablespoons (30 ml) of sugar together, pour over cabbage, toss well, and let stand. In a large stainless steel or enameled kettle, melt the butter. When it sizzles, add the chopped apples and sliced onions and sauté until both are limp and golden. Drain the cabbage and add to the kettle along with the whole onion stuck with the cloves and bay leaf (secure the bay leaf with the cloves). Bury the spiced onion in the cabbage, pour the boiling water and wine over all, cover, and bring to a simmer. Stir and taste occasionally, adding salt, sugar, and the malt vinegar as well as some additional water when necessary. Cook slowly until the cabbage is very soft, about 2 hours. Remove the spiced onion. Add the jelly (more if you wish) and stir until it dissolves. Serve the cabbage warm.

Greek-Style Cucumber and Tomato Salad

Makes 4 to 6 servings

This must be chilled thoroughly for the best texture and flavor. It is a fine accompaniment for grilled chicken and lamb. And because the taste improves with time, it is a wise choice for a buffet or picnic.

2 large, ripe tomatoes
1 large, crisp cucumber
1 sweet white onion
¼ pound (112 g) Greek Calamata olives (optional)
½ cup (125 ml) olive oil or other vegetable oil
3 tablespoons (45 ml) red wine vinegar
1 teaspoon (5 ml) crushed, dried sweet basil, or
2 teaspoons (10 ml) minced fresh basil
¼ teaspoon (1.5 ml) crushed rosemary
Salt and freshly ground pepper

Wash the tomatoes and slice into ⅜ inch (9 mm) thick rounds. Peel the cucumber and slice diagonally into ¼ inch (6 mm) thick ovals. Peel the onion and slice ¼ inch (6 mm) thick, then separate into rings. Arrange all of these vegetables attractively on a serving plate. Sprinkle with the black olives. Combine the oil, vinegar, herbs, salt, and pepper in a small container with a tight-fitting lid. Shake vigorously to blend the ingredients. Pour over the vegetables and let stand about 15 minutes undisturbed. Serve just slightly chilled.

VARIATION

Use chopped scallions instead of the onions. Vary the herbs according to your own taste: you might include tarragon, thyme, summer savory, garlic, etc.

Fried Eggplant

Makes 6 to 8 servings

Select fresh, firm eggplants that are not bruised or scarred. They should be deep in color with glossy skins and bright green stem tops. Use the eggplants as soon as possible.

2   large eggplants
    Salt
    Plenty of vegetable oil for frying

Trim the ends off the eggplants and peel them if you wish. Slice lengthwise into 3/8 inch (9 mm) thick pieces. Stand upright in a large colander and salt liberally. Let the eggplant stand for at least 30 minutes over a plate to catch the drippings. Heat about an inch (25 mm) of oil in a large skillet. Take as many slices of eggplant as will fit in the skillet comfortably and pat dry on both sides with a paper towel. When the oil is hot enough to sizzle when the eggplant is added, lay the slices in the skillet. Fry to a deep golden brown on both sides, turning once. Transfer to a warm platter lined with paper toweling to absorb excess oil. Keep the earlier ones warm until all the slices have been cooked in this manner. Add oil to the skillet between batches of the vegetable, and let it heat before you add more eggplant. Otherwise, the cooked vegetable will be greasy and soggy. Never add oil while eggplant is cooking.

🌺 Greek Garlic Sauce

SKORDALIA (SKOR-THAH-LEE-AH)

This creamy, robust garlic sauce is always served cold like mayonnaise. It is an exotic touch on broiled fish, fried zucchini and fried eggplant, and it makes a marvelous dip for crudites.

In the old days, *skordalia* was made in a wooden bowl, hand-pounded, and beaten to make a stiff sauce. Today, a blender or food processor produces satisfactory results in a fraction of the time.

    6   or 7 cloves of garlic, peeled and minced
    2   or 3 medium-sized boiled potatoes, peeled and riced
    ½   cup (125 ml) blanched, ground almonds
    2   cups (500 ml) fine quality imported olive oil
    ½   cup (125 ml) vinegar
        Salt and white pepper to taste

Pulverize the garlic and add the riced potatoes. Add the almonds and blend these ingredients into a paste. Gradually, with the blender or food processor running, add the oil and vinegar, alternately. Process until the sauce has enough body to hold its shape. Season with salt and pepper and refrigerate, tightly covered.

🌺 Greek Orange and Olive Salad

Makes 6 to 8 servings

Freeing ourselves from the notion that all salads include lettuce and tomatoes, one discovers how delightful "offbeat" combinations can be. Many ethnic groups combine all sorts of fresh available produce to create some divine combinations.

5 to 6 sweet, fresh oranges, chilled
1 large sweet, flat white onion
½ pound (225 g) Greek Calamata olives
½ cup (125 ml) olive or other vegetable oil
1 tablespoon (15 ml) cider vinegar or lemon juice
½ teaspoon (3 ml) crushed dried oregano
   Salt to taste
   Freshly ground pepper

Peel the oranges and remove as much of the white membrane as possible. Slice carefully using a very sharp knife, into 3/8 inch (9 mm) thick round slices. Remove all seeds. Lay the slices in a glass salad bowl. Peel the onion and slice 1/4 inch (6 mm) thick. Separate the slices into rounds and lay over the orange slices. Sprinkle olives over all. Combine oil, vinegar or lemon juice, herbs, salt, and pepper in a container with a tight-fitting lid. Shake briskly to combine all ingredients. Pour over the oranges, onions, and olives. Cover and refrigerate for a couple of hours before serving.

 **Greek Salad**

Serves 6 to 8

The Calamata olives needed for this recipe are firm, glossy, brownish-black, and shaped like a minute football. They are packed in brine and/or olive oil and have a characteristic lengthwise slit. The variety sold in supermarkets under the label "Greek olives" are mushy, and bitter, and not in any way comparable to Calamata olives. Look for these in Greek import food stores, sold loose out of a barrel, or bottled by certain Greek importers.

Feta, the salty goat's milk cheese, is also available in Greek import groceries, as well as Italian and Middle Eastern markets and most cheese shops. If the cheese is too saline, rinse it under cold water before you use it.

1   large head of Romaine lettuce, rinsed, drained,
      and chilled
1   large ripe, firm tomato, seeded and cut into ½ inch
      (12 mm) wedges
1   large cucumber, peeled and cut into ¼ inch (6 mm)
      slices
1   large green pepper, rinsed, seeded, and cut into 1 inch
      (25 mm) chunks
1   bermuda or sweet white onion, peeled and sliced
4   stalks celery, rinsed, drained, and cut diagonally into
      1 inch (25 mm) chunks
¼   pound (112 g) Greek feta cheese, crumbled
¼   pound (112 g) imported Calamata olives
      Olive oil dressing (recipe below)

Into a large wooden salad bowl, tear the lettuce into bite-sized pieces, discarding the tough lower stems. Add tomato, cucumber, pepper, onion which has been separated into rings, celery, feta, and olives. Pour olive oil dressing over all and toss well. Serve immediately, with crusty sesame-seeded bread, a pot of sweet butter, and a hearty red table wine.

OLIVE OIL DRESSING

½   cup (125 ml) imported olive oil
2   tablespoons (30 ml) lemon juice
2   tablespoons (30 ml) red wine vinegar
1   small garlic clove, minced
½   teaspoon (3 ml) crumbled dried oregano
      Several grindings of black pepper

Place all ingredients in a jar or salad cruet, cover tightly, and shake well to blend. Refrigerate until use. Shake well before using.

Hungarian-Style Brussels Sprouts
Makes 8 servings

Fresh brussels sprouts in a sour cream sauce embroidered with touches of dill, scallions, and smoked bacon is a heavenly, make-ahead casserole.

Assemble it hours ahead to bake just before serving; or bake it in advance and simply reheat. In either case, it's a perfect preparation for take-along suppers and buffets.

2	pounds (900 g) fresh brussels sprouts
4	thick slices smoked bacon, diced
6	green onions, finely chopped
	Salt to taste
½	teaspoon (3 ml) dried dill weed
	Freshly ground pepper to taste
16	ounce (450 g) container sour cream
½	cup (125 ml) diced bread crumbs
2	tablespoons (30 ml) butter
	Sweet Hungarian paprika

Choose small, firm brussels sprouts, uniform in size and free from yellow or bruised leaves. Trim away the stalks on each, but not so close that the leaves fall off. Rinse under cool water and pull away any damaged leaves. Bring a kettle of salted water to a boil. Drop in the brussels sprouts and boil for 5 to 10 minutes (watching carefully) just until they are tender when the stalk end is pierced with the tip of a small sharp knife. Drain well. Sauté the bacon in a skillet until the pieces are lightly browned but not hard. Add the green onions and sauté until the onions are just soft. Add the well drained brussels sprouts along with the salt, dill weed, and a few grindings of pepper to the skillet and sauté for another minute. Transfer all contents of the skillet to a shallow baking dish. If the bacon was very fatty, you can spoon off most of the excess fat. Cover first with the sour cream, then sprinkle the bread crumbs over all, dot with butter, and sprinkle with the paprika. Bake in a 325° F. oven for 20 to 25 minutes until the top is lightly browned. Serve hot.

🌹 Hungarian Cucumber Salad
Makes 6 to 8 servings

This wonderfully simple salad is found on almost every Hungarian dinner table. It serves as a refreshing contrast to those richly seasoned main dishes. Make it hours ahead and chill it thoroughly for supreme flavor.

     2   large firm cucumbers, peeled and thinly sliced
    ½   cup (125 ml) white vinegar
    ½   cup (125 ml) cold water
     1   tablespoon (15 ml) sugar
         Salt to taste
         Couple of grindings of black pepper

Several hours before serving, slice the cucumbers as thin as you possibly can. Place them in a glass bowl. Mix remaining ingredients together and pour over cucumbers. Toss them gently to coat. Cover tightly and refrigerate until serving time.

🌹 Irish Peas
Makes 6 to 8 servings

This is a simple dish that's a favorite addition to many Irish menus. It is surprising how a drizzle of fresh lemon, a crush of mint leaves, and curls of butter elevate the flavor of sweet green peas.

     1   cup (250 ml) water
     2   tablespoons (30 ml) sugar
     3   or 4 sprigs of fresh spearmint leaves, or 1 teaspoon
            (5 ml) dried mint
    ½   teaspoon (3 ml) salt
         Few drops fresh lemon juice
    20   ounces (560 g) packaged frozen sweet peas
     3   to 4 tablespoons (45 to 60 ml) sweet creamery butter

Combine the water, sugar, mint leaves, salt, and lemon juice in a saucepan and bring to a boil. Add the frozen peas. When the water returns to a boil, cover and simmer slowly until the peas are just tender—about 3 or 4 minutes. Separate the peas gently with a fork as they cook. Drain the peas thoroughly and toss with the butter. Serve immediately garnished with more fresh mint sprigs.

Anchovy and Chick Pea Salad
Makes 6 to 8 servings

This Italian salad tastes best at room temperature, so it's perfect for buffet entertaining.

Test the anchovies for salinity. If they are too strong for your taste, soak them in cold water for about 30 minutes and rinse them in several changes of cold water. Pat dry with a paper towel before you put them in the salad.

1	tablespoon (15 ml) minced fresh parsley
½	cup (125 ml) olive oil
	Juice of 1 lemon
	Salt and freshly ground black pepper
⅛	teaspoon (.5 ml) ground sage
2	cloves of garlic, peeled and bruised
16	ounce (450 g) can of chick peas, drained
1	small tin of anchovy fillets, drained
1	large sweet white onion, peeled and thinly sliced
1	tomato, cut in wedges

Combine the parsley, olive oil, lemon juice, salt, pepper, sage, and garlic in a jar with a tight fitting lid. Shake well to blend and refrigerate for a couple of hours. Arrange the chick peas, anchovies, and onion separated into rings in a shallow serving platter. Discard the garlic from the dressing. Shake the dressing and pour it over the salad. Garnish with wedges of fresh tomato and sprigs of herbs. Serve at room temperature.

🌺 Deep-Fried Artichoke Hearts with Egg and Lemon Sauce
Makes 6 to 8 servings

Heaped hot and crisp on a platter with a bowl of sauce on the side for dipping, these are luscious appetizers. They are equally divine drizzled with some of the sauce as a side dish for meats, fish, and poultry.

Like other fried vegetable dishes, these must be served immediately.

The egg and lemon sauce is simple and versatile enough to enhance a myriad of other steamed or fried vegetables as well.

20 ounces (560 g) packaged frozen artichoke hearts, thawed and drained dry
 2 eggs, well beaten
   Flour for breading
¾ cup (180 ml) fine bread crumbs
 3 to 4 tablespoons (45 to 60 ml) finely grated Kefalotyri or Parmesan cheese
   Vegetable oil for deep-frying
   Egg and lemon sauce (recipe follows)
   Salt and white pepper to taste

Dip the artichoke hearts first in egg, then in flour, then in egg again and coat well with the bread crumbs mixed with the grated cheese. Heat about 3 inches (75 mm) of oil in a deep fryer or heavy pan. When it is hot enough to sizzle the artichokes immediately, add a few of the breaded vegetables at a time and cook, turning gently, until they are nicely browned. Remove with a wire scoop and drain momentarily on paper toweling. Repeat this process with the remaining artichoke hearts. Salt and pepper lightly.

EGG AND LEMON SAUCE
3 egg yolks, at room temperature
   Strained juice of 1½ lemons, at room temperature

Salt and white pepper to taste
Pinch of herbs (dried, crushed rosemary, oregano,
   sage, tarragon, marjoram, etc.) (optional)

With a wire whisk or the beaters of an electric mixer, whip the egg yolks until they are thick and lemon-colored. Add the strained lemon juice a teaspoon (5 ml) at a time, whipping continually. Season to taste with salt, white pepper, and herbs, if desired. Use immediately over any fried or steamed vegetable.

Oven-Roasted Onions

Makes 6 servings

This Italian specialty is as simple and earthy as it is delicious.

6   whole yellow onions (1 per serving)
4   to 5 tablespoons (60 to 75 ml) soft butter
     Salt and pepper to taste
1   teaspoon (5 ml) ground rosemary
1   teaspoon (5 ml) ground oregano

Clean the onions with a slightly damp towel, but do not peel. Make a paste with the butter, salt, pepper, and herbs. Rub the onions well with the butter and place in a shallow baking dish. Roast at 325° F. for about 2½ hours or until the onions are soft inside. Serve hot like a baked potato, with additional butter and seasonings if desired.

Fried Peppers

Makes 4 to 6 servings

Here is my husband's contribution to a good home-cooked Italian meal. Using premium olive oil and the biggest, greenest bell peppers he can find, he hovers patiently over a slow skillet, turning, stirring, and shaking the pan so that not one piece scorches—the key to perfect peppers.

Larry's attentive technique pays off with fabulously flavorful peppers that literally melt in your mouth.

Fried peppers are especially good with spaghetti and most grilled or roasted meats.

>   1   cup (250 ml) good imported olive oil
>   2   crisp green bell peppers, peeled, seeded, and
>   cut into strips about 1 inch (25 mm) wide
>   2   cloves of garlic, peeled and bruised

Heat the oil in a large skillet and add the peppers and garlic. Cook very slowly, turning the peppers often until they are soft, but not too brown. Discard the garlic and serve the peppers either hot or at room temperature.

Roast Pepper Salad with Anchovies and Capers
Makes 4 to 6 servings

A fine buffet salad that is best when left to marinate for nearly 24 hours. It is a delicious offering with Italian, French, or Greek menus.

>   4   large bell peppers (red or green or a combination)
>   ½   cup (125 ml) good olive oil
>   Fresh lemon juice to taste
>   Salt and freshly ground pepper
>   2   cloves of garlic, peeled and bruised
>   1   tablespoon (15 ml) fresh minced parsley
>   1   teaspoon (5 ml) fresh minced sweet basil
>   Capers, drained
>   1   small can anchovy fillets, drained
>   Lemon wedges

Place the peppers on a baking sheet and roast in the oven at 450° F. until the vegetables are soft and the outer skin is blackened. Cool enough to handle, then slip off the skins, remove the stems and seeds, and cut into 1½ inch (37 mm) wide strips. Combine olive oil, lemon juice, salt and pepper, garlic cloves, parsley, and basil in a cruet and shake well to blend. Place the peppers in a glass casserole and pour the dressing over. Marinate from 5 to 24 hours. To serve, bring to room temperature. Discard the garlic cloves. Arrange the peppers on a platter lined with leaves of butter lettuce. Sprinkle with capers and garnish with anchovy fillets and wedges of lemon.

🌺 Potato Kugel

Makes 6 servings

My husband says his mother made a *kugel* so glorious that anyone who ever tasted it said it was the best he'd ever eaten. His family fondly remembers its magnificently crisp brown crust and the tender pudding underneath. But sadly, no one ever obtained Mom's formula.

According to all who loved her, Gertie Wildman's ethereal kugel has never been duplicated. But, if you have to settle for the next best thing, here's a fine recipe.

1	large onion
3	large potatoes
	Lemon juice
3	eggs, beaten
⅓	cup (85 ml) potato starch or flour
1	teaspoon (5 ml) baking powder
	Salt and white pepper to taste
4	tablespoons (60 ml) melted butter or chicken fat
1	tablespoon (15 ml) butter (unmelted)

Peel and finely grate the onion. Peel the potatoes and submerge them in a bowl of cold water with a few drops of lemon juice to prevent them from oxidizing. Finely grate the potatoes and drain off all the liquid. Combine the potatoes, onion, and eggs in a large mixing bowl. Sift the potato starch and baking powder together and add to the potatoes. Mix well. Add the salt and pepper and chicken fat or melted butter. Blend all ingredients. Pour into a well greased 10 inch × 10 inch × 2½ inch (250 mm × 250 mm × 62 mm) baking dish. Dot with 1 tablespoon (15 ml) butter. Bake in the center of a preheated 375° F. oven for about 1 hour, or until the top is crusty and very brown. Serve immediately.

Potato Latkes

Makes 6 servings

This is the Jewish version of potato pancakes as passed down in the Mellman family. Dr. Jim Siedel learned this recipe from his mother, Esther Mellman Siedel.

Jim says it was always up to the men in the family to grate the potatoes and onions—a job that he has now relegated to his food processor. But some things never change: Jim can still put away enough *latkes* (*lot*-kahs) to feed the entire Israeli army.

5	medium to large potatoes (Idaho or white rose)
1	large onion
2	eggs, lightly beaten
	Salt and pepper to taste
2	tablespoons (30 ml) bread crumbs
	Vegetable oil for frying

Place the potatoes in a bowl of cold water as each one is peeled. Grate the potatoes finely, draining off all the liquid that collects. Grate the onion finely, and mix with the potatoes. Add the eggs, salt, pepper, and bread crumbs and mix well. Heat about 1 inch (25 mm) of vegetable oil in a large skillet. You may want to add some butter for flavor. Place the latkes into the hot oil—one heaping tablespoon(15 ml) per latke, draining off any excess liquid as you go. Flatten each latke with a spatula and fry on both sides until crisp and golden brown.

Remove to a paper towel to drain and keep warm until the rest of the latkes are cooked. Serve immediately and pass plenty of sour cream and Homemade Applesauce (*see* index).

Tzimmes

The literal translation of *tzimmes* is "mixture." In this case, tzimmes is a richly flavored Jewish "stew," marrying various combinations of fruits, vegetables, and meats by careful, slow simmering.

Comprised of merely fruits and vegetables, tzimmes is a delightful side dish to be served with roasted or braised beef or poultry. When beef or poultry are added to the stew, tzimmes becomes a hearty main dish.

It seems that no two cooks make the same tzimmes. Let your taste and imagination guide you to yet unexplored combinations. Raisins, pineapple, apples, dried fruits, pears, potatoes, yams, brisket of beef, and turkey parts are all intriguing options.

After trying for years to make the tzimmes like my husband remembers from his childhood, this is my favorite combination. It's the kind of *haimische** recipe for tzimmes that would make a *mavin†* *kvell*.‡§

1   pound (450 g) pitted prunes
5   large carrots, peeled and cut on the bias into 2 inch
       (50 mm) pieces, then parboiled
3   medium-sized sweet potatoes, peeled and quartered
⅓   cup (85 ml) orange blossom honey
¼   teaspoon (1.5 ml) nutmeg
      Juice of ½ lemon, strained
      Very light sprinkling of salt
¼   cup (60 ml) fresh orange juice

* *haimische*—homestyle.
† *mavin*—connoisseur.
‡ *kvell*—marvel, gush, dote on.
§ Not bad for a Greek girl from Wyoming.

Combine all ingredients in a deep baking dish. Cover and bake at 250° F. for 4 to 6 hours, stirring occasionally, until the vegetables are very soft (not mushy) and the juice is thick. Serve warm with Stuffed Breast of Veal or Braised Brisket of Beef (*see* index).

 ## Polish Creamed Mushrooms
Makes 4 to 6 servings

Poles have a penchant for the flavor of mushrooms. Here is an especially popular version.

    2   pounds (900 g) fresh mushrooms, cleaned and sliced
    4   or 5 scallions, chopped
    6   tablespoons (90 ml) butter
        Juice of 1 lemon, strained
    1   teaspoon (5 ml) minced parsley
    2   tablespoons (30 ml) flour
    1   cup (250 ml) sweet cream
    1   egg yolk, beaten
        Salt and white pepper to taste
    1   slice buttered rye toast per serving

Sauté the mushrooms and scallions in 4 tablespoons (60 ml) of the butter with lemon juice added. When mushrooms shrink and liquid is nearly absorbed, sprinkle with parsley. In another small skillet, melt the remaining butter and stir in the flour. Cook, stirring until the mixture loses its floury taste (2 or 3 minutes over fairly low heat). Add this to the mushrooms and stir. Slowly pour in the sweet cream and bring to a slow simmer. Remove from heat. Whisk in the egg yolk, adjust the seasoning, and serve hot, spooned over buttered crisp rye toast.

Norwegian Herring and Apple Salad
Makes 6 to 8 servings

This traditional buffet salad is truly meant for fish devotees
. . . they seem to devour it.

The apple takes the bite off the pickled fish and the creamy
dressing serves to meld these seemingly unlikely ingredients into a
mellifluous melange.

1	cup (250 ml) pickled herring tidbits
1	large onion, finely chopped
1	large, tart apple, peeled, cored, and chopped
½	cup (125 ml) diced celery
	Lemon juice
1	teaspoon (5 ml) sugar
2	tablespoons (30 ml) apple cider vinegar
½	cup (125 ml) stiffly whipped cream
	Salt and white pepper to taste

Combine herring, onions, apples, and celery in a deep bowl.
Sprinkle lightly with lemon juice. Dissolve the sugar in the vinegar.
Fold into the whipped cream and season with salt and pepper. Fold
the cream dressing into the herring salad. Cover and chill for several
hours until serving. Buttered chunks of cracker bread or black
pumpernickel are a fine accompaniment to this buffet-style salad.

Swedish Savory Potato Casserole
JANSSON'S TEMPTATION
Makes 6 to 8 servings

Breathes there a Swedish cook who doesn't have a version of
this famed smörgåsbord casserole?

Feel free to adjust the quantity of anchovies. I like to serve this
with a crisp, tart green salad, knackbrod with butter, and icy *aquavit*
with cold beer chasers.

3   to 4 tablespoons (45 to 60 ml) butter
3   large onions, peeled and chopped
3   pounds (1350 g) red potatoes, peeled and
        thinly sliced
     Salt and freshly ground pepper to taste
2   small cans of anchovy filets, drained, or 8 smoked
        link sausages, thinly sliced
1½   cups (375 ml) grated jack cheese
2   cups (500 ml) whipping cream, milk, or half-and-half
¼   cup (60 ml) fine dry bread crumbs
     Butter

Melt the butter in a large skillet and sauté the onions in the butter until they are limp and golden brown. Arrange about ⅓ of the potatoes over the bottom of a baking dish, about 15 inches × 9 inches × 3 inches (375 mm × 225 mm × 75 mm). Spread half the onions over this and sprinkle with salt and pepper. Arrange half of the anchovy filets or sausage over the onions. Repeat these layers and top with the last third of the potatoes. Top with the grated cheese and pour the cream over all. Sprinkle with bread crumbs and dot with butter. Bake in a 350° F. oven for about 1 hour until the potatoes are very tender and the top is nicely browned.

 ## Swedish Marinated Tomatoes

Makes 8 servings

A good make-ahead salad is hard to find. But now that you've found one, be sure to pick the best possible tomatoes—firm, ripe, bright red, and home-grown, if possible.
This salad is especially suited for buffet entertaining.

8   tomatoes about 2½ inches to 3 inches
        (62 mm × 75 mm) in diameter
¾   cup (180 ml) corn oil
⅛   cup (30 ml) wine vinegar
2   cloves of garlic, peeled
     Salt and freshly ground pepper to taste

½ teaspoon (3 ml) dried dill weed
Pinch of sugar
¼ teaspoon (1.5 ml) prepared Dijon mustard
½ cup (125 ml) snipped fresh chives

Bring a kettle of water to a rolling boil. Skewer a tomato on a fork and hold it under the boiling water for about 30 seconds. Remove from the water immediately and plunge it into a bowl of ice water. The skin will peel off very easily. Repeat with the rest of the tomatoes. Cut each tomato in half lengthwise and use your finger to scoop out all of the seeds and juice, but leave the halves intact. Rub the bottom of a shallow glass baking dish well with the cut side of one of the cloves of garlic and place the tomatoes, cut side down, in the dish in one layer. In a cruet with a tight fitting lid, combine the oil, vinegar, whole garlic cloves, salt, pepper, dill weed, sugar, mustard, and about half of the chives. Shake vigorously until creamy and well blended. Pour over the tomatoes, cover, and chill for several hours, gently shaking the dish occasionally to evenly distribute the dressing. To serve, arrange the tomatoes attractively on a layer of crisp butter lettuce. Remove the garlic from the dressing and discard. Spoon the remaining dressing over the tomatoes and sprinkle with the rest of the snipped chives.

VARIATIONS

1. Sprinkle the finished tomatoes with chilled bay shrimp.

2. Garnish the tomatoes with narrow strips of anchovy filets.

Wilted Lettuce Salad

Makes 4 servings

My mother's side of the family, the Smiths, and the Daniels came to Wyoming and Colorado from the South in the mid-1800's. They were farm folks with lots of kids . . . and all of them, even the boys, were good country cooks.

This is a favorite salad from my childhood. My twin great-aunts, Jessie and Bessie, made wilted lettuce for all our family get-togethers. They'd use giant colanders of washed salad-bowl lettuce from their summer vegetable gardens, along with fresh picked scallions. And it was so good, that no matter how much they made, there never seemed to be enough.

    1   large head of garden lettuce (salad bowl or romaine)
    4   or 5 scallions, cleaned and chopped
    3   or 4 slices of smoked bacon
    ¼   cup (60 ml) vinegar
         Pinch of sugar
         Salt and pepper to taste

Wash and drain the lettuce and tear it into pieces. Add the chopped scallions. Fry the bacon until it is brown and crisp in a skillet. Remove the bacon, crumble, and add to the salad. Add the vinegar and a pinch of sugar to the bacon fat and bring to a boil. Pour this over the salad, add a little salt, if needed, and some pepper. Toss and serve immediately.

Deep-Fried Okra

Makes 4 to 6 servings

Fried fresh okra is delicious with fried chicken or fish.

    1½   pounds (675 g) fresh okra
         Salt and pepper to taste
         Fine ground corn meal for breading
         Peanut oil for deep-frying

Wash okra and remove stems. Slice crosswise into ⅜ inch (9 mm) rounds. Drop into a kettle of boiling salted water and parboil for about 5 minutes. Drain in a colander. Spread okra out on a sheet of waxed paper and sprinkle with salt and pepper. Roll each piece in corn meal and place on more waxed paper. Let the pieces dry for about 30 minutes. Heat about 2 inches (50 mm) of oil in a heavy kettle. Fry okra in small batches until the pieces are golden brown. Drain on paper toweling and keep warm. Repeat with remaining okra. Strain oil to keep bits of corn meal from burning.

Russian Chicken Salad with Sour Cream Dressing

SALAT OLIVIER
Makes 6 to 8 first course servings

This is a Russian standard. It's understandable. For a make-ahead, refreshingly cool hot weather dish, there's hardly an equal.

2   whole chicken breasts, skin and bones included
1   large onion, peeled and chopped
½   cup (125 ml) chopped celery
    Few peppercorns
2   tablespoons (30 ml) dill weed
3   medium-sized potatoes, boiled until tender, thinly sliced, and cooled
3   hard-boiled eggs, shelled and sliced
6   green onions, cleaned and chopped, including green tops
1   large garlic dill pickle, chopped
½   cup (125 ml) diced celery
    Sour cream dressing (recipe follows)

Place the chicken breasts in a stainless steel saucepan and cover with cold water. Add 1 chopped onion, ½ cup of chopped celery, the peppercorns, and the dill weed and simmer gently for about 20 minutes until the chicken is cooked through. Set aside to cool in the water. Remove the bones from the chicken breasts and discard. Strain the stock, discard the vegetables, and reserve the stock for another purpose. Cut the chicken meat into ½ inch (12 mm) strips. Combine the chicken with the sliced potatoes, eggs, green onions, pickle, and celery. Pour half of the dressing over all, mix well, and chill thoroughly.

SOUR CREAM DRESSING
¾   cup (180 ml) mayonnaise
¾   cup (180 ml) commercial sour cream
1½   teaspoons (37 ml) dried dill weed

Pinch of dried tarragon leaves, crumbled
2 tablespoons (30 ml) drained capers
1 teaspoon (5 ml) vinegar or pickle juice
Salt and white pepper to taste

Blend all ingredients well and chill.

TO ASSEMBLE
Fresh lettuce leaves, washed and dried
2 ripe, red tomatoes, cut in wedges
1 lemon, cut in wedges
½ pound (225 g) good black olives

Line a round serving platter with lettuce leaves. Mound the chicken salad in a pyramid shape in the center of the plate. Spoon the remaining dressing over the top of the chicken and let it run down the sides. Surround the chicken mound with tomato wedges, lemon wedges, and black olives.

Russian Eggplant with Walnut and Pomegranate Sauce

Makes 8 servings

Piquant and pretty—this dish is an extraordinarily delicious use of firm, fresh eggplant.

1 cup (250 ml) fresh walnut meats
3 or 4 sprigs of fresh coriander leaves
1 clove of garlic, minced
Unsweetened pomegranate juice
Salt and ground red pepper to taste
1 recipe Fried Eggplant (*see* index)
(use vegetable unpeeled)

Combine the nuts, coriander, and garlic in a blender, food processor, or food grinder. Process to a thick, coarse paste. Add pomegranate juice gradually and blend until you have a thick liquid, or to suit your taste. Add salt and pepper to taste. You can dilute the sauce if you wish, with a little water. Refrigerate for a few hours before using. Arrange the fried eggplant on a shallow serving platter and spoon the sauce over all. Garnish with sprigs of fresh coriander. Serve with a roast or with grilled lamb or chicken.

Sweets, Holiday Fare, & Drinks

Contrary to custom in our culture, rich desserts are seldom offered after a meal in most ethnic homes. Instead, fruit and cheese are the usual finales. Sweets and pastries are savored as between meal snacks with tea, coffee, or water.

We are probably much too cavity- and calorie-conscious to ever adopt that style of eating entirely. But fruit for dessert is one idea that is gathering momentum.

This chapter represents the best of both worlds. There are luscious fresh fruit desserts as well as a paradise of eye-popping pastries, tortes, and pies. Here are sweets for every occasion. There are breakfast baked goods, like buttery *Danish pastries* and *fruit kuchen*, through more elaborate holiday treats like the *Sicilian Christmas cake* and even *strudel* from scratch.

For simple fruit and cheese offerings, select ripe fruits in season. You may have to shop a few days in advance to let the fruit ripen to full sweetness. A local cheese merchant can recommend the right cheeses for specific fruit. (See the Ethnic Bazaar at the back of the book for additional cheese sources.)

For certain occasions, you might consider this: keep dinner to a bare minimum, then offer a splendid dessert buffet; have an assortment of fruits, cheeses, and pastries; set out a tray of liqueurs and brew an exotic coffee or tea.

🌸 Basque Sponge Cake

Follow the recipe and directions for the Traditional Passover Sponge Cake (*see* index), omit the matzo cake meal and potato starch and substitute 2 cups (500 ml) sifted cake flour.

Sponge cake is the favored dessert at many Basque celebrations. Its lightness and delicate flavor is the perfect foil for the preceding highly seasoned feasts.

ALMOND SPONGE CAKE

Add 1 teaspoon (5 ml) almond extract to batter and fold in ½ cup (125 ml) ground blanched almonds with the stiff egg whites. Bake in a 10 inch (250 mm) tube pan. Sprinkle top of cooled cake with sifted powdered sugar.

ORANGE SPONGE CAKE

Add finely grated rind of 1 orange. Bake in a large rectangular cake pan lined with butter and waxed paper. Serve cut in squares with powdered sugar.

RUM SPONGE CAKE

Bake a 10 inch (250 mm) plain sponge cake (flavored like the Passover Sponge Cake). Cut crosswise into three even layers. Spread rum filling between layers and reassemble cake. Dust with powdered sugar and chill before serving.

RUM FILLING

2½	cups (625 ml) milk
1	vanilla bean
3	egg yolks
½	cup (125 ml) granulated sugar
½	teaspoon (3 ml) cinnamon (optional)
3	tablespoons (45 ml) cornstarch
	Rum to taste
2	tablespoons (30 ml) sweet butter

In a saucepan, scald the milk and vanilla bean and set aside to cool. In a mixing bowl, beat the egg yolks. Combine the dry ingredients and gradually whisk them into the beaten yolks until the mixture is thick and lemon-colored. Pour into the top of a double boiler over hot water, and stir in the milk (discard vanilla bean). Cook the custard until it thickens, stirring constantly. Remove from heat and stir in the rum and butter until well blended. Stir until cool, to prevent a skin from forming on the top. The cake should be completely cool before you fill it.

Frozen Banana Cream

Makes 6 to 8 servings

This thick, dreamy dessert has its roots in many Latin American countries. Its flavor can be varied with the addition of coconut milk, rum, crushed pineapple, or mango or papaya pulp.

Here is the simplest version.

```
1    cup (250 ml) very ripe, mashed banana (about 3)
     Juice from 1 lime, strained
½    cup (125 ml) granulated sugar
1    pint (250 ml) heavy cream
     Pinch of salt
```

Combine banana, lime juice, and sugar and mix thoroughly. Using an electric mixer, whip the cream with the salt until it is very stiff. Fold bananas into the cream and spread into a large shallow baking dish. Freeze solid. Remove from the freezer and soften slightly. Cut into cubes and process in a food processor fitted with a steel blade, until the consistency of ice cream. Pack into airtight containers and either serve immediately or refreeze. Let frozen cream stand in the refrigerator about 1 hour before serving.

Bananas Flambé

Makes 6 servings

Glistening flamed bananas permeated with an array of exotic-flavorings is a spectacle befitting the end of a colorful Latin dinner. Make it at the table for unparalleled drama.

        6   tablespoons (90 ml) sweet butter
        ½   cup (125 ml) packed brown sugar
             Juice of 1 lemon
             Juice of 2 oranges
        1   teaspoon (5 ml) grated lemon peel
        1   tablespoon (15 ml) grated orange peel
        6   firm, green bananas
        ½   cup (125 ml) finely chopped pineapple
        ½   cup (125 ml) rum
             Freshly grated coconut (optional)

In a large, heavy skillet, melt the butter and stir in the sugar until it melts. Add all the juice and rind and allow the mixture to simmer over medium heat until it starts to thicken. Stir occasionally. Place the peeled bananas in the skillet along with the chopped pineapple and spoon the sauce over the bananas until they are well coated. Simmer over low heat just until the bananas have had a chance to warm through. Add the rum and continue to heat for another 15 to 20 seconds. Ignite the rum and serve as soon as the flame begins to fade. Sprinkle with fresh coconut if you wish.

Sweet Potato Pudding

Makes 4 to 6 servings

Sweet Potato Pudding, in one form or another, is traditional fare in many Latino homes. Its variations incorporate mashed bananas, freshly grated coconut, mashed, cooked pumpkin, red yams, and a wide array of spices and flavorings.

1   pound (450 g) sweet potatoes, scrubbed,
      trimmed, and quartered
⅔   cup (170 ml) cream of coconut
¼   cup (60 ml) sweet sherry
½   cup (125 ml) flour
½   cup (125 ml) granulated sugar
4   large eggs, well beaten
¼   teaspoon (1.5 ml) salt
1   teaspoon (5 ml) ground cinnamon
¼   teaspoon (1.5 ml) ground cloves
2   teaspoons (10 ml) grated orange zest (no white)
¼   pound (112 g) sweet butter, melted
½   cup (125 ml) packed light brown sugar

Place the sweet potatoes in a large saucepan and cover with
water. Add a bit of salt and bring to a rapid boil. Cook until the sweet
potatoes are tender. Drain and peel if you wish. Sometimes the peel is
used in the pudding—it's entirely up to you. Mash the potatoes
through a food mill. Don't use a food processor for this or the texture
will be too fine. Combine the sweet potatoes with the cream of
coconut, sherry, flour, sugar, eggs, salt, spices, orange zest, and melted
butter and mix well. In a heavy saucepan, melt the light brown sugar
and cook until it caramelizes. Pour into a 10 inch (250 mm) pie plate
and swirl to coat the plate and cool. Spoon the sweet potato mixture
into the pie plate and spread evenly, being careful not to disturb the
caramel coating. Set the pie plate inside a larger baking dish with
about 1 inch (25 mm) of water. Bake in a 350° F. oven until the pudding is set and a toothpick comes out of the center clean. When
slightly cooled, unmold the pudding onto a serving plate. Carefully
run the edge of a small sharp knife around the edge of the pudding, invert the serving plate over the pudding, then turn the pie plate over so
that the serving plate is on the bottom and carefully lift off the pie
plate. Serve warm as a vegetable side dish or as a dessert with toasted
coconut, whipped cream, or heavy cream.

Fresh Applesauce

Makes about 1 quart (1000 ml)

To me, nothing makes a better applesauce than fall-fresh giant golden delicious apples. They are juicy and full of natural sweetness so you need add no sugar. However, most any apple that's firm and ripe will make a far better sauce than you've ever had from a can or jar.

Try to use natural unfiltered, unsweetened apple juice for double apple flavor. Or, if you can buy fresh pressed cider in the fall, use it in applesauce.

Fresh applesauce is perfect with so many different dishes, from Potato Latkes (*see* index) to a German Country Breakfast Skillet (*see* index). It's even good as a dessert, served warm with fresh sweet cream.

You may never settle for "store-bought" again.

3½   to 4 pounds (1575 to 1800 g) fresh apples,
        peeled, cored, and chopped
1   tablespoon (15 ml) lemon juice
½   to ¾ cup (125 to 180 ml) apple juice or cider
        Sugar to taste
¼   teaspoon (1.5 ml) cinnamon to taste (optional)

As soon as the apples are peeled, chop them and put them into a large stainless steel or enameled kettle containing the apple juice and lemon juice. Over medium heat, bring the apples to a boil. Cover, turn the heat down to a slow simmer, and cook until the apples are very soft, adding a bit of liquid when necessary. This process takes about 45 minutes. Stir frequently and taste for sweetness as you go along, adding sugar and cinnamon, if you wish, to your liking. If you like a finer textured sauce, run the sauce through a food mill when it is done. Place in a sterile jar, with a tight lid, and store in the refrigerator up to 10 days. May be warmed before serving.

🌸 German Gingerbread

Makes about 9 servings

Oh, the wonderfully heady fragrance of gingerbread right out of the oven!

Delectable for dessert, but consider it as a bread to accompany dishes of pork, ham, or goose as well.

Dripping with sweet butter, it is a divine winter breakfast treat with mugs of freshly brewed tea.

½	cup (125 ml) molasses (light or blackstrap, according to your preference)
½	cup (125 ml) filtered orange blossom honey
⅔	cup (170 ml) hot water
	Juice of 1 lemon
	Grated zest of 1 lemon (no white)
2½	cups (625 ml) sifted all-purpose flour
½	teaspoon (3 ml) salt
1½	teaspoons (8 ml) baking soda
1½	teaspoons (8 ml) ground cinnamon
1	teaspoon (5 ml) ground cloves
1½	teaspoon (8 ml) ground ginger
¼	teaspoon (1.5 ml) ground nutmeg
¼	teaspoon (1.5 ml) ground cardamom
½	cup (125 ml) sweet butter, softened at room temperature
½	cup (125 ml) granulated sugar
1	egg, beaten
	Whipping cream for topping

Combine molasses, honey, hot water, and lemon juice together in a saucepan and bring to a slow boil. Remove from heat immediately, stir in grated lemon zest, and cool. Sift together all dry ingredients. In a large mixing bowl, cream butter and sugar until light and fluffy. Beat in egg. Alternately add dry ingredients and molasses mixture, beating well after each addition. Pour into a greased 9 inch (225 mm) square cake pan and bake in a preheated 350° F. oven for 50 to 60 minutes until the top springs back when pressed lightly with your finger. Serve warm topped with cream either slightly beaten or whipped.

 Fresh Fruit Kuchen
Makes about 12 servings

This delicious and easy German fruit tart is so simple to prepare that you can easily whip it up in time for breakfast. Have it warm with butter or cream drizzled over each piece.

In the winter, I like to make a simple dinner of homemade soup, bread and wine, then for dessert a freshly baked apple *kuchen* served with ice cream. If you'd like to try kuchen for dessert, add a dash more spice to the topping, and even a splash of liqueur.

DOUGH
- 2 cups (500 ml) all-purpose flour
- 4 tablespoons (60 ml) sugar
- 1 teaspoon (5 ml) baking powder
- ½ teaspoon (3 ml) salt
- ¾ cup (180 ml) softened butter
- 1 egg, well beaten
- 2 tablespoons (30 ml) milk

Sift dry ingredients into a mixing bowl. Add the softened butter and work in with your hands until the mixture is crumbly. Beat the egg and milk together and stir into the flour with a fork to mix, then blend well with a wooden spoon, or your hands. Cover tightly with plastic wrap and chill completely. In the meantime, make the filling.

FILLING
- 3½ cups (875 ml) sliced fruit (apples, pears, peaches, plums, apricots, pitted prunes, each individually or in any combination), peeled, stemmed, cored, pitted, etc.
- ½ teaspoon (3 ml) ground cinnamon

¼   teaspoon (1.5 ml) ground nutmeg
1   cup (250 ml) packed brown sugar
½   cup (250 ml) softened butter
½   cup (125 ml) finely chopped walnuts
1   teaspoon (5 ml) finely grated lemon zest (no white)

Toss the fruit slices with the cinnamon, nutmeg, and about 2 tablespoons (30 ml) of the brown sugar, just to coat. Crumble brown sugar, butter, walnuts, and lemon zest and set aside.

TO SERVE

Press the chilled dough into an oblong baking dish. Arrange fruit over the dough and sprinkle with the brown sugar and nut mixture. Place in a preheated 350° F. oven and bake until bubbly, about 40 minutes. Cut in squares and serve warm.

🌺 Phyllo Dough

Makes about 1 pound (450 g)

Greek *phyllo* is one of the wonders of the pastry world. Thin, crisp, and buttery, its multilayers bake to a richly golden crackle that encases meats, nuts, custard, cheeses, and fresh vegetables. In baking, phyllo is used in much the same way as puff pastry and pie dough.

Phyllo is the Greek word for "leaf." Sometimes spelled "filo" or "fillo," it is sold ready-made in many Greek, Middle Eastern, and Jewish (strudel leaves) specialty stores. Commercial phyllo is uniformly thin and comes in sheets 16 inches × 18 inches (400 mm × 450 mm) . . . and while it's good, it's no match for the fresh, homemade version. Handmade phyllo offers a deeper color, a more delicate pastry and it is much easier to handle than store-bought.

Now don't be intimidated. You don't have to be from the old country or even be a gifted baker. But you will have to employ patience, gentleness, a bit of finesse, and time to make your first great batch of phyllo—and indeed it can be done the first time out. Come to think of it, those are the same requirements for doing anything worthwhile.

One caution: once you've tasted homemade phyllo, you'll never again want to settle for store-bought.

    3   cups (750 ml) white bread flour
    ½   cup (125 ml) gluten flour
    1   teaspoon (5 ml) salt
    1¼   cups (310 ml) warm water (110° F. to 115° F.)
         Cooking oil
         Sifted cornstarch

Sift flours into a mixing bowl. Mix in salt. Make a well in the center and add only 1 cup (250 ml) of the water to start. Mix with your hands until the dough begins to stick together. If necessary, add more water a bit at a time until the dough is cohesive. Turn the dough out onto an unfloured surface (use a marble slab if you can) and knead the dough with oiled hands until it is like stretchy satin and the surface blisters (in about 10 minutes of vigorous kneading). Keep a small dish of oil handy to keep your hands well lubricated. Occasionally lift the dough and slap it down hard onto the work surface.

Cover the dough with a slightly damp (not wet!) kitchen towel, cover with a bowl large enough not to touch the dough and let it rest for about an hour until the dough loses its elasticity (a pinch of dough when pulled out will not rebound). While the dough is resting, make your filling.

Next, cover a square or rectangular work table with a clean patterned sheet and dust it lightly and evenly with flour. Cut the dough in half. Leave one half covered with the damp towel and bowl. Place the other half in the center of the sheet and roll out in all directions as far as you can using a rolling pin. If the dough resists rolling, cover it with a dry cloth and let it rest until it is no longer elastic (15 to 20 minutes). Give it the "pinch and pull" test to see if it's ready. When the dough no longer resists stretching, begin to work it. Placing the backs of your hands *under* the center of the dough, work carefully and slowly to stretch and pull the dough out to a size that will eventually hang over the sides of the work table. Walk around the table as you work, stretching the dough evenly in all directions with the backs of your hands, up and over your forearms. This takes patience and care, if the finished dough is to be thin and transparent as tissue. Stretch the dough until it hangs over the edges of the work table. Trim the edges to make a neat square or rectangle. Dust the entire top of the dough very lightly with some of the sifted cornstarch. Using a very sharp knife, cut the dough down the center lengthwise, then cut each half into six even rectangles. Stack the 12 pieces cornstarch side up, one on top of the other. Wrap them well with plastic wrap until they are virtually airtight. Place them flat into a plastic bag and refrigerate up to 4 days, or freeze indefinitely. Be sure to keep them flat or they will wrinkle and become harder to work with. Repeat with remaining dough.

TO USE FROZEN PHYLLO
Defrost completely in refrigerator. Keep tightly wrapped and chilled until you are ready to use.

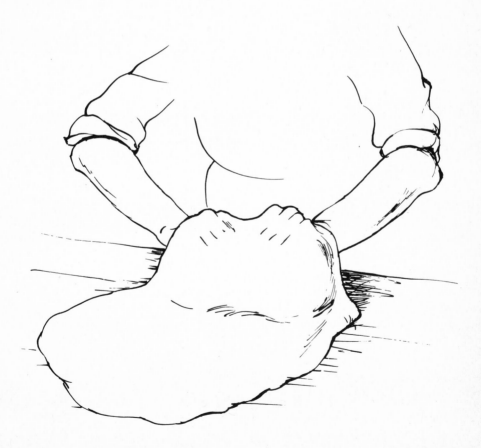

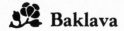 **Baklava**

Makes about 24 pieces

Baklava (bahk-lah-*vah*) is layers of crackling pastry encasing a spicy nut filling, then steeped in fruit-tinged honey. It is probably the most famous and adored of all Middle Eastern sweets. So prevalent is this pastry that Greeks, Bulgarians, Rumanians, Turks, Armenians, and Lebanese all claim it as their own invention. There are endless versions—some shockingly sweet, some highly spiced, and some that incorporate fruits in the filling.

This Greek recipe is more spicy than sweet, and the distinct flavor of imported Hymettus Greek honey gives the flavor added character. Clover or orange honey can be substituted, but the flavor will be noticeably different.

Baklava is best when made a day in advance. Serve it at room temperature accompanied by strong, freshly brewed coffee and a glass of ice water.

Greeks rarely have anything more than fruit for dessert, so Greek pastries and baked goods are normally savored as between-meal-snacks. But to American palates, a small diamond of baklava is a most welcome ending to a Greek feast.

Make sure the nuts you use are the freshest and that your honey is of premium quality. Use creamery butter, not margarine, on the phyllo dough. Phyllo dough may be purchased at Greek, Middle Eastern, or Jewish specialty stores, and it can be found in many grocer's frozen food cases. If you have the time and the inclination, make your own Phyllo (see preceding recipe) for the most divine taste sensation you can imagine.

4	cups (1000 ml) finely chopped blanched almonds, walnuts, or pecans, or any combination of these
⅔	cup (170 ml) sugar
1	teaspoon (5 ml) ground cinnamon
¼	teaspoon (1.5 ml) cloves
2	small tart apples, peeled, cored, and finely chopped (optional)
1	pound (450 g) unsalted sweet butter, melted over hot water in the top of a double boiler

1½   pounds (675 g) phyllo, either commercial or
        homemade (see preceding recipe)
      Honey syrup (recipe follows)

TO PREPARE

In a mixing bowl combine the nuts, sugar, spices and apples if
you wish. Using a wide pastry brush, butter the bottom, corners, and
sides of 12 inch × 7½ inch × 2 inch (300 mm × 187 mm × 50 mm)
baking dish. On a large work surface, lay out the sheets of phyllo flat
on a piece of plastic wrap. Cover with another sheet of plastic wrap to
keep it moist and pliable. Place a slightly damp kitchen towel over all.
Assembled on your work surface, close at hand, should be the baking
dish, the phyllo (completely covered), the melted butter in the top of a
double boiler over hot water to keep it warm, the filling, and your
pastry brush. First, brush the top sheet of phyllo all over on one side
with some melted butter and lay it crosswise, butter side up, over half
of the baking dish, allowing the edges to hang over the sides of the
dish by a couple of inches (50 mm). Next, brush a second sheet of
phyllo with butter and overlapping the first sheet, cover the other half
of the dish, again allowing at least a couple of inches (50 mm) of the
dough to hang over the edges. Continue in this fashion until you have
ten complete layers on the bottom of the dish. Re-cover the stack of
phyllo with the plastic wrap and damp towel after each sheet of phyllo
is removed to keep them moist and pliable. Sprinkle the tenth layer
evenly with ½ to ⅔ cup (125 to 170 ml) of the filling and top with two
layers of buttered phyllo laid out flat over the filling. Continue this

process alternating filling with two layers of phyllo, until all of the filling is used up. Butter each remaining sheet of phyllo on one side and layer butter side up over all. Brush the edges of the dough that are hanging over with the remaining butter and roll them up and over to make a neat roll around the inside edge of the pan. Score the top of the baklava, through just the top couple of layers of phyllo, using the tip of a very sharp small knife. Do this to aid in cutting later and to help the syrup penetrate. Score it three squares across and four squares down, 12 squares in all. Then score each square in half diagonally from one corner to the opposite corner to make 24 diamond-shaped pieces. Sprinkle with a few drops of warm water.

TO BAKE AND ASSEMBLE

Bake in a preheated 350° F. oven for 50 to 55 minutes until the top is a deep golden color. While the baklava is baking, make the syrup and let it cool. When the pastry comes out of the oven, pour about half of the *cooled* syrup over the top very slowly—by cupfuls (250 ml at a time)—to let it soak in. About 20 minutes later, slowly pour on the remaining syrup in the same manner. Let the baklava stand undisturbed for several hours before cutting to serve. Cut along the scored lines using a sharp knife. Cut through all of the layers completely. Lift out gently with a flexible spatula and a fork.

TO FREEZE

Baked baklava can be frozen if wrapped tightly in plastic wrap and foil. Let it come to room temperature before serving. To freeze *unbaked* baklava, assemble according to the above directions but do not bake. Cover tightly with layers of aluminum foil and freeze. To bake, place the frozen baklava, uncovered, directly into a preheated 350° F. oven and bake for about 1½ hours. Turn the heat down to 325° F. and continue to bake for another hour until the top is golden brown and the filling is hot throughout. Proceed with the syrup as directed above. After frozen baklava has been baked it can be refrozen.

SPICED HONEY SYRUP
    2   cups (500 ml) sugar
    1   cup (250 ml) imported Greek Hymettus honey
    1   cup (250 ml) water

Juice of 1 lemon, strained
Scrubbed rind of ½ lemon
2   sticks of cinnamon about 3 inches (75 mm) long
4   to 5 whole cloves
1   teaspoon (5 ml) rose water or orange flower water

Place all ingredients in a saucepan and bring to a boil. Reduce heat and simmer for 10 minutes. Cool completely and strain before using.

Greek Butter and Nut Balls

Makes about 48 cookies

These rich, delicate cookies are holiday treats for Greeks. They are served at Christmas and New Years as well as weddings and christenings. With coffee, they make a scrumptious dessert all by themselves. With fruit and cream, they are sinful. Handle them gently, follow the rules for the powdered sugar coating, and you'll have perfect cookies every time.

1   pound (450 g) sweet butter, at room temperature
½   cup (125 ml) powdered sugar
3   teaspoons (15 ml) Ouzo or fine cognac
1   teaspoon (5 ml) pure vanilla extract
4   cups (1000 ml) sifted all-purpose flour
3½   cups (875 ml) *finely* chopped walnuts
     Plenty of powdered sugar for coating

Using an electric mixer, whip the butter. Add the ½ cup (125 ml) of powdered sugar and beat well. Mix in the liquor and vanilla. Add flour gradually, mixing well after each addition. Fold the nuts into the dough. Using your hands, shape the dough into balls about 1½ inches (37 mm) in diameter. Place side-by-side (they do not rise during baking) on an ungreased cookie sheet. Bake in a preheated 350° F. oven for about 15 minutes. Since these cookies don't brown, break one open to test for doneness. If no butter line shows in the center, they're ready. Have a large baking sheet or dish with raised edges ready with about ½ inch (12 mm) of sifted powdered sugar covering the bottom. When the baked cookies have cooled enough to handle, place them side-by-side in one layer on the bed of powdered sugar. Sift a thick coat of powdered sugar over the tops and sides of all of the cookies. Let them stand *undisturbed* overnight. Repeat this procedure with the remaining dough, using a new powdered sugar-covered pan as needed. The next day the cookies can be stored in bags or in covered containers. To serve, you can stack them in mounds on a lovely plate and sprinkle the tops with more powdered sugar. They can be flash frozen on a cookie sheet, then placed together in an airtight plastic bag. To thaw, place them in one layer at room temperature. Unbaked dough can be frozen, as well. Wrap it tightly in plastic and freeze. To thaw, place in the refrigerator for several hours.

 Greek Nut Cake in Fragrant Syrup

RAVANIE
Makes 24 pieces

This mellifluous cake is best if made well in advance to give the flavors a chance to bloom. Use the very freshest nuts you can obtain. Instead of using a combination of nuts as this recipe indicates, you may want to use all of one kind. This formula produces a pleasantly sweet, subtly spiced cake, but you can adjust the level of sweetness and the spices to suit your own taste.

    12 eggs, separated
    1½ cups (375 ml) sugar
     1 teaspoon (5 ml) vanilla extract
     3 cups (750 ml) ground walnuts
     3 cups (750 ml) ground almonds
    16 pieces zwieback, finely ground
        Finely grated zest of 1 orange and 1 lemon

Put the egg whites in a large mixing bowl (not plastic). With electric beaters, start to beat the egg whites at a fairly low speed until big bubbles form on top. Gradually increase the speed and whip until the egg whites are stiff. Set aside. In another mixing bowl, using clean beaters, beat the egg yolks with the sugar until the mixture is light and lemon-colored. Add the vanilla during the beating process. Mix nuts, zwieback, and rind together. Gradually and gently, fold the stiff egg whites into the beaten yolks. Then, gently fold in the nut mixture. Pour the batter into a greased 16 inch × 13 inch × 3 inch (400 mm × 325 mm × 75 mm) cake pan. Bake in a preheated 350° F. oven for 1 hour until the top is lightly browned and a test toothpick comes out clean. Remove the cake from the oven and immediately pour one of the honey syrups below over the cake, by the cupful (250 ml at a time), until all the syrup has been absorbed. Let the cake stand undisturbed for a few hours, then cut into 24 serving pieces—either diamonds or squares—and serve at room temperature. See the illustration in the recipe for Baklava to cut into diamond shapes.

RUM SYRUP
- 2 cups (500 ml) sugar
- 4½ cups (1125 ml) water
- 2 or 3 cinnamon sticks, each about 3 inches (75 mm) long
- 1 thick slice of lemon with rind
- ½ cup (125 ml) rum

Bring sugar and water to a boil in a saucepan and stir until all of the sugar is dissolved. Add lemon rind and cinnamon sticks and simmer gently for about 10 minutes. Remove from heat and stir in rum. Let cool. When ready to use, remove cinnamon and lemon.

HONEY-ORANGE SYRUP
- 2 cups (500 ml) Greek Hymettus honey, or other fine quality honey
- 1 cup (250 ml) water
- 3 or 4 cinnamon sticks, each about 3 inches (75 mm) long
- 3 or 4 whole cloves
  Scrubbed rind from 1 orange
- 2 tablespoons (30 ml) orange extract

Combine all ingredients in a saucepan and bring to a boil. Simmer for about 10 minutes. Remove from heat and cool. Strain before using.

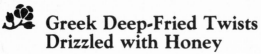

Greek Deep-Fried Twists Drizzled with Honey

KSEROTIGNA (KZERO-*TEEG-A-NAH*) OR DIPLESS (*THEE-PLESS*)
Makes about 3 dozen

In my mind's eye, I can see my mother's kitchen on many Christmas Eves past. Thick frost of the Wyoming winter etched the kitchen windows. Our table was dusty with flour and draped with *kserotigna* dough waiting to be cut, crisply fried, and drizzled with honey. The platters were piled with glimmering *loukoumades*, puffy and golden with soft, syrupy centers. And Mom, happily, patiently, cutting and cooking mountains of these wonderfully simple Greek sweets.

4	eggs, well beaten
1	cup (250 ml) lukewarm water
¼	teaspoon (1.5 ml) salt
1	teaspoon (5 ml) anise seed (optional)
2	tablespoons (30 ml) oil
3	to 4 cups (750 to 1000 ml) sifted all-purpose flour
	Plenty of vegetable oil for deep-frying
	Honey syrup (see succeeding recipe, Greek Honey Doughnuts)
¼	cup (60 ml) sesame seeds, toasted until they are lightly browned (optional)
	Ground cinnamon (optional)
	Finely chopped nuts (walnuts, pecans, almonds, etc.) (optional)

Combine the beaten eggs and water in a large mixing bowl. Add salt and oil plus the anise seed if you like the licorice flavor. Stir to blend well. Add flour gradually, mixing well after each addition until the dough is workable and not too sticky. Divide into three or four separate balls. Cover each with plastic wrap until use. Roll each ball out on a lightly floured board until it is as thin as pie dough. Cut the dough in strips about 1 inch (25 mm) wide and anywhere from 5 to 8 inches (125 to 200 mm) long. The strips need not be uniform in length. Twist each piece into shapes: figure-eights, loose bows, loops, etc. In a deep kettle or deep-fryer, heat a few inches (50 mm) of oil to 360° F. and drop a few cookies at a time into the hot fat. Cook, turning each piece carefully with tongs until the twists are crisp and lightly golden. Drain briefly on layers of paper towel. Dip momentarily in the ice-cold honey syrup and transfer to a large platter, or place drained cookies on a platter and drizzle the syrup over them. Sprinkle lightly with toasted sesame seeds or cinnamon and finely chopped nuts.

Freshly made kserotigna are incomparable, but they are still delectable up to 24 hours after they are cooked.

Greek Deep-Fried Honey Doughnuts

LOUKOUMADES (LOO-KOO-*MAH*-THES)
Makes about 3 dozen

1   cup (250 ml) milk
1   cup (250 ml) water
1   package dry yeast
¼   teaspoon (1.5 ml) salt
3   eggs, separated
1   teaspoon (5 ml) vanilla
1   to 2 cups (250 to 500 ml) sifted all-purpose flour
    Vegetable oil for deep-frying
    Honey syrup
3   to 4 tablespoons (45 to 60 ml) sesame seeds toasted in the oven until lightly browned

Heat the milk and water to 110° F. to 115° F. Add salt and yeast and stir until dissolved. Add slightly beaten egg yolks plus the vanilla and mix well. Add flour gradually, mixing after each addition to make a semithick mixture. In a separate mixing bowl (not plastic) beat the egg whites with electric beaters until the whites stand in peaks. Fold the stiff egg whites into the batter. Cover the bowl and let stand in a warm place until the dough has risen to double its original size. In a deep, heavy kettle or a deep fryer, heat a few inches (50 mm) of vegetable oil to 375° F. Drop the dough by teaspoonsful (5 ml at a time) into the hot oil, turning to brown them on all sides. Don't crowd them in the pan—too much dough at once will lower the cooking temperature making the *loukoumades* absorb excess fat. Also, if the temperature is too high, the little doughnuts will brown too quickly on the outside, but the inside will be doughy. Lift the loukoumades out with a wire basket or slotted spoon and drain them momentarily on layers of paper towel. Then plunge them immediately into the bowl of icy syrup. Transfer within a few seconds to a platter and sprinkle with toasted sesame seeds. Make the loukoumades the same day you intend to serve them.

HONEY SYRUP
2 cups (500 ml) honey
1 cup (250 ml) water

Blend the honey and water thoroughly in a mixing bowl. Keep the syrup ice-cold by setting this bowl inside a bigger bowl containing ice cubes.

Italian Cafe Ricotta

Serves 6 to 8

Cafe ricotta is so rich and thick it has to be spooned from demitasse cups in tiny bites. Cool mocha-and-rum-flavored whipped ricotta is sandwiched between layers of rich, melted chocolate, then flourished with sweet whipped cream and toasted almonds.

This dessert lover's fantasy is a grand finale for a memorable Italian dinner.

3 tablespoons (45 ml) instant coffee
¼ cup (60 ml) granulated sugar
¼ cup (60 ml) boiling water
½ pound (225 g) ricotta cheese
½ pound (225 g) sour cream

Rum to taste
6   ounces (168 g) semisweet chocolate bits, melted
Almond whipped cream (recipe below)
Chocolate curls or shavings
Roasted, unsalted almonds for garnish

Combine the instant coffee and sugar in a small mixing bowl. Add the boiling water and stir to dissolve. Set aside to cool. With a blender or electric mixer, whip the ricotta and sour cream together until the mixture is smooth. Add the cooled coffee mixture and rum and blend well. Cover and refrigerate for at least 4 hours. To serve, spoon some of the melted chocolate into the bottom of a demitasse cup. Fill about ¾ full with the ricotta mixture. Add another bit of melted chocolate, a dollop of whipped cream, and garnish with chocolate curls and almonds. Serve immediately.

ALMOND WHIPPED CREAM
½   pint (250 ml) whipping cream
Sugar to taste
½   teaspoon (3 ml) almond extract

Pour the cream into a chilled mixing bowl and beat at medium speed until the mixture begins to thicken. Add the sugar and almond extract and continue to whip until the cream is quite stiff. Refrigerate until serving.

Molly Custrini's Italian Cream Puffs with Ricotta Filling

These tender, airy pastries are filled with whipped ricotta cheese which gives them the character and tang needed to crown a lusty Italian meal.

CREAM PUFF SHELLS
½   cup (125 ml) water
½   cup (125 ml) salad oil
¼   cup (60 ml) all-purpose flour
3   eggs, at room temperature

Combine the water and oil in a saucepan and bring to a good boil. Remove from the heat and immediately beat in the flour with a wooden spoon. Return the mixture to the stove, cooking and stirring until the batter leaves the sides of the pan. Do not overdo the cooking or stirring or the shells will not puff. Remove the batter from the stove and cool for a minute or two. Then one at a time, add the eggs, beating vigorously with a wooden spoon. The batter is ready when it will stand in a peak on the end of the spoon. Spoon dollops of the batter on an ungreased baking sheet, allowing space between each one for the shells to puff. Bake in a preheated 375° F. oven, for 30 minutes, until firm, puffed, and golden brown. Cool in a draft-free space. Meanwhile, make the filling.

RICOTTA FILLING
1½   pounds (675 mg) creamy ricotta cheese
        Sugar to taste

Using electric beaters, beat the ricotta until it is smooth and creamy. Gradually add sugar to your liking. Cut off the tops of cream puff shells with a sharp bread knife. Fill each shell with some of the ricotta mixture. Replace the top of the shell and dust with powdered sugar or ground cinnamon. You may chill before serving.

VARIATIONS
To the filling you may add:

1. Melted semisweet chocolate to taste

2. 1 teaspoon (5 ml) vanilla extract

3. ½ teaspoon (3 ml) almond extract

🌹 Italian-Style Fruit Compote

An Italian home-cooked meal rarely includes any kind of dessert other than cheese and ripe seasonal fruits. This combination of fruits and liqueur is usually reserved for honored guests and special occasions.

Fresh ripe fruits in season, peeled, seeded, and cut
  into bite-sized pieces (plums, cherries, peaches,
  melons, apples, grapes, etc.)
Fresh ripe berries in season, washed, stemmed, and
  drained (blackberries, blueberries, raspberries, etc.)
Chopped nuts to taste (pistachios, walnuts,
  pecans, etc.)
Sugar to taste if needed
Liqueur of choice to taste (Amaretto, Galiano,
  Kirsch, etc.) or a good, chilled champagne
Lightly sweetened whipped cream flavored with a little
  matching liqueur or vanilla or almond extract

Select a combination of fruits that is both appetizing and
colorful, allowing about 1 cup (250 ml) of compote per serving. Combine the chopped fruits, nuts, sugar, and liqueur in a glass mixing
bowl, cover, and chill thoroughly. Serve the compote at the table
from an iced serving dish (a giant clear glass snifter is beautiful).
Spoon fruit and liqueur into stemmed sherbet glasses and top each
with a mound of whipped cream.

🌸 ITALIAN ICES

Italians are very fond of fruity desserts. Unlike ice cream or
sherbet, these old-fashioned tasting ices let the true flavor of the
fresh, ripe fruit shine through.

With the advent of the food processor, fresh homemade ices
are better than ever. A good machine will produce fine, velvety
textured—almost creamy—results in very short order.

Start with the sweetest ripest fruits you can find, and add only
enough sugar to make the ice pleasing. Three fine varieties are
followed here by instructions for processing and serving.

Lemon Ice

    1   cup (250 ml) freshly squeezed lemon juice
    2   cups (500 ml) water
    1   packet unflavored gelatin
    1   cup (250 ml) sugar, or to taste
        Finely grated lemon zest from 1 lemon
    2   egg whites, stiffly beaten

    Place the lemon juice in a large mixing bowl. Place the water in a saucepan and add the gelatin to soften. Bring to a boil. Stir in the sugar and lemon zest. Pour this mixture into the lemon juice and blend well. Fold in the beaten egg whites. Pour into a shallow glass baking dish and freeze solid. Process and serve according to directions given under Fresh Melon Ice.

Orange Ice

    2   large sweet oranges, peeled, seeded,
            membranes removed
    ½   cup (125 ml) frozen orange juice concentrate, thawed
    1   cup (250 ml) water
    1   packet unflavored gelatin
    1   cup (250 ml) sugar, or to taste
    ⅓   cup (85 ml) freshly squeezed lemon juice, strained

    Purée the orange meat. Combine with the orange concentrate in a mixing bowl and set aside. Soften the gelatin in the water in a saucepan. Bring to a boil and stir in the sugar to dissolve. Pour this into the orange mixture and add the lemon juice. Stir to blend. Pour into a shallow glass baking dish and freeze solid. Process and serve according to directions given under Fresh Melon Ice.

Fresh Melon Ice
Makes about 2 quarts (2000 ml)

    6   cups (1500 ml) melon purée (peeled, seeded meat from
            ½ medium watermelon; 2 large cantaloupes; or 1½ to
            2 honeydew melons)
        Sugar to taste
        Juice from 1 large lemon, strained
    ½   cup (125 ml) water
    1   packet unflavored gelatin

Scoop the meat out of the melon and remove all of the seeds. Purée the big chunks of meat in a blender until you have about 6 cups (1500 ml) of smooth purée. Add enough sugar to make the mixture pleasing, plus the lemon juice. In a small saucepan, soften the gelatin in the water and bring to a boil. Pour into the melon mixture, and blend. Pour into a large shallow, glass baking dish (or two smaller ones) and freeze solid. Process and serve according to directions given below.

TO PROCESS AND SERVE

Remove from the freezer and thaw until soft enough to cut with a knife. Cut into cubes. With the food processor running, drop the cubes into the machine and process with the steel blade until smooth and creamy. Serve immediately, or refreeze in airtight containers. Remove frozen ice from the freezer and thaw in the refrigerator for about 1 hour before serving. Scoop into small balls and serve in iced sherbet glasses.

Sicilian Christmas Cake

CASSATA
Makes about 12 servings

The exotic combination of flavors—rum, rose water, rich chocolate, almonds, cherries, and creamy ricotta—elevate the sponge cake to new heights.

Rose water and orange flower water can be found in many Italian grocery stores, as well as Greek and Middle Eastern markets. I've found that they make luscious and interesting flavor additions to fresh and dried fruit compotes as well.

Make this Sicilian specialty in plenty of time to chill completely before you slice it.

CAKE

10   inch (250 mm) homemade Sponge Cake (*see* index), baked in a tube pan
Rum
Rose flower water

Cut the cake crosswise, using a good bread knife or an electric knife, into three round layers. Sprinkle the top of each layer with a little rum and flower water and set aside.

FILLING

1½   pounds (675 g) ricotta cheese
⅓   cup (85 ml) sugar
¼   cup (60 ml) sour cream
3   to 4 tablespoons (45 to 60 ml) rose flower water
½   teaspoon (3 ml) almond extract
1   ounce (28 g) good semisweet chocolate, chopped
½   cup (125 ml) candied cherries, chopped
½   cup (125 ml) roasted, unsalted almonds, chopped

Combine the ricotta, sugar, sour cream, flower water, and almond extract with electric beaters. When the mixture is smooth and creamy, fold in the chocolate, cherries, and almonds with a wooden spoon. Cover and chill while you make the frosting.

FROSTING

2½   cups (625 ml) powdered sugar
1   egg white
1   teaspoon (5 ml) almond extract
Fresh strained lemon juice
Candied cherries, roasted unsalted almonds, and chocolate shavings for garnish

Combine the powdered sugar, egg white, and almond extract and beat until smooth. Add the lemon juice a bit at a time until you have a spreadable frosting.

TO ASSEMBLE

Place the first layer of cake on a serving plate. Cover with half the filling. Add the second layer of cake and top with the remaining filling. Top with the final layer of cake. Frost top and sides with the frosting and decorate with cherries, almonds, and chocolate. Refrigerate for a couple of hours until serving. Serve chilled, sliced in wedges.

VARIATIONS

1. Substitute orange flower water and candied orange peeling for the rose water and cherries.

2. Use mixed chopped candied fruit instead of cherries or orange peel.

3. Melt 1 ounce (28 g) of dark or semisweet chocolate with 2 tablespoons (30 ml) of sweet butter and beat into the ricotta. Increase the sugar to taste.

Passover Charoses

(HAR-O-SES)
Makes 15 to 20 servings

Charoses is a traditional part of the Jewish Passover Seder meal. It represents the mortar used by Jewish slaves to build the Egyptian pyramids.

There are endless variations of the ingredients used in charoses, but basically it consists of finely chopped nuts and fruit which are seasoned with fragrant spices and bound together with sweet kosher wine.

Charoses should be made a few hours in advance and chilled thoroughly in an airtight container. It is a wonderful accompaniment for roasted or braised beef.

    4   tart apples, peeled and finely chopped
       Sprinkling of fresh lemon juice
1½ cups (375 ml) roasted unsalted almonds,
       finely chopped
       Sweet kosher Concord grape wine
       (I prefer Manischewitz)
    1   teaspoon (5 ml) cinnamon, or to taste
    1   teaspoon (5 ml) allspice, or to taste
    2   tablespoons (30 ml) honey, or to taste

Finely chop the apples. You can do this with a food processor or blender, but don't over-process them to mush. Put the apples in a large mixing bowl and sprinkle with a little lemon juice to prevent them from turning too dark. Finely chop the almonds. Again, you can use a food processor or blender, but don't over-process. Add the nuts to the apples and mix well. Sweeten with the wine a teaspoonful (5 ml) at a time. Mix well after each addition. Add only enough wine to make the charoses thick (like mortar) but not too juicy. Season with spices and honey to taste and mix well. Cover tightly and refrigerate until serving. Just before serving, stir in a little more wine.

🌸 Honey Cake

Makes one 16 inch × 11 inch × 4 inch
(400 mm × 275 mm × 100 mm) cake

This fragrant, richly spiced cake is so entwined with the ritual of Jewish family cooking, that it nearly always conjures up a happy memory—a favorite aunt, a long-ago holiday, the beckoning aroma of mama's kitchen before the Sabbath.

The intensity of the spices varies from cook to cook so let your palate be your guide. Premium, filtered honey works best here, and the coffee should be freshly brewed and *very* strong.

Honey cake freezes well. Wrapped tightly in plastic wrap and foil it will keep for months. In the refrigerator, properly wrapped, honey cake lasts for a couple of weeks.

5	cups (1250 ml) sifted all-purpose flour
1½	teaspoons (8 ml) baking soda
2½	teaspoons (13 ml) baking powder
1	teaspoon (5 ml) allspice
½	teaspoon (3 ml) cinnamon
½	teaspoon (3 ml) nutmeg
2	cups (500 ml) dark honey, warmed
1	cup (250 ml) hot, strong coffee (no grounds)
5	large eggs
1	cup (250 ml) sugar
⅓	cup (85 ml) vegetable oil
	Grated zest of 1 lemon (no white)
	Grated zest of 1 orange (no white)
1	cup (250 ml) shelled almonds or walnuts

Sift the flour, baking soda, baking powder, and spices together. Mix the honey and hot coffee together and stir to dissolve the honey. In a large mixing bowl, beat the eggs until they are frothy, thick, and lemon-colored. Gradually beat in the sugar, then the oil. Gradually add the flour and honey-coffee mixture alternately beating well after each addition. Chop most of the nuts, reserving enough whole nuts to arrange on the top of the cake. Mix the chopped nuts in about 1 teaspoon (5 ml) of flour to coat. Fold the floured, chopped nuts into the batter along with the grated lemon and orange zest. Grease and flour a 16 inch × 11 inch × 4 inch (400 mm × 275 mm × 100 mm) baking pan, shaking out the excess flour. Line the bottom with a piece of waxed paper. Pour the cake into the pan, smoothing batter into the corners evenly. Arrange the remaining whole nuts attractively on the top of the cake. Place on the center rack of a preheated 325° F. oven and bake for 60 to 70 minutes until the cake springs back when pressed lightly with your finger or a straw inserted into the center of the cake comes out clean. Cool the cake in the pan set on a wire rack. Invert onto a flat surface, peel away the wax paper, then place the cake on a large flat platter to serve. Cut into 3 inch to 4 inch (75 mm to 100 mm) squares.

Hilda's Rugelach

(RUG-A-LUKH)

Makes about 6 dozen cookies

Never has there been a man fussier about his food than famed comedy writer-producer Milton Josefsberg. Years ago when he and his petite, vivacious bride Hilda were first married, she set about having Milt's mother teach her to make his favorite dishes.

None of these recipes was written down, of course, so Hilda was taught to make *rugelach* (Jewish rolled cookies) the traditional way, using a yeast dough with all the ingredients measured by handfuls and pinches.

Back in her own kitchen, this method was a dismal flop. Hilda's hands were half the size of her mother-in-law's. After many a tear and failure, she resorted to making rugelach her own way. Using the traditional filling and method, Hilda substituted her own smooth, rich dough.

Well, the new rugelach were so spectacular that even Milt loved them—and has been requesting them now for nearly 50 years.

DOUGH
- 3 ounce (84 g) package cream cheese, at room temperature
- ¼ pound (112 g) butter, at room temperature
- 1 cup (250 ml) sifted all-purpose flour

FILLING
- 1 cup (250 ml) sugar
- 1 tablespoon (15 ml) cinnamon
- ¾ cup (180 ml) raisins
- Boiling water
- ¾ cup (180 ml) finely chopped walnuts

COATING
- 4 tablespoons (60 ml) sugar
- 1 tablespoon (15 ml) cinnamon

Cream the butter and cream cheese together until light and fluffy. Add the flour a little at a time, mixing well after each addition. Form the dough into a ball, wrap tightly in plastic wrap, and refrigerate until thoroughly chilled. The dough can also be frozen for later use. Simply allow the dough to unthaw completely in the refrigerator. Pour boiling water over the raisins to cover them and soak for about 30 minutes. Drain completely and dry on paper toweling. Combine the raisins, sugar, nuts, and cinnamon and mix well. Divide the chilled dough in half. Rewrap one half and refrigerate it while you prepare the other half. On a lightly floured surface, roll the dough out into a large rectangle about ¼ inch (6 mm) thick. Spread half the raisin-nut filling evenly over the dough. Starting at one of the narrow ends, begin to roll the dough over itself pinwheel fashion about 1½ revolutions. Slice that long roll off with a sharp knife, press the seam closed, and cut into pieces about 2 inches (50 mm) long. Roll each cookie in the cinnamon-sugar coating and place on an ungreased cookie sheet seam side down. Continue this procedure with all the remaining dough and filling. Bake the rugelach in the center of a preheated 350° F. oven for 12 to 15 minutes until the cookies are golden brown.

Rugelach are sinfully tempting when they are warm. But if any survive, they freeze beautifully if kept in an airtight container. Rugelach can also be refrigerated for a few weeks.

🌸 Traditional Passover Sponge Cake
Makes 1 cake

This delicious sponge cake was given to me by Faye Teischmann who brought the recipe from her native Austria. While the matzo cake meal and potato starch are out-of-the-ordinary ingredients, they do make a difference in the cake's flavor. You can find these items in the kosher section of your supermarket or in many Jewish delicatessens.

12   eggs, separated
1   large, ripe lemon
¼   cup (60 ml) freshly squeezed orange juice, strained

1   cup (250 ml) matzo cake meal
1   cup (250 ml) potato starch
½   teaspoon (3 ml) salt
2   cups (500 ml) granulated sugar
1   teaspoon (5 ml) cream of tartar

TO PREPARE

About 1 hour before you plan to put the ingredients together, remove the eggs from the refrigerator. Separate the eggs while they are still cold. (Be careful not to get even a speck of egg yolk into the whites or they will not whip up properly.) It's wise to separate each egg over a small dish, one at a time, so if one egg yolk breaks, you haven't spoiled the whole batch of whites. Place the whites in a deep mixing bowl (not plastic) that is scrupulously clean and free from any grease. Grate the zest (yellow only) from the lemon, then juice the lemon and strain. Have all ingredients come to room temperature before you begin to put them together.

THE BATTER

Combine the cake meal, potato starch, and salt, and sift together a few times. Using an electric mixer, beat the egg yolks on high speed until they are frothy. Little by little add all the sugar except for 2 tablespoons (30 ml), and continue to beat the yolks until they are very thick and creamy. This will take a few minutes. *Be sure not to add the sugar all at once.* When the yolks are thick enough to mound softly, add the lemon zest, lemon juice, and orange juice and mix well. Sift the dry ingredients into the yolk mixture a little at a time, folding lightly after each addition until no traces of the dry ingredients are visible. Wash the beaters of your electric mixer with warm water and soap, rinse, and dry thoroughly. They must be meticulously clean before you begin to beat the egg whites. Using the electric mixer at high speed begin to beat the egg whites. Beat until big bubbles form then stop the mixer, add the cream of tartar and the 2 tablespoons (30 ml) of reserved sugar. Resume beating the whites at high speed until they form soft peaks and are foamy white. *Do not over-beat, or beat until the whites are stiff or glossy.* Immediately fold the whites into the batter, gently, using a wire whisk or spatula.

TO BAKE

Pour the batter either into an ungreased 10 inch (250 mm) tube pan or into a 14 inch × 9 inch (350 mm × 225 mm) baking dish which has been lined on the bottom with a square of wax paper. Spread the batter evenly around the pan, cutting through it with your spatula to break any large air bubbles. Bake in the bottom third of a preheated 350° F. oven for 45 minutes or until the cake springs back when pressed with your finger. Do not open the oven. If you use a tube pan, invert the pan to cool either on the pan's own supports or place it upside down over the neck of a bottle. Cool the rectangular cake by inverting it on a wire rack. You may have to run the thin blade of a sharp knife around the edges to help it out of the pan.

Serve this sponge cake with a compote of fresh fruit and thick whipped cream to which a little vanilla has been added for flavor.

🌺 STRUDEL

A delicate, homemade strudel has just the right flavor and texture to top almost any Hungarian, Jewish, Russian, or Polish meal. Even the heartiest eaters always seem to have room for a warm slice of this buttery wonder.

It's a pity that so many cooks are intimidated by the art of making fresh strudel dough. Actually, with care and patience, a beginner can make an excellent dough. With practice, one can stretch flawless, tissue-thin dough with very little time and effort.

SOME TIPS

1. Keep the butter warm in the top of a double boiler.

2. If the dough resists rolling and stretching, cover it with a dry cloth and let it rest.

3. Don't start rolling the dough before it's lost all of its elasticity. It simply will not be rushed.

Strudel freezes beautifully so you can make it well ahead of time and reheat it before serving.

Happy strudeling!

🌸 Homemade Strudel Dough

Makes one 3 foot (91 cm) strudel

        2   cups (500 ml) sifted all-purpose flour
        ½   teaspoon (3 ml) salt
        1   teaspoon (5 ml) white vinegar
        1   large egg at room temperature, slightly beaten
        ½   to ¾ cup (125 to 180 ml) warm water (110° F. to
               115° F.)
            Cooking oil for hands
            Flour for kneading
        ½   pound (225 g) butter, melted, kept warm in the
               top of a double boiler
        ½   cup (250 ml) dried bread crumbs
        2   tablespoons (30 ml) butter

Sift the flour into a mixing bowl. Add the salt and mix well. Make a well in the center of the flour. Add the vinegar to the egg and blend. Pour egg mixture along with ½ cup (125 ml) of warm water into the flour well. Stir with a wooden spoon and then mix with your hands until the dough sticks together. Add a little more warm water if necessary to keep it cohesive. Turn out onto a lightly floured board and, using oiled hands, knead the dough for several minutes until it is like elastic satin and the surface begins to blister. It is helpful to keep a small dish of oil and a small dish of flour handy to use as you work. When the dough is sufficiently kneaded, pick it up and slap it down hard onto the board. Do this for about 5 minutes (at least 100 times). Then place the dough on a lightly floured surface, brush liberally with melted butter, and cover with a warm, heavy mixing bowl large enough not to touch any part of the dough. Let it rest for at least an hour or until the dough loses all elasticity. Test it by pulling out a pinch of the dough. If it rebounds it's not ready. While the dough is resting, make the filling. Spread a clean patterned sheet over a work table measuring roughly 3 feet × 3 feet (90 cm × 90 cm). Rub small amounts of flour into the sheet with your hands until the surface is completely covered. Place the dough in the center of the sheet. Roll it out with a rolling pin as far as you can in all directions. Brush with more melted butter. If the dough resists rolling or begins to rebound, cover it with a dry cloth and let it rest a few more minutes. Using the backs of your fists, start underneath the dough's center and stretch the dough out slowly and carefully until it eventually covers the entire work table. Walk around and around the table as you work to keep the dough stretched evenly in all directions. Continue to stretch-pull the dough from the center with the backs of your hands, up and over your forearms. If the dough resists, cover it with a dry cloth and let it rest. The dough should be stretched thin as onion skin with a margin of dough hanging over the edge of the table. You should be able to see the pattern of the sheet through the dough. Brush the entire surface with melted butter. Trim off the hanging edges with a sharp knife (save the thinnest parts to patch any holes) and let the dough rest for a few more minutes. Expert strudel makers rarely tear the dough. But if you are just mastering this art, you may not be so fortunate. Not to worry. Cut the thinnest pieces of the scraps to fit over any holes. Brush them with butter and place over the tears. Press edges gently with your fingers. Sauté the bread crumbs in 2 tablespoons (30 ml) of butter, until they are lightly browned. Cool slightly, then spread crumbs evenly over about ¾ of the dough leaving a 2 inch (50 mm) margin on the edges. This will prevent the filling from seeping into the dough. Spread the filling over the bread crumbs. Fold the margins in then. Starting with the filled end, lift the sheet up so the strudel will roll over itself. Continue pulling the sheet back and up to roll the strudel over and over much like a jelly roll. Cut the strudel into lengths that will fit your cookie sheet, or bend it gently into a "U" shape. Slide it onto the cookie sheet and brush with remaining melted butter. Place in the center of a preheated 450° F. oven for 10 minutes. Turn the heat down to 400° F. and continue to bake for 25 or 30 minutes until the strudel is crisp and golden brown. Cut into 2 inches (50 mm) slices and serve warm. To reheat, place on a cookie sheet in a slow oven for about 15 minutes.

TO FREEZE
Wrap tightly in plastic wrap and foil and freeze up to 4 months.

TO SERVE
Place frozen strudel on a cookie sheet and set into a 400° F. oven for 30 minutes, until center is piping hot and dough is crisp.

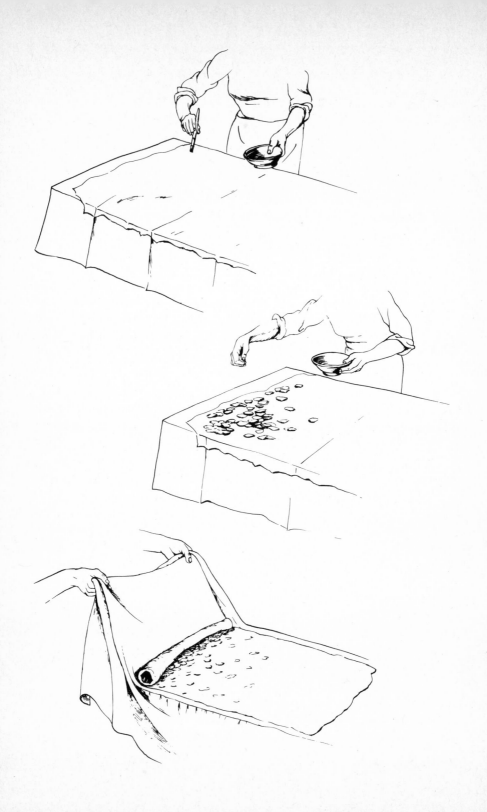

✿ Apple Strudel

    6   to 7 cups (1500 to 1750 ml) tart cooking apples,
            peeled, cored, and thinly sliced
    1   tablespoon (15 ml) cinnamon
    ½   cup (125 ml) sugar
    ½   cup (125 ml) seedless raisins (optional)
    ¼   cup (60 ml) currants (optional)
    1   teaspoon (5 ml) grated lemon rind
    1   teaspoon (5 ml) grated orange rind
    2   tablespoons (30 ml) butter
    1   recipe Strudel Dough (preceding recipe)
    1   cup (250 ml) *finely* chopped almonds or walnuts
        Sifted powdered sugar

Combine apples, cinnamon, sugar, raisins, currants, lemon rind, and orange rind in a mixing bowl. Sprinkle strudel dough with chopped nuts over buttered bread crumbs as directed in strudel dough recipe. Using the directions in the strudel dough recipe, spread apple mixture over nuts. Dot with 2 tablespoons (30 ml) of butter and roll according to the strudel dough recipe. Brush top liberally with melted butter left from strudel dough. Bake according to instructions for strudel dough. Sprinkle with sifted powdered sugar. Cut into 2 inch (50 mm) slices and serve warm, with lightly whipped or heavy cream.

✿ Cherry Strudel

    7   to 8 cups (1750 to 2000 ml) fresh pitted cherries
            (if using canned cherries, make sure they are
            thoroughly drained)*
    2   cups (500 ml) sugar (more or less depending on
            the sweetness of the cherries and the degree of
            sweetness you desire)

*You can use sweet or sour cherries, but adjust sugar accordingly.

2   teaspoons (10 ml) freshly grated lemon peel
1   recipe Strudel Dough (*see* index)
1   cup (250 ml) finely chopped almonds

Mix cherries, sugar, and lemon peel together. Sprinkle strudel dough with the almonds (over buttered bread crumbs as directed in recipe for strudel dough), and spread cherries over all according to directions. Proceed according to strudel dough recipe instructions. Cut into 2 inch (50 mm) slices. Serve warm, with slightly sweetened whipped or heavy cream.

✿ Cheese Strudel

See index for Cheese Filling. Proceed as directed in recipe for Strudel Dough.

✿ Polish Cheese Cake

Makes about 30 squares

This wonderfully spicy cheese cake is traditionally served at Easter—one of the holidays Poles celebrate with greatest zeal. After having strictly observed 40 days of Lent, the sheer abundance of a Polish Easter feast can be mind-boggling.

The open house buffet might include a selection of cold meats—sliced veal, baked ham, pickled sausages, sliced roast turkey, sliced roast goose, roast beef, and a whole suckling pig.

The meats are accompanied by relishes, sauces, horseradish, baskets of bread, sweet butter, and a tureen of hot *barszcz*, a fermented beet soup (see index for Rusell Borscht). Hard-boiled eggs are eaten for good luck, health, and happiness.

And to top it off, there are enough pastries to put a bakery window to shame. *Krupnik* (*see* index), in this case a honey-flavored liquor, is sipped with the sweets.

As you can well imagine, this buffet goes on from morning 'til night . . . it takes that long just to try everything.

DOUGH

1½   cups (375 ml) all-purpose flour
1   teaspoon (5 ml) baking powder
½   teaspoon (3 ml) salt
½   cup (125 ml) sweet butter, softened
1   egg plus 1 egg white
¼   cup (60 ml) sour cream
½   cup (125 ml) powdered sugar

Combine flour, baking powder, and salt in a mixing bowl. Cut in the butter with two knives or a pastry blender. Combine egg and sour cream in a bowl and heat until smooth. Stir the egg mixture into the flour mixture. Add the sugar and mix well. Knead the dough in the bowl until it is smooth. Turn out onto a floured board and roll into a rectangle. Press into a 13 inch × 9 inch × 2 inch (325 mm × 225 mm × 50 mm) glass dish, and bring the dough about ¾ of the way up the sides.

FILLING

5   whole eggs plus 2 egg yolks
2   cups (500 ml) powdered sugar
1½   teaspoons (8 ml) vanilla extract
2   teaspoons (10 ml) fresh, strained lemon juice
1   pound (450 g) farmer cheese or ricotta
⅔   cup (170 ml) butter, melted
1½   cups (375 ml) unseasoned mashed potatoes
2   teaspoons (10 ml) baking powder
½   teaspoon (3 ml) nutmeg
½   teaspoon (3 ml) salt
¼   cup (60 ml) grated orange or lemon rind

Beat the eggs and yolks with the powdered sugar about 5 minutes at high speed with an electric mixer. Add the vanilla extract and lemon juice and beat at high speed for another 2 minutes until the mixture peaks softly. Press the cheese through a sieve. In a large mixing bowl, blend the cheese with the melted butter. Add the potatoes, baking powder, nutmeg, and salt and blend well. Stir in the citrus rind. Fold in the egg mixture. Do not overmix.

Turn the filling onto the crust and spread it evenly. Bake at 350° F. for about 45 minutes or until the filling has set. Cool the cheese cake thoroughly before you cut it into small squares.

Polish Walnut Torte

This is a spectacular yet fairly easy creation. Be sure the walnuts are as fresh as possible, though, or you might have a rancid spectacle on your hands.

CAKE
- 12   eggs, separated
- 1   cup (250 ml) granulated sugar
- ½   teaspoon (3 ml) salt
- ½   cup (125 ml) sifted all-purpose flour
- ½   pound (225 g) finely ground walnuts
- 1   ounce (31 ml) brandy

One hour before you plan to put the ingredients together, remove the eggs from the refrigerator and separate while cold. Let them come to room temperature. Using an electric mixer, beat egg yolks at high speed until they are thick and lemon-colored. Add ½ cup (125 ml) of the sugar gradually, beating continuously. Add salt, flour, ground walnuts, and brandy and blend well. Remove the electric beaters and wash thoroughly with soap and water and dry. In a separate bowl (not plastic) begin beating the egg whites at high speed. When big bubbles begin to form on the top, stop the mixer and add the salt and about 1 tablespoon (15 ml) of the remaining sugar. Return to high speed and gradually add remaining sugar until the whites stand in soft peaks. Do not over-beat. Gently fold egg whites into yolk batter. Pour evenly into two 10 inch (250 mm) round layer cake pans that have been well greased and floured and have bottoms lined with a circle of waxed paper. Bake in a preheated 350° F. oven for about 30 minutes until a toothpick inserted in the middle of each cake comes out clean. Cool cakes on a wire rack, then chill.

FILLING

½	pint (250 ml) whipping cream
1	cup (250 ml) powdered sugar
1	ounce (31 ml) brandy
½	pound (225 g) finely ground walnuts

Using an electric mixer, whip the cream in a chilled metal or glass bowl until it begins to thicken. Gradually beat in the powdered sugar and brandy and continue beating until the cream is stiff. Fold in nuts. Chill, covered tightly.

FROSTING

4	tablespoons (60 ml) sweet butter
1	egg yolk
2	ounces (62 ml) brandy
1½	to 2 cups (375 to 500 ml) powdered sugar

In an electric mixer, combine butter, egg yolk, and brandy and beat until smooth. Gradually beat in powdered sugar until you have a thick, fluffy frosting. Chill.

TO ASSEMBLE

Place one layer of the cake on a cake pedestal or plate, and spread the filling. Place the second layer of cake over this. Spread top with the frosting and garnish with whole, toasted walnuts. Chill until serving. Cut into thin wedges.

🌸 Danish Applecake

Aeblekage
Makes 6 to 8 servings

This is a light and luscious no-bake dessert that can be made well in advance.

4	tablespoons (60 ml) sweet butter

1½ cups (375 ml) fine dry pumpernickel crumbs or
    ground zwieback
 2 tablespoons (30 ml) sugar
12 soft macaroons
⅓ cup (85 ml) sweet sherry
 2 cups (500 ml) Homemade Applesauce (*see* index)
 2 teaspoons (10 ml) melted butter
 1 pint (500 ml) whipping cream, stiffly beaten
    Currant jelly

Melt 4 tablespoons (60 ml) of butter in a skillet and add the crumbs and sugar. Stirring continuously, cook until the crumbs are crisp. Set aside. Crumble the macaroons in the bottom of a glass serving bowl. Sprinkle sherry over them and let stand until the sherry is absorbed. Stir the melted butter into the applesauce and sweeten the applesauce to taste. Spread a layer of the applesauce over the soaked macaroons, then a layer of buttered crumbs. Proceed with these layers until all of the crumbs and applesauce are used, ending with the buttered crumbs. Top with a thick layer of whipped cream and dot with currant jelly. Chill until serving.

✿ Danish Chilled Apricot Dessert

Being partial to fruit desserts, Danes have devised numerous ways to turn fresh and dried fruits into sumptuous no-bake delicacies.

Make this several hours in advance and chill it completely. Serve it in frozen goblets or stemmed sherbet glasses and pass some delicate butter cookies at the table.

 1 pound (450 g) large, dried apricot halves
 2 tablespoons (30 ml) strained fresh lemon juice
 2 to 3 tablespoons (30 to 45 ml) apricot brandy
    Sugar to taste
¼ cup (60 ml) apricot jam
20 soft almond macaroons
½ cup (125 ml) sweet sherry
½ cup (125 ml) sliced almonds

1   pint (500 ml) whipping cream
2   tablespoons (30 ml) sugar
1   teaspoon (5 ml) vanilla, or ½ teaspoon (3 ml)
    almond extract

Place the apricots in a stainless steel saucepan and barely cover with boiling water. Let stand overnight. Add the lemon juice, brandy, and sugar and bring to a slow boil in the same water. Simmer about 20 minutes until the fruit is very soft. Stir in the jam and cool. In a glass serving bowl, crumble half the macaroons on the bottom, sprinkle with the sherry, and let stand until the liquor is absorbed. Cover with half the apricots, then the remaining macaroons and a few of the almonds, and finally a layer of the remaining apricots. Top with whipped cream and the rest of the nuts. Chill thoroughly before serving.

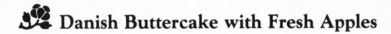 Danish Buttercake with Fresh Apples

Caramelized apples are the self-making "frosting" atop this light, buttery cake punctuated with fresh lemon.

½   cup (125 ml) sweet creamery butter
½   cup (125 ml) sugar
2   large eggs
1   teaspoon (5 ml) fresh lemon juice
1½   teaspoons (8 ml) grated lemon zest
1   cup (250 ml) sifted all-purpose flour
4   large apples (pippin, crisp golden delicious, etc.),
     peeled, cored, and thinly sliced, then sprinkled
     with ½ teaspoon (3 ml) fresh lemon juice
2   tablespoons (30 ml) sweet butter
¼   cup (60 ml) brown sugar

Cream butter and sugar together in a large mixing bowl. Add eggs one at a time, beating well after each addition. Mix in 1 teaspoon (5 ml) lemon juice and the lemon zest. Gradually stir in the flour. Pour the batter into a buttered 9 inch (225 mm) spring-form cake pan.

Layer the sliced apples on the top. Combine the remaining 2 tablespoons (30 ml) of butter and brown sugar to make a crumbly mixture. Sprinkle over all. Bake in a 350° F. oven for about 50 minutes, or until a toothpick inserted in the middle of the cake comes out clean. Serve the cake while it is still slightly warm and spoon sweetened thick or whipped cream over each slice, or offer créme fraiche for a topping.

🌸 Danish Pastry
WIENERBROD

The making of these flaky, buttery pastries, like good croissants, undeniably takes time. But anybody who has tasted homemade Danish will agree that it's an uncommonly delicious experience.

These pastries can be made in bountiful batches and frozen for later use. I have found that they freeze best when each pastry is wrapped individually in plastic wrap and foil. Then I place them into large plastic food bags and tie them securely. Give them about 2 hours thawing time at room temperature. If you'd rather have them warm, wrap in foil (be sure to remove the plastic) and heat in a 200° F. oven for about 30 minutes or until the centers are heated through.

1	package active dry yeast
¼	cup (60 ml) warm water (110° F. to 115° F.)
¼	cup (60 ml) scalded milk
2	eggs at room temperature, lightly beaten
¼	cup (60 ml) sugar
½	teaspoon (3 ml) salt
¼	cup (60 ml) soft sweet butter
2	to 2½ cups (500 to 625 ml) sifted all-purpose flour
12	tablespoons (180 ml) frozen sweet butter
	Choice of fillings (recipes follow)

Dissolve the yeast in the warm water. In a large mixing bowl, combine the milk, eggs, sugar, salt, and soft butter. Stir until everything is well blended. Cool to lukewarm. Stir in the dissolved yeast and about 1¾ cups (430 ml) of the sifted flour. Turn the dough out onto a floured board and knead in more flour to make a light, springy, elastic dough. Cover the dough with a large mixing bowl and let it rest for 30 minutes. On a floured board, roll the dough out again into a rectangle about ⅜ inch (9 mm) thick. Slice the frozen butter as thin as possible and place half of it down the center of the dough. Fold the right third of the dough (long side) over the middle third. Place the rest of the butter down the center of this section, then fold the left third of the dough over it. You now have one long piece of dough in three layers with butter in between each. Pinch the ends together to prevent the butter from oozing out. From now on the object is to blend the butter into the dough, slowly, without puncturing the dough or allowing the butter to seep out. To begin with, the dough must be kept very cold. First, press the long three-layered piece lightly with your hands or with a rolling pin to indent the butter into the dough. Place the dough on a cookie sheet and chill in the freezer (it's faster) for about 20 minutes. Chill the rolling pin as well. If you have a marble pastry slab, use it as your rolling surface, because it will stay cooler than a wooden board. Remove the dough from the freezer and place it on a lightly floured rolling surface with the open edge toward

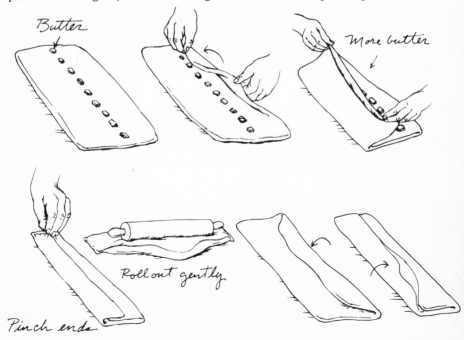

Butter

More butter

Roll out gently

Pinch ends

you. Working quickly with gentle up and back strokes, roll out the dough to make a ⅜ inch (9 mm) thick rectangle. Fold the right third of the dough over the center and fold the left third over this, to make a three-layered long piece of dough as before. Turn so that the open edge is toward you and continue in this manner, rolling very gently, folding and turning until all of the butter is absorbed in the dough. If the butter begins to ooze out, place the dough back in the freezer for a few minutes. Fold the dough, cover with plastic wrap and chill for about 1 hour while you prepare the filling.

TO SHAPE INTO A RING

On a lightly floured surface, roll out the dough into a rectangle about ¼ inch (6 mm) thick. Spread the filling out over the dough leaving about a 2 inch (50 mm) margin on the long sides. Roll up, starting with a long side, in pinwheel fashion. Bring the ends together, moisten each with a little water, and seal. Place on a greased baking sheet. With a sharp knife, make slashes at even intervals about every 2 inches (50 mm) all around the top outer edge of the dough. This will let steam escape in baking and give the finished ring an interesting teardrop design. Brush the top with a little wash made with a beaten egg and a little water. Sprinkle with cinnamon sugar or slivered nuts if desired. Cover with a clean kitchen cloth and let rise in a warm (80° F.) spot until it's double in size. Place in a preheated 400° F. oven and bake for 20 to 25 minutes, until flaky and lightly browned.

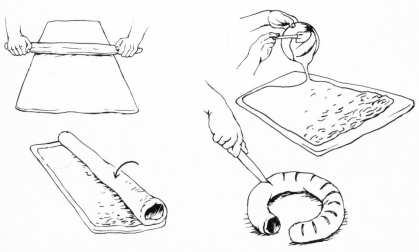

TO MAKE INDIVIDUAL DANISH PASTRIES

On a lightly floured surface, roll out the dough into a large square, ¼ inch (6 mm) thick. Use a sharp knife to cut the dough into 16 even squares. Spoon a portion of the filling into the center of each square. Fold each of the corners up and in, almost to the center. Leave a space for the filling to peek through in the center. Place on a greased baking sheet, about 2 inches (50 mm) apart. Brush the tops with an egg wash made by beating one egg with a little water. Sprinkle with sugar, cinnamon, and/or nuts if desired. Cover with a clean kitchen cloth and set in a warm spot to rise until about double in size, 20 to 25 minutes. Bake in a preheated 375° F. oven for about 20 minutes until flaky and lightly browned. If the tops were left plain, you may drizzle with a thin frosting made by combining powdered sugar and water to a thin, smooth liquid. Frost while the pastries are slightly warm.

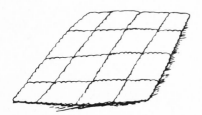 

🌺 Danish Pastry Nut Filling

    ½   cup (125 ml) softened butter
    ½   cup (125 ml) chopped nuts (almonds, walnuts, or
         filberts)
    1   cup (250 ml) powdered sugar
    1   teaspoon (5 ml) cinnamon (optional)

Combine all ingredients in a small mixing bowl. Top the finished pastry with some additional nuts, granulated sugar and cinnamon if desired.

🌺 Danish Pastry Prune Filling

20   large, dried pitted prunes
      Water
 1   tablespoon (15 ml) strained fresh lemon juice
 4   tablespoons (60 ml) currant jelly
 1   teaspoon (5 ml) butter

Place the prunes in a stainless steel saucepan and barely cover with water. Simmer over low heat until the fruit is very soft. Drain off the water, mash the fruit, and stir in the lemon juice, jelly, and butter. Blend well.

🌺 Danish Pastry Apricot Filling

20   large, dried apricot halves
      Water
 4   to 5 tablespoons (60 to 75 ml) apricot jam
 1   tablespoon (15 ml) strained fresh lemon juice
      Sugar to taste
 1   teaspoon (5 ml) butter
      Powdered sugar
      Chopped nuts

Place the dried apricots in a stainless steel saucepan and barely cover with water. Simmer over low heat until the fruit is very soft. Drain off the water and mash the fruit. Add the apricot jam, lemon juice, sugar to taste, and butter and blend well. After the apricot Danish have been baked and are just barely warm, sift the powdered sugar over the top of each, and sprinkle with chopped nuts.

Danish Pastry Cheese Filling

See index for Cheese Filling for Blintzes. Before baking, sprinkle the tops of the Danish with a little granulated sugar and sliced almonds.

 ## Finnish Cardamom Cream Cookies

Makes about 4 dozen cookies

The sweet pungency of cardamom gives these easy drop cookies a fine fragrance. They're good right out of the oven with mugs of hot chocolate.

4	eggs
1	cup (250 ml) sugar
1	cup (250 ml) sour cream
2	cups (500 ml) sifted all-purpose flour
1	teaspoon (5 ml) baking soda
½	cup (125 ml) melted butter
½	teaspoon (3 ml) pulverized cardamom seeds

Beat the eggs and sugar until thick and lemon-colored. Beat in sour cream. Sift flour and soda together in a large mixing bowl. Gradually pour in the egg mixture, mixing well after each addition. Stir in the melted butter and cardamom seeds. Drop by teaspoonsful (5 ml at a time) onto a greased baking sheet. Bake at 350° F. for about 12 minutes, until the cookies are light brown. Cool on a wire rack and store in an airtight container.

 ## Norwegian Gingered Apple Rings with Almonds

Makes 4 servings

According to so many recipes that incorporate apples, tart pippins are the only decent apples for cooking.

I disagree. Last fall I bought a lug of sweet golden delicious apples that were freshly picked from an orchard in Northern California. Without a doubt, those firm green beauties made the finest tasting applesauce, apple butter, strudel, pie, cobbler, and gingered apple rings we've ever eaten. In fact, they were so sweet that I added only a trace of sugar.

For this wonderfully spicy dessert, choose sweet, firm, ripe apples in the late fall or early winter and keep them refrigerated until use.

½   cup (125 ml) packed light brown sugar
1   to 1½ teaspoons (5 to 8 ml) ground ginger
4   to 5 tablespoons (60 to 75 ml) butter
½   cup (125 ml) slivered or chopped almonds
4   firm apples, peeled, cored, and cut into ¼ inch
      (6 mm) rings
      Cream topping: crème fraiche, sour cream,
        whipped cream, or thick cream
      Ground mace

Combine the sugar and ginger and mix well. Melt about 2 tablespoons (30 ml) of butter in a small skillet and sauté the almonds until they are toasted. Stir in about half the sugar mixture and stir to melt. Set aside. Melt the remaining butter in a large skillet and add the apple rings when the butter sizzles. Cover and cook over low heat until the apples are tender, about 10 minutes. Using a spatula, carefully turn the apples over and cook on the other side for a couple of minutes. Sprinkle the remaining sugar mixture over the apples and let it melt. To serve, place a quarter of the warm apples in a shallow fruit dish. Spoon some of the almonds and their syrup over the apples and top with crème fraiche, sour cream, lightly sweetened whipping cream, or thick cream and dust sparingly with some ground mace.

Swedish Spiced Christmas Cookies

PEPPARKAKOR

Makes about 5 dozen cookies

A beloved gingersnap of sorts, these ultra-spicy cookies are made in various ways: they can be rolled out thinly on a lightly floured surface, then cut into different shapes; or they can be rolled into "logs" which are thinly sliced and each cookie topped with an almond half; or, as in this version, the cookies are shaped by hand, then coated with sugar while still hot from the oven. While the yield will vary, the basic dough recipe will work with any of these methods.

¾	cup (180 ml) hard frozen butter, diced
¼	cup (60 ml) water
1¼	cups (310 ml) firmly packed brown sugar
1½	teaspoons (8 ml) ground cinnamon
1½	teaspoons (8 ml) ground cloves
2	teaspoons (10 ml) ground ginger
½	teaspoon (3 ml) ground cardamom
2	cups (500 ml) sifted all-purpose flour
¼	teaspoon (1.5 ml) baking soda

Put the diced butter in a large mixing bowl. In a small heavy saucepan, combine the water, brown sugar, and spices and bring to a boil. Cook and stir continually about 1 minute. Pour the hot liquid over the butter and stir with a wooden spoon to melt the butter. Sift the flour again with the baking soda. Gradually stir into the spice mixture, mixing well with a wooden spoon after each addition. Form the dough into a ball and wrap tightly in plastic wrap. Refrigerate for several hours or overnight. Keep the dough chilled as you work. Only make as many cookies as will fit on the cookie sheets at one time. Pinch off teaspoonsful (5 ml) of dough and roll into little balls in your hands. Flatten slightly. Bake on greased cookie sheet in a 375° F. oven for 10 to 12 minutes. Drop the hot cookies into a paper bag with granulated sugar and give them a shake to coat them. Cool on a wire rack. Repeat with the rest of the dough. Store the cookies in airtight containers or in the freezer. They will keep for several weeks.

🌺 Swedish Fresh Raspberry Tart
Makes 6 to 8 servings

This dessert has been referred to as "raspberry cloud" which is, I think, the best way to describe its ethereal quality. Delicately sweet, the toasted nutty flavor of the meringue shell complements the natural tartness of fresh raspberries and lightly sweetened whipped cream. It's light and luscious . . . in my book, the perfect dessert.

You can vary the nuts, the flavorings, and even the fruit. I've used fresh blueberries, strawberries, and even a touch of liquor and orange zest.

For best results with the meringue shell, separate the eggs while they are cold, then let the whites come to room temperature before beating.

While the tart must be assembled at the last possible moment, you can bake the shell hours ahead. Keep it at room temperature or cover it loosely and refrigerate. The raspberries and the whipped cream must be kept as cold as possible up to the last minute.

4	egg whites, at room temperature
	Pinch of cream of tartar
½	teaspoon (3 ml) almond or vanilla extract
1	cup (250 ml) sifted powdered sugar
1½	cups (375 ml) walnuts or roasted, unsalted almonds, very finely chopped or coarsely ground in a blender or food processor
10	ounces (280 g) fresh or thawed, drained raspberries (approximate)
1	pint (500 ml) whipping cream
½	teaspoon (3 ml) vanilla or almond extract
2	teaspoons (10 ml) sugar
	Thinly sliced almonds or finely chopped walnuts

Place the egg whites in a deep mixing bowl (not plastic) that is scrupulously clean and free from any grease. Using electric beaters, begin to beat the whites at high speed until big bubbles form. Stop the beaters and add a pinch of cream of tartar and ½ teaspoon of extract. Start the mixer again at high speed and begin to add the powdered sugar, 1 tablespoon (15 ml) at a time, until all the sugar is used. Beat the whites until they stand in stiff peaks on the beaters. Gently fold the nuts into the stiff whites. Spread into a round 9 inch or 10 inch (225 mm or 250 mm) spring-form pan with a lightly oiled circle of waxed paper on the bottom. Bake in a 350° F. oven for about half an hour, or until the meringue shell is lightly browned and firm in the middle. Carefully remove the sides of the pan and cool on a wire rack for about 15 minutes, then invert the shell and peel off the paper. Cool thoroughly on the rack. Whip the cream until it is stiff, flavoring with sugar and extract if you wish, while it is being whipped. Chill thoroughly. Place the shell on a flat serving dish. Spoon the raspberries over the top of the tart shell, reserving some nice, whole berries for the top. Spread the whipped cream over all and garnish with the reserved berries and nuts. Chill and serve immediately.

Old Fashioned Pound Cake

Makes two 9 inch × 5 inch × 3 inch (225 mm × 125 mm × 75 mm) loaf cakes or one 3 quart (3000 ml) fluted bundt cake

For best flavor, always use premium creamery butter and farm eggs if you can get them, because deep yellow yolks add both color and richness to the finished product.

Additional flavorings such as liquors and spices should be added with discrimination, considering the toppings you'll be using and the fact that pound cake's honest ingredients should shine through.

To serve up to 24 people, use a large bundt pan. For smaller gatherings, bake the pound cake in two loaf pans, freezing one loaf for later use.

1	pound (450 g) butter, softened at room temperature
1	pound (450 g) granulated sugar
10	eggs, separated
1½	teaspoons (8 ml) vanilla extract
4	cups (1000 ml) all-purpose or cake flour

VARIATIONS

Add any of these optional flavorings:

1. 1 teaspoon (5 ml) mace

2. 1 teaspoon (5 ml) almond extract

3. 1 teaspoon (5 ml) lemon extract

4. 1 teaspoon (5 ml) orange extract

5. 3 tablespoons (45 ml) good brandy

6. 3 tablespoons (45 ml) light rum

In the large bowl of an electric mixer, cream the butter until light and fluffy. Gradually add sugar, beating continually until the mixture is creamy. One by one, beat in the egg yolks, mixing well after each addition, until the batter is thick and lemon-colored. Mix in the flavorings of your choice and blend. With the mixer on low speed, gradually beat in the flour until the batter is smooth. Do no overbeat. Set the batter aside and wash and dry the beaters. In a clean mixing bowl (not plastic), beat the egg whites until they are stiff. Fold into the batter well. Pour into two loaf pans that have been buttered, floured, and lined on the bottom with waxed paper. Or use a fluted bundt pan that has been buttered and floured. (Before it is floured, I spray the pan with nonstick vegetable spray as well.) Bake in a preheated 325° F. oven for about 1 hour until golden. The bundt pan will take about 15 minutes longer. Test with a straw for doneness. Cool in the pan, on a rack, for 15 minutes before unmolding. If tightly wrapped in waxed paper and foil, this cake will keep in the freezer for months.

🌸 Southern Peach Brandy Shortcake

Makes 12 servings

9   inch × 5 inch × 3 inch (225 mm × 125 mm × 75 mm) Homemade Pound Cake (preceding recipe), flavored with vanilla, mace, and homemade Peach Brandy (*see* index)

3   cups (750 ml) sliced peaches from the Peach Brandy, or fresh or frozen sliced peaches, flavored with **sugar, brandy, and a drop of almond extract**

1   pint (500 ml) whipping cream, stiffly whipped and
        flavored with a little sugar and vanilla extract

Slice the cake into 12 pieces. Place each on a serving dish.
Spoon some of the peaches over each slice, sprinkle with some of the
peach brandy, and top with whipped cream. Serve immediately.

Spanish Cream Sherry Cake
Makes one 1 quart (1000 ml) mold

Use a tall, pretty cake mold for the most striking results. This
cake is a lovely, refined contrast to an otherwise earthy Basque
dinner.

Serve small slices of cake with glasses of good Spanish sweet
sherry.

CAKE MIXTURE
1¼   cups (310 ml) granulated sugar
 ¾   cup (180 ml) water
 9   inch × 5 inch × 3 inch (225 mm × 125 mm ×
        75 mm) Homemade Pound Cake (*see* index),
        flavored with vanilla, or almond extract, 3
        tablespoons (45 ml) Spanish sweet cream sherry
 ¾   cup (180 ml) Spanish sweet cream sherry

FILLING MIXTURE
 1   cup (250 ml) pecans or roasted almonds
 4   egg yolks at room temperature, well beaten
 1   teaspoon (5 ml) almond extract
     Pinch of salt

Combine the sugar and water and stir to dissolve over medium
heat. Bring to a boil and cook for about 10 minutes. Cool completely.
Cut the pound cake into cubes and sprinkle with the sherry. Pour half
the cooled syrup over this, mix lightly, and let stand while you

prepare the filling. Grind the nuts in a blender or food processor. Whip together with the egg yolks, almond flavoring, salt, and remaining syrup until well blended. Butter a 1 quart (1000 ml) fluted mold. Layer ⅓ of the cake mixture and the ⅓ of the filling alternately, starting with the cake and ending with the filling. Place in a preheated 350° F. oven for about 1 hour until the cake tests done and is nicely brown on the top. Let the cake cool in the mold, on a rack, for about half an hour, then unmold on a pretty serving plate. Cover tightly with plastic wrap and foil and let stand at room temperature for up to 3 days before serving. Serve slices of cake with sweetened almond-flavored whipped cream.

 ## Aunt Jessie's Special Blueberry Cobbler

Makes one 8 inch (200 mm) cobbler

All the family knows that Aunt Jessie is a fabulous cook. The jars upon jars of pickles, preserves, and relishes she makes from the vegetables in her summer garden are legendary.

When the family gets together for a big shebang, Aunt Jessie's specialties are sure to be at the heart of things.

This cobbler is one of her summertime specialties.

BLUEBERRIES
- 3   tablespoons (45 ml) butter
- 3   cups (750 ml) fresh blueberries, washed, stemmed, and picked over
- ⅔   cup (170 ml) sugar
- 3   tablespoons (45 ml) fresh lemon juice
- 3   tablespoons (45 ml) all-purpose flour

Combine all ingredients in a saucepan and heat to boiling. Pour into an 8 inch (200 mm) [2 inches (50 mm) deep] square pan. Set aside while you make the batter.

BATTER
- 1⅓   cups (335 ml) all-purpose flour
- ¼   cup (60 ml) sugar

2   teaspoons (10 ml) baking powder
⅓   cup (85 ml) butter
½   cup (125 ml) milk
1   egg, beaten

In a mixing bowl, combine flour, sugar, and baking powder. Cut butter into "small peas" and add to bowl. Add milk and egg and stir quickly with a fork, mixing thoroughly. Drop by spoonfuls over the hot blueberries. Bake at 350° F. for 35 minutes until the cobbler is lightly browned. Serve warm. Offer heavy cream or homemade vanilla ice cream with each serving.

FRESH PEACH COBBLER
Substitute 3 cups (750 ml) of fresh sliced ripe peaches for the blueberries. Add a dash of cinnamon or nutmeg to the fruit if you wish. When baked, pour homemade Peach Brandy (*see* index) over each serving and offer sweetened whipped cream or homemade vanilla ice cream.

FRESH APPLE COBBLER
Substitute 3 cups (750 ml) of apples for the berries and ½ teaspoon (3 ml) cinnamon, ½ teaspoon (3 ml) ground cloves, and a dash of nutmeg to the fruit. Serve warm with whipped cream, ice cream, or thin slices of cheddar cheese.

🌺 Grandma Ruth's Roaster Spice Cake
Makes 1 large cake

Ruth Daniels Modlin was born in Laramie, Wyoming to a Swedish immigrant father and a mother whose family has been traced back to the Old South.

Her natural knack for baking saw her family through some meager times. In fact, she sold loaves of her delicious homemade bread to pay for my mother's music lessons.

Today, I still get awfully hungry for a slice of the roaster spice cake she made for us at Christmas . . . dark, moist, rich, and just bursting with raisins and nuts.

3 cups (750 ml) boiling water
2 cups (500 ml) granulated sugar
2 cups (500 ml) lard
2 cups (500 ml) seedless Thompson raisins
2 teaspoons (10 ml) ground cinnamon
½ teaspoon (3 ml) allspice
½ teaspoon (3 ml) nutmeg
  Pinch of salt
4 cups (1000 ml) all-purpose flour
1 rounded teaspoon (5 ml) baking soda
1 cup (250 ml) coarsely chopped walnuts

In a large heavy saucepan, add the sugar, lard, raisins, spices, and salt to the boiling water and stir until dissolved. Boil slowly for 10 minutes. Remove from heat and cool completely. Slowly mix in the flour, baking soda, and nuts with a wooden spoon. Butter and flour a small oval or round roasting pan with a lid. Pour the cake into the pan and put the lid on tightly. Set in a 300° F. to 325° F. oven and bake for about 1½ hours, until a straw comes out clean. Cool with the lid on. Do not frost. Keep cake wrapped tightly in layers of foil. This cake will keep for weeks if properly wrapped.

 **Chess Pie**

Makes one 9 inch or 10 inch (225 mm or 250 mm) pie

Made with a few staple ingredients, this pie is believed to have originated sometime during the Civil War when there was a severe food shortage in the South. It is said that a Black mammy on a nearly abandoned Louisiana plantation offered a slice of this sweet to a passing Union soldier. When he asked the name of her delicious pastry she shrugged, "Ah don' know, suh, it's 'jes' pie." Hence the name.

Today there are literally dozens of versions, some very fixed-up and fancy. But this simple rendition is as luscious as can be . . . a light, sort of pecan pie.

Chess pie is so rich that you can probably get twice as many slices from one pie, because thin slivers are so incredibly satisfying.

Make it for holidays instead of the obligatory pumpkin and mincemeat. Serve it on the day it is baked.

FLAKY PIE CRUST
1½ cups (375 ml) sifted all-purpose flour
½ teaspoon (3 ml) salt
½ cup (125 ml) Crisco shortening
4 tablespoons (60 ml) ice water (approximate)

Sift the flour and salt together in a mixing bowl. Add about half of the shortening and mix with your hands until the mixture is crumbly. Add the other half of the shortening and cut in with two knives until there are pieces the size of large peas. Stir quickly with a fork as you sprinkle the ice water, a spoon at a time, over the mixture. Add just enough water to make a barely cohesive dough. Do not over-mix. Press the dough into a ball and refrigerate while you make the filling.

CHESS FILLING
½ cup (125 ml) butter
1½ cups (375 ml) sugar
1 tablespoon (15 ml) vinegar
3 eggs
1 teaspoon (5 ml) vanilla extract
Pinch of salt
¾ cup (180 ml) coarsely chopped pecans for topping

Melt the butter in a saucepan, stir in sugar and vinegar, and bring to a boil. Place eggs in a mixing bowl and beat well. Add the butter and sugar mixture, beating well. Stir in vanilla and salt.

TO ASSEMBLE
Place the chilled dough on a lightly floured board and flatten with your hand into a circular shape. Using a lightly floured, seasoned rolling pin, roll evenly in all directions with quick light strokes until the dough is a circle about ⅛ inch (3 mm) thick. Carefully fold the dough in half and, lifting the center of the crust along the fold, slide the pie plate under, gently, until the crust is draped over half the

plate. Unfold carefully to cover the pie plate. Trim the edges with a pair of kitchen shears leaving about 1 inch (25 mm) of dough hanging over the edges of the plate. Fold those edges under and flute all the way around. There must not be any holes in the crust, or the filling will seep through. Pour the filling into the crust and bake at 325° F. for 25 minutes. Sprinkle the pecans evenly over the filling and return to the oven for another 15 minutes until the crust is golden brown and the filling is set. Cool completely. Serve with big dollops of lightly sweetened whipped cream flavored with a little vanilla.

Southern Yam Pie

Makes one 9 inch (225 mm) pie

The brown sugar and pecan topping on this fresh yam pie makes the difference between a great pie and one that's a memorable experience. With big scoops of homemade ice cream, there's nothing comparable.

    1   Flaky Pie Crust (*see* index)

FILLING
    2   or 3 large red yams [you'll need 1½ cups (375 ml) mashed yams]
    3   tablespoons (45 ml) sweet butter
    ½   cup (125 ml) packed light brown sugar
    ½   teaspoon (3 ml) cinnamon
    ½   teaspoon (3 ml) nutmeg
    1   teaspoon (5 ml) ground ginger
        Dash of cloves
        Pinch of salt
    ¾   cup (180 ml) scalded half-and-half
    2   large eggs, well beaten
        Topping

Prepare the pie crust as directed. Line a 9 inch (225 mm) pie plate and flute the edges. Cover with a clean cloth and set aside. To cook the yams, wrap them individually in foil and bake until soft in a

350° F. oven, about 2 hours. Cool the yams, peel off the skin, and discard. Purée the yams and butter with a potato masher, food mill, or food processor. Add sugar, spices, and salt and blend well. Pour the hot milk into the yams and beat well. Add the beaten eggs and mix well. Pour cool filling into the unbaked pie shell and place in a 375° F. oven for 20 minutes. Remove the pie from the oven, sprinkle with topping, and return to the oven for an additional 25 minutes. Cool pie and serve with sweetened whipped cream.

TOPPING
- 4 tablespoons (60 ml) sweet butter, softened at room temperature
- ½ cup (125 ml) packed brown sugar
- 1 cup (250 ml) chopped pecans

Cream the butter and brown sugar. Mix in the chopped pecans and crumble the mixture over the pie. Spread gently with a spatula to even it up if necessary. Bake as directed above.

Christmas Plum Pudding

Makes 4 to 6 servings

My friend, Cindy Leonetti, a born Southerner, offers her favorite recipe for this traditional Yuletide treat. Each year she makes several puddings up to 3 months ahead of time to give as gifts.

- ½ cup (125 ml) butter
- ½ cup (125 ml) sugar
- 1 egg, beaten
- ⅓ cup (85 ml) milk
- ½ teaspoon (3 ml) baking soda
- ⅓ cup (85 ml) strong, freshly brewed coffee
- ½ cup (125 ml) brandy
- 3 cups (750 ml) day-old whole wheat bread crumbs
- 1 cup (250 ml) currants
- 1 cup (250 ml) raisins
- 1 cup (250 ml) chopped nuts (optional)

Cream the butter and sugar together. Beat in the egg. Mix the milk and baking soda together. Add the coffee and brandy. To the butter and sugar mixture, alternately beat in the liquids and bread crumbs until all are well incorporated. Fold in the fruits and nuts. Pour into a well buttered pudding mold. Cover tightly with aluminum foil and tie it in place with a string. Set on a rack in a deep kettle with lid. Fill the kettle with boiling water halfway up the sides of the pudding mold. Steam over slow heat for 3 to 4 hours, adding boiling water when needed. Serve warm with fresh thick cream.

 ## Piña Colada

A perfect, frothy beginning for a Cuban fiesta!

FOR EACH SERVING
- 2 ounces (62 ml) white Puerto Rican rum
- 1½ ounces (46 ml) cream of coconut
- 3 ounces (93 ml) pineapple juice
- ½ ounce (15 ml)) cream
- ½ ounce (15 ml) milk
- ½ cup (125 ml) chopped ice

Place chopped ice in a blender jar. Add remaining ingredients and blend at high speed until frothy—about 8 to 10 seconds. Pour into a frozen goblet, garnish with a stick of fresh pineapple, and serve immediately.

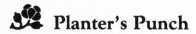 ## Planter's Punch

Makes 2 servings

The West-Indian formula for Planter's Punch goes like this: "One of sour, two of sweet, three of strong, and four of weak." Here it is translated:

- 1 jigger fresh lime juice, strained
- 2 jiggers sugar water

3 jiggers dark Jamaican rum
4 jiggers chilled pineapple juice
Plenty of crushed ice
Fresh pineapple sticks for garnish

Combine all ingredients. Fill two highball glasses half full of crushed ice. Pour half the drink into each glass, stir briefly, garnish with a pineapple stick, and serve.

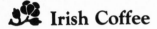 ## Irish Coffee

FOR EACH SERVING
1 ounce (31 ml) Irish whiskey
2 teaspoons (10 ml) sugar
Very hot freshly brewed coffee
Chilled whipped cream

Pour some boiling water into a 6 ounce (186 ml) stemmed goblet to heat it. Pour out the water and add the whiskey and sugar, stirring to dissolve the sugar. Pour in the hot coffee to fill the goblets ¾ full, then spoon on the whipped cream so that it floats on the coffee. Do not stir. The object is to sip the hot coffee through the cold cream.

Krupnik

Makes 1 quart (1000 ml)

This lovely drink combines two favored Polish flavors—honey and vodka. Krupnik (*kroop*-nik) can be served either hot or cold and is often offered with pastries or sweets, to be sipped slowly and savored.

The Polish Easter feast is traditionally capped by an array of sweets and a sparkling crystal decanter of this heavenly golden nectar.

2 cups (500 ml) orange honey
1 cup (250 ml) water

     1   vanilla bean
    ½   teaspoon (3 ml) nutmeg
     6   cinnamon sticks
     4   to 5 whole cloves
         Rind from ½ lemon
         Rind from ½ orange
    ⅘   quart (800 ml) vodka

Combine the honey, water, vanilla bean, spices, lemon, and orange rinds in a heavy kettle. Bring to a boil, cover, and simmer for 20 to 25 minutes. Remove from heat and stir in vodka. Strain and serve either hot or cold.

🌹 Swedish Glögg

Makes 20 cups (5000 ml)

This flaming punch is traditionally served around the Christmas holiday. Watch out, though. This is a mighty powerful brew!

     4   whole cardamom pods (about 25 seeds)
    ¼   cup (60 ml) broken cinnamon sticks
         Peel of 1 orange
    25   whole cloves
     2   quarts (2000 ml) port
     2   quarts (2000 ml) burgundy
    1½   cups (375 ml) seedless raisins
     1. cup (250 ml) whole blanched almonds
     2   cups (500 ml) sugar cubes
    ⅘   quart (800 ml) brandy
         Orange slices to garnish

Remove the seeds from the cardamom pods. Tie together in a cheesecloth bag the cardamom seeds, cinnamon sticks, orange peel, and cloves. In a large saucepan, combine half the port, half the burgundy, the raisins, and the spice bag. Simmer covered for 15 to 20 minutes. Add the remaining wines and the almonds and heat through. Place the sugar in another saucepan. Warm about ⅓ of the brandy, pour over the sugar, and ignite with a match. When the sugar has melted, extinguish the flame by pouring the remaining brandy over all. Add the sugar mixture to the wine mixture. Serve the *glögg* warm and float half an orange slice in each cup. Offer the traditional Swedish Spiced Christmas Cookies (*see* index) and fruit cakes.

🌸 Old Fashioned Mint Julep

Sipping a tall, frosty julep on the front porch swing is a summertime ritual that everyone should experience at least once. But, lacking a wrap-around veranda and a cooling magnolia-scented breeze, it is still possible to enjoy a julep so authentic that it can truly coax the fuzz right off of the peach.

FOR EACH SERVING
1   teaspoon (5 ml) sugar
1   teaspoon (5 ml) water
1   big jigger of bourbon
    Several nice sprigs of fresh mint, washed and
        drained
    Lots of crushed ice

In the bottom of a big glass mixing cup (or in a pitcher if you are making a batch), stir the sugar and water until dissolved. Add the bourbon and stir again. Choose a few sprigs of mint and bruise them or crush them in the bourbon mixture and let stand for several minutes. Fill each glass with crushed ice, keeping the outside of each glass dry. Pour a portion of the bourbon mixture over the ice and stir briskly. Add more ice to the glass to keep the glass full. A thick frost will form on the outside of the glass—the sign of a well made julep. Do not touch the frost or disturb it in any way. Garnish each glass with a sprig of mint and serve immediately.

❧ Southern Peach Brandy

Makes 3 quarts (3000 ml)

Make this with summer's ripest Freestone peaches, but don't drink it before Thanksgiving. In pretty bottles, it makes wonderful Christmas gifts.

- 1   dozen large, ripe Freestone peaches
- 2   pounds (900 g) granulated sugar (plus)
- 1   fifth good gin (plus)

Wash the peaches well and cut them in half. Discard the stones. In a sterile 1 gallon (4000 ml) crock with a lid, combine the sugar and gin. Stir to dissolve. Add the peaches and stir to coat. Cover with the lid plus a clean kitchen cloth to keep the dust off. Set in a fairly cool dark place where the brandy can ferment almost undisturbed for a few months. Several days later, check the brew and add more liquor to cover. In early October, check again and add more liquor if necessary. Taste for sweetness. You can add more sugar at this time. Keep the jar covered until late November. Any time after that you can strain the brew through a fine wire mesh sieve or through several layers of clean cheesecloth. Put the fruit into a large wide-mouthed jar with a lid, add some of the brandy and use to serve with sweetened whipped cream, pound cake, or vanilla ice cream for dessert. Bottle the liquor in pretty decanters to have on hand for the holidays, for gifts and parties.

THE ETHNIC MAIL ORDER BAZAAR

For those who live in major metropolitan areas, locating assorted ethnic specialties (food, spices, music, etc.) is not such a great task. Chances are the Yellow Pages can lead to hundreds of local sources.

But for the great number of Americans who populate small communities and rural areas, the quest for foreign goodies may be next to impossible.

If ethnic exotica is not accessible to you, the following list will open some doors.

I suggest that you write to these companies first, explain what you're looking for, and request a current catalog or price list.

Greek & Middle Eastern

C & K Importing Company
2771 West Pico Blvd., Los Angeles, CA 90006
Greek, Egyptian, Jewish, and Italian specialties: olive oils, cheeses, canned delicacies, phyllo, imported honey, etc.

Sahadi Importing Co., Inc.
187 Atlantic Ave., Brooklyn, NY 11201
Flower waters, spices, phyllo, olives and olive oil, dried legumes, syrups, condiments, tinned delicacies, and even costumes.

Hungarian, German, & Polish

Lekvar-By-The-Barrel
1577 First Avenue, New York, NY 10028
All sorts of Hungarian specialties: baking supplies, herbs, spices, tarhonya, plus a selection of foods from around the world, and novelty coffees and teas.

Paprikas Weiss Importer
1546 Second Avenue, New York, NY 10028
Hungarian, Polish, and German food stuffs: salamis, sausages, strudel leaves, tarhonya, spätetzle, spices, and canned goods.

Italian

Conte Di Savoia
555 West Roosevelt Road, Chicago, IL 60607
Specializing in cheeses, salamis, prosciutto, baked goods, preserved fishes, and a selection of international delicacies.

Manganaro Foods
488 Ninth Avenue, New York, NY 10018
An Italian grocery store offering cheeses, pasta, salamis, sausages, olive oils, and vinegars.

Latin American

Casa Moneo
210 West 14th Street, New York, NY 10011
Cuban, Mexican, South American, Portuguese, Puerto Rican, and Spanish specialties: cheeses, chiles, tortillas, sausages, spices and condiments, dried beans, and canned goods.

Scandinavian

Vander Vliet's Holland Imports
3147 West 111th Street, Chicago, IL 60655

Danish cheeses, candies, cookies, cakes, crackers, tinned fishes, sausages, pickles, and condiments, plus foods from other European countries.

Southern & Creole

Creole Delicacies Co., Inc.
533-H Saint Ann Street, New Orleans, LA 70116
Louisiana specialties: preserves, pickles, hams, baked goods, pecans, syrups, jams, herbs, and spices (gumbo filé powder), and New Orleans coffee blend.

Cheeses

Caravansary
2263 Chestnut Street, San Francisco, CA 94123
Specializing in cheeses and imported coffees and teas.

Cheeselovers International
Cheeselovers International Building,
Freeport, NY 11520

Cheese of All Nations
153 Chambers Street, New York, NY 10007

Sonoma Cheese Factory
2 Spain Street, Sonoma, CA 95476
Cheeses, salamis, wines, and condiments.

Coffee & Tea

D. M. Enterprises
Box 2452, San Francisco, CA 94126
"Specializing in North Beach Cappuccino."

Grains & Flours

Better Foods Foundation, Inc.
300 North Washington Street, Greencastle, PA 17225

The Birkett Mills
P.O. Box 440-A, Penn Yan, NY 14527

Whole Grain Sales
Route 2, Waunakee, WI 53597

Herbs & Spices

Armanino Marketing Corp.
1970 Carroll Ave., San Francisco, CA 94124

The Spice Market
94 Reade Street, New York, NY 10013

Specialty Spice Shop
2757 152nd Ave., N.E., Redmond, WA 98052

Green Mountain Herbs
P.O. Box 2369, Boulder, CO 80302

Ethnic Recordings

Festival Records
2769 West Pico Blvd., Los Angeles, CA 90006
"Folk Music from Around the World."

Hataklit
436 North Fairfax, Los Angeles, CA 90036
"Music of All the World."

Musica Latina, Inc.
2360 West Pico Blvd., Los Angeles, CA 90006
*Specializing in Cuban, Puerto Rican, South American, Spanish, and
    Mexican LP's.*

MEASURING METRICALLY

Volume

⅛ teaspoon	.5 milliliter (ml)
¼ teaspoon	1.5 milliliter
⅓ teaspoon	1.7 milliliter
½ teaspoon	3 milliliters
1 teaspoon	5 milliliters
⅛ tablespoon	1.5 milliliters
¼ tablespoon	3 milliliters
⅓ tablespoon	6 milliliters
½ tablespoon	8 milliliters
1 tablespoon	15 milliliters
⅛ cup	30 milliliters
¼ cup	60 milliliters
⅓ cup	85 milliliters
½ cup	125 milliliters
1 cup	250 milliters
1 fluid ounce	31 milliliters
1 quart	1000 milliliters [1 liter (l)]
1 gallon	4 liters

Weight

⅛ ounce	3 grams (g)
¼ ounce	7 grams
⅓ ounce	9 grams
½ ounce	14 grams
1 ounce	28 grams
⅛ pound	56 grams
¼ pound	112 grams
⅓ pound	150 grams
½ pound	225 grams
1 pound	450 grams

Length

⅛ inch	3	millimeters (mm)
¼ inch	6	millimeters
⅓ inch	8	millimeters
½ inch	12	millimeters
1 inch	25	millimeters
1 foot	300	millimeters
		[30 centimeters (cm)]

🌺 RECIPE INDEX

319

❀ ETHNIC INDEX

331

Turkey Scaloppine with
Fresh Lemon, 188

Veal and Peppers, 190
Veal and Sausage Loaf, 191

JEWISH

Blintzes, 116
  blueberry, 118
  cheese, 118
Borscht, 59
  basic, 60
  Rusell, 61
Braised Brisket of Beef, 192
Charoses, Passover, 273
Chopped Liver, 21
Clear Chicken Soup, 62
Dairy Noodle Pudding, 147
Gefilte Fish, 22
Gribbenes, 22
Groats with Bow-Tie Noodles
  (Kasha Varnishkas), 142
Honeycake, 274
Knishes, 143
  appetizers, 144
  dinner size, 144
  liver, 145
  potato, 145

Kreplach, 145
Lox, Eggs and Onions, 118
Matzoh Balls, 146
Matzoh Brie, Pancake-style, 119
Mushroom and Barley Soup with
  Boiled Flanken, 63
Pirogen
  basic dough, 149
  cheese, 151
  fruit, 153
  potato, 151
Potato Kugel, 236
Potato Latkes, 237
Rendered Chicken Fat, 22
Rugelach, Hilda's, 276
Rusell Beets, 61
Stuffed Breast of Veal, 193
Traditional Passover Sponge
  Cake, 277
Tzimmes, 238

NORWEGIAN

Gingered Apple Rings with
  Almonds, 295
Herb-Nut Bread, 94
Herring and Apple Salad, 240

Pork Chops with Caraway
  Apples, 204
Skillet Chicken with Lemon
  and Fruit, 201

POLISH

Beet Relish, 25
Braised Chicken with Sauerkraut, 195
Cheese Cake, 284
Cheese Spread, 25
Cold Beet and Cucumber Soup
  (Chlodnik), 65
Creamed Mushrooms, 239

Hunter's Stew, 197
Krupnik, 309
Mustard Butter, 102
Pickled Eggs, 26
Pickled Mushrooms, 27
Pickled Watermelon Rind, 28
Pierogi, 148